An OPUS book

THE HARVEST OF THE SIXTIES

Patricia Waugh teaches in the School of English at the University of Durham. Her publications include *Feminine Fictions: Revisiting the Postmodern* (1989), *Practising Postmodernism/ Reading Modernism* (1992), and *Postmodernism: a Reader* (1992).

D0141298

THE HARVEST
OF THE SIXTIES

ENGLISH LITERATURE AND ITS
BACKGROUND 1960–1990

Patricia Waugh

Oxford   New York

OXFORD UNIVERSITY PRESS

1995

Oxford University Press, Walton Street, Oxford OX2 6DP

Oxford New York
Athens Auckland Bangkok Bombay
Calcutta Cape Town Dar es Salaam Delhi
Florence Hong Kong Istanbul Karachi
Kuala Lumpur Madras Madrid Melbourne
Mexico City Nairobi Paris Singapore
Taipei Tokyo Toronto
and associated companies in
Berlin Ibadan

Oxford is a trade mark of Oxford University Press

British Library Cataloguing in Publication Data
Data available

Library of Congress Cataloging in Publication Data
Waugh, Patricia.
    The harvest of the sixties : English literature and its
background, 1960–1990 / Patricia Waugh.
        p. cm.
    'An OPUS book'—P. preceding t.p.
    Includes bibliographical references and index.
    1. English literature—20th century—History and criticism.
2. Politics and literature—Great Britain—History—20th century.
3. Literature and society—Great Britain—History—20th century.
4. Great Britain—History—Elizabeth II, 1952– I. Title.
820.9′00914—dc20 PR471.W34 1995 94–24111
ISBN 0–19–289226–6

10 9 8 7 6 5 4 3 2 1

Typeset by Graphicraft Typesetters Ltd., Hong Kong
Printed in Great Britain
by Biddles Ltd.,
Guildford and King's Lynn

For Seán

ACKNOWLEDGEMENTS

MANY people have contributed in a variety of ways to the writing of this book. In particular I would like to thank David Fuller for his careful reading of the manuscript and his support throughout and also many thanks to Christopher Butler for some extremely perceptive editing (if there are any remaining mixed metaphors I must carry the entire blame!). I am very grateful too for some helpful advice and thorough editing by Hilary Walford and the staff at Oxford University Press. Intellectual support and friendship have been provided as ever by Irving Velody, Denise Brown, Harold Sykes, Bert Nutter, John Wakeley, and Philip Best. My interest in contemporary writing first flourished, as a graduate student of David Lodge and I remain especially grateful to him. To my family, Eric, Eileen, Rob, and Jane, and my children Mathew and Jessie, many thanks for continuing love and support. And for all of this and more, to Seán Burke, who clearly shares my belief in the author.

P. W.

CONTENTS

1. Discontinuities: Politics, Crisis, and Change
   1960–1990   1
2. Continuities: Culture and Change 1960–1990   22
3. Keeping our Metaphysics Warm: Sacred
   Impulses in a Secular Age   58
4. Planners, Politics, and Poets: Intellectual
   Culture and the Limits of Reason after 1960   107
5. Nation and New Identities   149
6. Post-Consensus Fictions   179
   Conclusion   208

   Notes   214
   Appendix   218
   Chronology   220
   Further Reading   228
   Index   235

1 DISCONTINUITIES

POLITICS, CRISIS, AND CHANGE
1960–1990

> A moment comes, which comes but rarely in history, when we
> step out from the old to the new, when an age ends.
>
> (David Edgar, *Destiny*, 1.1 (1976))

The year 1960, in popular consciousness at least, has come to be represented as one such threshold in modern political and cultural history. For the contemporary cultural historian attempting to describe the nature of such apocalyptic moments, however, the first consideration must be one not so far removed from the theme of that historically somewhat remote meditation on the passage of time, Augustine's *Confessions*. Like the deconstructionist or phenomenologist philosopher of today, St Augustine recognized the overwhelming difficulties confronting anyone who attempts to understand the nature of temporal change. He saw that time exists for and can only be confronted by a consciousness which is itself immersed within time. St Augustine's answer to the problem—that time is an aspect of consciousness and that the past, present, and future are related only by an intentional act such as the writing of autobiography—is perhaps one way in which we can begin to think about Edgar's reflection upon history.

To write an account of a historical period through which one has lived is in some sense to write an autobiography where the past and future are necessarily and often mysteriously shaped by the writer's present situation. To write of 1960 in the mid-1990s is to be conscious of trying to define a legacy whose implications and ramifications are far from clear. We are still living the harvest of the sixties and to that extent we cannot entirely bring its meaning or significance to conscious articulation: to declare that it was an indubitably bad harvest or an unusually rich one seems premature. Which is why literature, operating in the mode of particularity, indirection, metaphor, and imaginative projection, complements the more global verdicts of rational political analysis as a means of facilitating the recognition of who and where we are. In a period of rapidly changing identities, new technologies, and a pluralization of aesthetic cultures, imaginative literature has been as important as ever in offering us narratives of recognition and the means to personal and social understanding. For St Augustine though, the attempt to stretch out present consciousness arrived at historical and self-understanding by coming to recognize its contrast with the eternal present of God. Yet in the period 1960–90, not only has there been a pervasive preoccupation with the loss of any transcendent sphere, but personal consciousness and history too have come to be defined rather by metaphors of discontinuity and crisis than by those of unification and continuity. Perhaps contemporary histories can only ever and at best be fragmented autobiographies. If so, then there is a curious logic in reading the age through its imaginative literature.

First of all though, some conventional background setting seems necessary. If the rest of the book prefers on the whole to approach culture through an emphasis on textual analysis, the first two chapters are designed to serve as a broad summary of some of the contexts, political and cultural, in which imaginative writing has been produced and read. This chapter examines some of the arguments, largely political, supporting a crisis or discontinuity view of the period, whereas the next will begin to indicate some of those cultural continuities, trends, and features gathering throughout the entire thirty years, which suggest a less apocalyptic reading of the times.

A Blissful Dawn? Political Myths and Countermyths of the Sixties

We might begin with another look at the quotation from David Edgar which prefaces this chapter. The reference within *Destiny* is actually to midnight 15 August 1947: the moment when India stepped out of colonial rule to become an independent nation. The moment precedes our period by thirteen years, yet it is one of a number of appropriate starting-points from which to begin to survey British culture from 1960 and to see that 1960 itself is far from being the radical watershed of popular myth. Few observers would quibble with Edgar's interpretation of the event as decisive for the future of world as well as British history. August 1947 ushered in a new era of decolonization, accelerating in the fifties and sixties and, particularly after the Suez crisis of 1956, propelling Britain by 1960 into a deepening confusion about its imperial identity and role as a world power. From the late fifties, despite growing consumer affluence and a 30 per cent increase in manufacturing output since 1950, and before the severe financial crises of 1961 (which would expose the relative world decline of the British economy), the Macmillan government had begun to look decidedly shifty behind its façade of aristocratic Edwardian nonchalance. The Cuban Missile crisis of 1962 dramatized and confirmed its actual dependency on the new superpower of the United States of America. The frustrated attempt at reorientation toward Europe with the refusal of entry into the Common Market in 1963 further prompted a rush of pessimistic commentary and even a special issue of *Encounter* entitled *Suicide of a Nation?*.

History, of course, is rarely truncated and refashioned in such a decisive manner as in 1947, but historical moments are frequently mythologized in popular consciousness as decisive breaks in identity. The year 1960 is clearly one such moment when Britain is supposed to have stepped out into a liberated and upbeat mood of optimistic abandon. In fact, from 1960 until 1963 a pervasive obsession with the decline of Britain occupied both the literary intelligentsia and the popular media, and this mood was to continue in the literary work and much of the intellectual thought throughout the decade. National consciousness was still coming to terms with the legacy of both 1945 and 1947, and, even without the crisis in imperial identity, internally too, the Keynesian pump-priming economics which continued to underpin the post-war settlement had failed to avert a series of balance-of-payment crises. Britain was falling behind other industrial nations in manufacturing output. The Profumo scandal of 1963 revealed the government to be seriously unaware of the activities of its members and the attitudes of the general public, and the satirical magazine *Private Eye* parodied its insouciant decadence in a fall-of-Rome cartoon in the June issue. A prominent spokesman for the British New Left, Perry Anderson, castigated the nation as 'sclerotic' and a key figure in the US administration, Dean Acheson, had famously announced that Britain 'has lost an empire and not yet found a role'.

In political terms, in fact, 1964 might seem to be a more appropriate official birthday for the sixties. The year was marked first of all by Harold Wilson's accession to office. He arrived, bestriding the ancient world of what had been dubbed 'the Establishment' in his Gannex raincoat, and immediately adopted a posture of classless and no-nonsense social rationalization summed up in Kennedy-style promises of 'new frontiers' to be reached through the 'white heat of technological revolution'. His appointment of a new minister for the arts, an increase in Arts Council funding, promises of educational expansion, and an avowed commitment to science were offered as manifestations of the 'good society' to be planned from a technologically harnessed enlightened modernity: an equal world where each would partake of 'culture, beauty, leisure'. Though this phrase is actually taken from Anthony Crosland's social democratic plea for a new emphasis on cultural planning in the influential *The Future of Socialism* (1956), Wilson's promises seemed to echo Crosland's words and indeed to respond to a number of cultural declarations from the late fifties. In 1959 C. P. Snow had delivered the lecture entitled 'The Two Cultures' (reproving a complacent and declining upper-class literary culture for its blindness to the importance of developing science and technology) which subsequently provoked a wrathful accusation of philistinism from the Cambridge literary critic F. R. Leavis. Probably the most marked literary event of the immediately preceding years had been the production of John Osborne's *Look Back in Anger* at the Royal Court in 1956, an explosion of disgust at the Tory Establishment and what was portrayed as the bewildering lassitude and flexibility of the consensus politics of welfare capitalism. Jimmy Porter had railed, if ineffectually, at what he saw as a meretricious array of neurasthenic attitudes represented by institutionalized bureaucrats who 'spend their time looking forward to the past . . . cut right off from the ugly problems of the twentieth century altogether'. It looked for a time as though Wilson might be the answer to Crosland's plea for Hellenic light, Snow's for a modernization of the dark Satanic mills, and Jimmy Porter's anguished 'Oh heavens, how I long for a little ordinary human enthusiasm'.

At the economic and political level at least, however, it was not to be. The second half of the sixties saw continuous economic crises, an increase in industrial unrest, and an abandonment of the projected National Plan for 25 per cent growth. There was a prevailing sense of disaffection with Britain's domestic government and in particular the failure to condemn American aggression in Vietnam. Yet this was supposedly the era of newly commercialized 'swing' and utopian and anti-capitalist counterculturalism. Were the 'swinging sixties' simply a myth projected by commercial interest and youth idealism and without any foundation in political or social structures? In fact, despite the economic gloom, between 1964 and 1968 there was undoubtedly much radical and popular optimism about the potential dawn of a new social order. The decade witnessed enormous transformations in attitudes to authority, sexuality, censorship, and civil liberties. Relative affluence; a new consumerism feeding off technological innovation; the rise of youth subcultures around varieties of popular music, philosophy, and fashion; the massive expansion of education; increased arts funding; television; and a marked development of the genre of political satire, all helped finally to bring to an end the more deferential and consensual culture which had been gradually eroded since the early fifties.

Aside from the somewhat tawdry glamour of the commercial youth culture of 'swinging London', one of the major sources for the construction of a myth of the New Age was the idea of 'the counterculture'. This reached its apogee in the student protests of the late sixties and was given retrospective and definitive identity in Theodore Roszak's 1970 book *The Making of a Counterculture*. Its subtitle (*Reflections on the Technocratic Society and its Youthful Opposition*) gives some sense of the countercultural ethos and of the composition of its adherents. These ranged from R. D. Laing, David Cooper, and Aaron Esterton, the most distinctive voices of the anti-psychiatry movement, to the radical philosopher Herbert Marcuse, and included an assortment of co-opted or fellow-travelling voices as diverse as

Timothy Leary speaking for the drug culture, the poetry of Allen Ginsberg, the theology of Martin Buber, and the visionary sociology of Paul Goodman. Yet a question which must be addressed more thoroughly once we come to examine the literature of the sixties is why the more heady utopianism of the counterculture was kept generally at arm's length by a British intelligentsia largely sympathetic to the retreat from total commitment to scientific progress and social planning? Suffice it to say here that the ideological impact, particularly of the popular arm of the counterculture, was curiously muted or treated with suspicious irony in many of the prominent literary works of the sixties and seventies.

Both the intellectual and the more popular branches of the counterculture launched a critique of technocracy which was anchored in a Rousseauistic belief in the possible liberation of an essentially whole but repressed self. For the student movement, as for radicals such as Herbert Marcuse and Norman O'Brown, salvation would only be found in a return to the Romantic and German Idealist belief in spiritual liberation. For most of these thinkers, such ideals had been sacrificed in subsequent anti-humanist and 'scientific' misreadings of the works of Karl Marx by socialist ideologues. For the counterculturalists, barricades must temporarily go up in order that what Marcuse described as the one-dimensional barriers of 'repressive tolerance' might come down. Only then might the full human spirit (and body) be liberated from a narrow confinement to the dictates of a functionalist rationality.

By 1968 the radical psychiatrist R. D. Laing had moved away from his earlier work and toward a psychedelic mysticism, but his idea of the self continued to carry an important force for most counterculturalists. His notion that insanity is not an abandonment of the real but a potentially intelligible attempt to achieve ontological security through the expression of a self fragmented by the pressures and violences of a competitive and exploitative society was one of the most influential theses to come out of the radical movements of the sixties. It would influence a number of writers during the decade, including the dramatist Edward Bond and the novelist Doris Lessing. Laing's early ideas were in fact shaped by his reading of the first volume of Sartre's *Critique de la raison dialectique* published in 1960 and by a number of case histories written by

Sartre in the years before its publication. These included an analysis of the chameleon-like shifts of identity in the writer Jean Genet, which were viewed as a means of dealing with the engulfment and terror exercised over him by an oppressive and cannibalistic society. If society traps the self in false boundaries, then the self must respond by continuously shifting or breaking down those boundaries.

Barriers, thresholds, and doorways, which must be blown up or broken down, are pervasive metaphors throughout the countercultural manifestos of the time: William Blake was invoked so that the doors of perception might be cleansed (whether through drugs or poetry); followers of Laing at the Tavistock Clinic analysed the false and conformist ego produced through the internalization of a repressive social 'reality principle' and promised liberation through the breakdown of the 'divided self' into a purifying madness. Herbert Marcuse added his influential voice to a continuing European dissident tradition. Since the work of the Frankfurt school of critical theory in the thirties, this movement had developed a critique and analysis of what it saw as the violence and political exclusion perpetrated in the name of a social rationalization dedicated to planning the good society supposedly founded on the principles of liberty and equality.

Though the counterculture was to be short-lived and, as we shall see in a later chapter, to fall prey to commercial appropriation, New Left critique, and later right-wing exploitation (social breakdown in the eighties was continually blamed on the seeds sown by the libertarianism of the sixties), it has remained a powerful aspect of the popular mythologization of the decade. In popular consciousness at least, its utopian image has tended to overshadow the pervasive economic and political pessimism of the period as well as the profound dystopianism of much of the highbrow and middlebrow literature. We shall see almost a Jacobean Faustianism in many literary works of the time, perhaps reflecting the dominant mood of the liberal intelligentsia that it had indeed seen the best of its time and that ruinous disorder must follow inevitably to the grave. Literary culture was rife with disaffection at the inadequacies of the Welfare State, the contradictions of a sagging liberalism, the apocalyptic legacy of Hiroshima, the evil incarnate of Auschwitz and Belsen, the perceived threat from technologized mass cultures. Both traditional religion and rationalized secular culture appeared to have failed to provide a foundational value-system which could anchor a fragmenting society whose new technologies had unleashed unprecedented horrors and thrown up unresolvable ethical dilemmas.

So, despite Macmillan's famous reminder in the late fifties that Britons had never had it so good, W. H. Auden expressed a view rather more representative of the literary intelligentsia on the eve of the new decade when he wrote, in April 1959, that 'there has never been a time, I believe, when the present and the future of the whole human endeavour on this earth have seemed questionable to so many people'.[1] The American economist Galbraith had already, in 1958, summed up the time as one of 'public affluence and private squalor'. Even by 1964, and despite Harold Wilson's promises of gustier trade winds which would sweep up the dead leaves and Edwardian debris of the Macmillan years, it became increasingly apparent that the post-war settlement had failed to establish the promised golden age of prosperity, national unity, and economic equality. In 1945 Beveridge had announced a commitment to a welfare state which would crown that sense of national unity achieved during the Second World War. His report of 1942 had enshrined the ideal of common citizenship and the universality of newly framed individual and social rights, including provision of healthcare, education, housing, leisure and arts funding, support for the unemployed, and childcare facilities. This superstructure would rest on an economic base, broadly Keynesian, with a commitment (in theory at least) to intervention from the constitutionally elected state in a forwardly planned economy in pursuit of an ideal of full employment with low inflation and a welfare state supported by a mixed economy.

Macmillan had declared in 1959 that the class war was over thanks to a national unity achieved through the so-called 'Butskellite' Labour–Conservative consensus of the fifties. Once again, though, a rather different story will emerge once we come to examine some of the literature of the sixties. Richard Hoggart's picture of the consumer-driven erosion of working-class community in *The Uses of Literacy* (1957) would be echoed in the writing of Arnold Wesker, Nell Dunn, David Mercer, David Storey, John Arden, and many others. Even by the late sixties, less than 10 per cent of the population would still own more than 80 per cent of the wealth (a fact enshrined in the title of the agitprop theatre company 7 : 84). More-over, not only did the old class divisions persist under the guise of new appearances; other forces actually unleashed by the economic and social settlements of 1945 were producing what seemed un-avoidably, by the sixties, to be effects of cultural fragmentation rather than those of national unity. From the mid-sixties the youth culture which fed off the new commercialism and fed into the countercultural utopianism was gathering force with an impetus enabled by the social and educational reforms of welfare capitalism. The comprehensiv-ization of schooling was well under way by the mid-sixties, by 1966 seven new universities had been founded, the Open University would begin teaching in 1971, and older universities expanded steadily after the Robbins report on higher education. The student generation which was the progeny of the Welfare State reforms, however, seemed set on playing the role of prodigal child. Politicians were seen to embody that Victorian paternalism which must be flouted, and to be young was such very heaven that 'hope I die before I grow old' began as a pop song and ended as a teenage homily.

The very forces liberated by the welfare capitalist compromise and stimulated by the growth of technologized consumerism would eventually fragment from within its commitment to the long front of a universal culture where a consensually validated High Art would be made available to all, on the understanding that, in the words of the dramatist Arnold Wesker, it might give to people the feeling 'that they are part of a whole group, which is humanity'.[2] What seems evident in retrospect is that, whether one sees the legacy as a morbid threat to social unity or as a curative boost to cultural health, the harvest of the sixties included a number of hybrids, variegated strains, and exotic new fruits which simply did not fit into any of the old categories. In later chapters we will see how the categories them-selves had to change in order to accommodate the new goods. The sixties provided less the opportunity to cement social unity through participation in a national culture than the chance to pursue indi-vidual or subcultural paths to liberation from it: consumer liberation from post-war austerity; cultural liberation from leisure-class values; sexual liberation from Victorian mores; and a celebration and mak-ing of the new, of youth, technology, design, and fashion.

Writers, however, tended to dwell on the negative aspects of such fragmentation: realists explored the failure of successive governments to address the underlying contradictions of the post-war settlement and fantasists exposed the spiritual bankruptcy of a Western consciousness caught between the rationalist utopianism of the planners and the anti-rationalist excesses of counterculture, swing, and underground. As we shall see in the next three chapters, absurdism, Gothic, the grotesque, extremism, the theatre of cruelty, the poetry of diminished expectation, apocalyptic fantasy, self-reflexivity, empty ritual, and absurd repetition were just some of the literary modes explored and developed in this writerly expression of the Faustian side of the sixties. Any brief survey of the key texts written between 1959 and 1964 will confirm that there is certainly not much swing or utopianism in evidence. There is the impersonalized violence of *A Clockwork Orange* (1962); the social and personal fragmentation of *The Golden Notebook* (1962); the territorial atavism of *The Caretaker* (1960); fantastic apocalyptic xenophobia in *The Old Men at the Zoo* (1961); the class conflicts or anger in the work of Wesker, Storey, and Arden; deflated urban pastoral in Larkin's welfare-world Waste Land; the savage *danse macabre* of Murdoch's high bourgeois intelligentsia in *A Severed Head* (1961); brute Darwinian survivalism in the poetry of Hughes; and gender anger with no available politically formulated vehicle for its expression in the linguistic extremism of Plath. Though anger and apocalypse subside somewhat by the end of the decade, they are simply mitigated by nihilistic anarchism in Orton; philosophical relativism in Stoppard; continuing aetiolated minimalism in Beckett; tortured sexuality in Golding; and an increasingly self-conscious awareness of the dangerously Fascistic political implications of the uses of myth and fictionality in the analysis of power in works by Edward Bond, Muriel Spark, Iris Murdoch, and John Fowles.

New Times: 1976 and the 'Break-up' of Britain

Rather than pursue imaginary moments of absolute crisis and change, however, it may be more useful to attempt some understanding of the interrelationships between the various political and cultural paradigms which shape the sense of a period. Clearly, there were both swinging and underground Londons between 1964 and 1968 (Carnaby Street, the Rolling Stones, the Beatles, Andy Warhol imitators, pop art, the poetry of the 'The Children of Albion', *Oz*, and the drug scene) and there was undoubtedly too a marked shift in social mores and lifestyles which partly arose out of this consumer-driven individualism but equally out of a collectivist resistance to it. Outside this largely hedonistic commercial culture and the newly urgent libertarianism, however, persisted a rather more austere, still influential if modified, dissident culture of middle-class liberal disaffection with roots in an Arnoldian and Leavisite belief that literature, as the best that has been thought and said, might still save us. And behind each of these emergent, oppositional, or dissident cultures continued an official adherence to economic, political, and cultural assumptions about consensus which, though fragmenting since the fifties, would not be fundamentally challenged until the mid-seventies.

The literature of the period both reflects and is a constitutive factor in the shaping of these various stories of the age, and the stories themselves tend to be reordered pragmatically by later storytellers making sense of their own histories. Any period of history is always in part a construction from within an age of its own sense of itself: a number of explanatory paradigms across the spheres of politics, economics, culture, and society will compete for dominance. In turn, such paradigms inevitably come under the scrutiny of later historical commentators who are themselves in part (and unconsciously too) determined by what they survey. Any attempt to understand an age from within will unavoidably be implicated in a never-ending and finally impossible unravelling of theorizations and myths which operate as much to constitute the identity of a time as to offer a commentary upon that identity. Moreover, to write a history of one's own time is to be more than usually aware of the impossibility of any deistic perspective upon events.

Indeed, consciousness of such a condition of interiority and implication has in any case been peculiarly acute in the period under survey in this book. It has certainly been a major preoccupation of many writers and intellectuals to be examined here. Despite the transcendent claims of popular counterculturalists, it would seem that for the majority of writers there could be no liberating Ariadne's thread leading to certain points of exit from the dark labyrinth of theoretical hypothesis and into the bright light of historical fact or metaphysical truth. As we see from even this brief introductory historical survey, moments of resolution constructed for one paradigm (1947 as significant in world-historical terms) may seem less crucial for the next (1964 as the beginning of swing and the permissive era and an emphatic shift in social mores), or implicated in but subordinate to events in yet another (1976 as the final breakdown of the post-war domestic political culture of consensus). Perhaps the greatest virtue in approaching a period through its literature is that literary texts have always indirectly connected and confronted paradigmatic contradictions, fraying the trimmed and well-groomed positivistic account of history as a series of formulated periods or a unilinear chain of moments of crisis.

Works of literature facilitate a perspectival reading of the times even if they (consciously or otherwise) present as universal, experiences which arise out of the practices of particular social groups within a culture. Retrospectively, what seems exciting about the literature of 1960–90 (though for some no doubt depressing and threatening) is that there was an accelerating and dramatic expansion, particularly from the late seventies, of the range of social groups and voices demanding to be included within the category of the literary and thereby challenging its traditional representative democracy. The effect, as we shall see, has been to contribute to a feverish and florid condition diagnosed by Bernard Bergonzi as 'exploding English'. However, literary texts articulate their time through modes of indirection, metaphor, and counterfactuality, presenting the 'imaginary' hinterlands of everyday rationalized history. It would be pointless to read them as a diagrammatic map of the time or indeed to believe that one could reverse the relationship and entirely understand the history of a period simply by reading its literature.

The significant moment of one group or person may look very different through the eyes of another. The intellectual disenchantment of the period was variously expressed in ways specific to individual groups. As many post-1968 ex-'grammar-school-boy' male students went into 'post'-modern decline in the seventies, for example, the newly optimistic perspective from feminism seemed very different. Similarly, as feminism largely failed to broaden its class base in the eighties, some of the more heady utopian celebrations of *écriture féminine* came to seem historically blind and politically simplistic to socialists engaged in a critique of Thatcherism. Such perspectival disconnections represent both causes and effects of the gradual breakdown of cultural consensus, a process which in itself has been welcomed as liberationist by some and condemned by others as the symptom of a crippling cultural relativism. In this respect, and to pick up the earlier search for significant markers of history, we should now move on to the seventies and eighties and in particular to the year 1976. It is this year more than any other perhaps which emerges as the moment when the culturally diasporic effects of the sixties gathered into combustion with the individualism and rising monetarist economics of the mid-seventies to bring to an end the stable foundation of cultural assumptions upon which had rested the apparently unified ideals of post-war collectivist social reform. It is no coincidence that Edgar's play with which we began was first performed in September 1976.

The year 1976 was a troubled one in British politics, though its full significance would not become immediately apparent. Although heralded by the new scions of Friedmanite monetarism for some years, it was perhaps not until May 1979, when Margaret Thatcher was elected Prime Minister, that political commentators began to register that an era was indeed at an end and another historical threshold crossed. Actually, since the mid-seventies a steady theoretical rejuvenation of Conservative thought, which placed economic over personal liberties and rejected the market planning of Keynesianism, had been gathering force. In this new monetarism, the market was regarded as a self-correcting mechanism requiring minimal state intervention and planning. Poverty was conceived not as a correctable social evil but as a fact of life. Indeed, the pursuit of social justice was actually claimed by some theorists of the New Right to be destructive of morality, for, in eroding individual incentive, socialist policies were seen to remove freedom of choice and to allow one social group to impose its own criteria of redistribution on others.

With the election of Margaret Thatcher in 1979, the era of monetarism arrived. Although later to claim that she had 'always regarded individualism as a Christian mission',[3] she made no such announcement at this stage, but began immediately to identify heretics, the old Heathite Tory 'wets', and to eliminate them from her cabinet. In the spirit of one leading her children to the Promised Land, she gathered together her tabernacle and set about ridding the country of its plagues of corporate Fabian planners and oligarchies of Tory squires. If the sixties, in popular consciousness at least, had been the swinging years, the eighties were to be those of 'enterprise'. Yet even this apparent watershed carried with it as many continuities as discontinuities. It is arguable that Mrs Thatcher simply inherited and accelerated political and social trends well under way before 1979. Two years earlier Tom Nairn had announced the final 'break-up of Britain',[4] the end of a post-war consensus whose mosaic pieces had finally become absolutely unstuck. By 1975 unemployment figures were the highest since the war. In 1976 James Callaghan had taken over as Prime Minister, inheriting the industrial fall-out from the Heath years (the miners' strike, the three-day week, the oil crisis, inflation, and growing unemployment), an IMF crisis which paraded to the world the limitations of Keynesianism, a nineteenth-century concept of the nation state now increasingly untenable in the face of global technologies and international finance, racial tensions and inner-city breakdown, devolutionary crises in Scotland and Wales, the Troubles in Northern Ireland, an irreconcilable split in the Labour Party as divisive as that of the Old and New Right within the Conservative, and a 'national culture' fragmented not only into the divisions of labour and capital, but also into contestatory subcultures, classes, and groups, representing seemingly incommensurable value-systems, lifestyles, ideals, and beliefs. A 'total eclipse' seemed finally to have obliterated from view that vision of a common culture projected by the planners of 1945, the liberal middle classes of the fifties, and the New Left of the sixties. Britain had entered new times, and the mood was and has remained one of transition.

The Rise of the New Right

Edgar's play *Destiny*, performed in 1976, uncannily grasped the deep undercurrents of political change gathering at that time, though it was possible only for the Angel of History to foresee the profound impact which Mrs Thatcher's particular brand of personal conviction politics was to have on the legacy of the political disaffections of the mid-seventies. *Destiny* is prefaced with two excerpts from Conservative statements of the fifties. The first is from the Party Manifesto of 1950, declaring itself to be 'by long tradition and settled belief . . . the Party of the Empire' and proclaiming an 'abiding faith in its destiny'. The second is a quotation from Peregrine Worsthorne, a Conservative commentator, written some nine years later: 'The Right is acutely aware that the kind of Britain it wishes to preserve very largely depends on Britain remaining a great power . . . Everything about the British class system begins to look foolish and tacky when related to a second-class power on the decline.'

The play proceeded to examine the frustrations and disappointed hopes which were the legacy of the disintegration of the imperialist myth and which fed into the rise of National Front politics as into the new brutal commercialism. It plots the fortunes of three ex-army members of different rank as they respond to the loss of Britain's imperial image after 1947 within the social and political constraints of the post-war Welfare State. The midnight stroke which ushers in the new India simultaneously removes from its old colonialist masters the very foundations of their national identities. Each character is in turn brought to recognize that the old imperial dream can no longer continue to function as the mainstay of British national unity, but that the emotions invested in such dreams require new objects of attachment: these are provided in the shape of an unbridled entrepreneurialism, racial hatred, hardnosed international financial transactions, and a realigned and commercially driven class war. One of the three central characters, Colonel Chandler, is an example of what, in the eighties, would be seen by the New Right as one of the old wets. Faced with 'another England | Rough and Raw | Not gentle, sentimental as before,' he stands up at the beginning of the play, offers a panegyric to a lost world, and bows off the stage of history: 'Colonel Chandler, past his prime: | Dignified. Worthy. Out of time. | Colonel Chandler, oyster-eyed, | One fine summer morning, died.' Major Rolfe, meanwhile, 'condemns the mindless comforts of a flaccid, sponger's state' and 'despairs of trendy idiocies repeated as a rote', blaming the paralysis as much on the 'whole social-democratic demonology of workers good and bosses bad' as on the Chandlers of England who still have the 'knot of old school tiredness . . . tight round England's throat'. Rolfe sums up the mood of disaffection and the fears of social breakdown of a considerable proportion of the British population in the mid-seventies.

Wage control collapses, unemployed take over factories, council tenants massively refuse to pay their rents, in name or not, another General Strike, the pound falls through the floor, the English pound, the English river's burst its English banks . . . So what d'you do? You either let the deluge, deluge, or you build a dam against it. Mmm?

Another dramatic work of the mid-seventies which analysed the drift of the times even before the appearance of Mrs Thatcher, was David Hare's *Teeth N' Smiles* first performed in 1975. An ironic elegy to a counterculture now seen to have been bought off by commercial interest, the play marked the beginning of that recognition of the effectiveness of capitalism in subsuming and negating oppositional ideologies. Within the left, it was partly this recognition which would precipitate the post-modern crisis of the left in the New Times eighties. If the early sixties had seemed, for a short time, to be the blissful dawn of a new age when to be young was indeed presented as a celestial state, then the stern rise of the New Right might be seen as the return of an admonishing Yaweh come to remind the recreational children of Albion that it is the doers and not the dreamers who shall inherit the land. If the counterculture had spoken an anti-corporate libertarian individualism which always sat uneasily with its avowed collectivist egalitarian sentiments, then the new monetarists could congratulate themselves for their foresight in trusting to the market to expose the lurking contradictions in the welfare capitalist compromise. Youth revolt was good for business, and libertarianism itself was a spur to an economic blueprint dependent on the encouragement of individualist impulses which could be rechannelled into a manifesto of 'no ideas but in money'.

Hare's play, published in the year of the subcultural and anarchic explosion of punk (1976), satirized the tainted utopianism of a jaded protest rock band in the countercultural year of 1969. The band are seen to be exploited by their entrepreneurial manager Serafian for whom they are 'just merchandise' but are also victims of the similarly nihilistic and rhetorically empty revolutionism of the drug culture. The only character, Maggie, who sees beyond and explicitly repudiates the rhetoric knows that to see is not necessarily to reach. She sings a final 'last orders on the Titanic', knowing that those who are most hydrogenated with empty eloquence will be the same ones who are kept afloat by it when that ship which is Great Britain finally sinks.

Indeed, part of the success of the New Right lay in its effective appropriation of the rhetoric of libertarianism inherited from the sixties. A vocabulary of freedom and individualism had been expanded in the sixties and, even as the utopianism of the decade faded, its rhetoric could be exploited by transference from the context of counterculturalist critique to that of monetarist *realpolitik*. At the very absent heart of the New Right war against the social engineers of the post-war consensus (and in particular the defensive corporatism of Edward Heath) was an avowedly moral appeal (based on F. A. Von Hayek's *The Road to Serfdom*) against economic planning as a threat to individual liberty. An off-the-peg vocabulary of libertarianism was there for the taking, and the only effort required was in prising it away from the earlier counterculturalist roots by castigating the 'permissive' sixties (and thus hardening the myth) as the source of every evil which increasingly beset civil society in the acquisitive individualist eighties: terrorism, football hooliganism, racial violence, escalating crime, rising divorce rates, homelessness. Once the libertarian vocabulary had been safely regrafted onto monetarist economic theory, then it could be put on the back shelf in order that the more substantial package of Victorian values might be brought on full display. For here was another ready-made vocabulary to be recycled as packaging for an authoritarian populism now deemed essential to hold together a society destabilized by the arrantly unpredictable energies of the ubiquitous Market.

If things were not to appear to be falling apart, the Thatcher thinktank precipitately recognized in the early eighties that the abandonment of macroeconomic planning (as a commitment to redistribution of incomes and resources) must entail a shift from corporate economic planning to authoritarian civil manangement. If the market was to be given a very long leash, civil society must be kept on a correspondingly short one. Nineteenth-century liberalism was fine in the economic sphere, but sixties' civil-rights libertarianism could only bring about the 'decay of the fabric of society', giving rise to dangerous critiques of the family and of law and order and an impertinent assumption of civil rights previously regarded as the gift of the state (or its reward offered for good behaviour). If the Beatles had been the 'unacknowledged legislators of populist revolt',[5] then Margaret Thatcher claimed to be the long overdue, corrective, and acknowledged legislator of populist authoritarianism: the 'Iron Lady' who had, as she put it, 'changed everything' and broken with the 'debilitating consensus' of the nanny state.[6]

By the time of her second term of office, contradictions were apparent between an economic libertarianism committed to the dismantling of welfare corporatism and a revitalized social authoritarianism bent on curbing opposition to state control (these were the years of Trade Union Acts, Local Government Acts, conflict with the BBC over the nature of its independence, the *Spycatcher* incident, and the tussle over GCHQ). It was also the moment when the sixties were most forcibly dragged back from the grave and that shibboleth of the New Right laid down: that the social breakdown of the eighties was the harvest reaped from the defective seeds of the sixties. In March 1982 Mrs Thatcher announced: 'We are reaping what was sown in the 1960s . . . The fashionable theories and permissive claptrap set the scene for a society in which the old virtues of discipline and self restraint were denigrated.'[7]

In the same month the British task force was sent into the Falkland Islands. The British popular press responded by reviving the sort of myths of imperial greatness which Edgar had analysed as so culturally and socially crippling to the nation after 1947. With Big Bang not far away and Margaret Thatcher's second term of office now secured, a new and gleaming current would flow more freely through the land: no more the quiet pastoral streams of rural England, but instead the rapid and unpredictable undertows of international money. From the war in 1982 arose the image of the new Boadicea, and with a shrewd pragmatism tempering the radical economic theory, Mrs Thatcher began to recognize the importance of mythic construction and the value of publicity. She continued to bend her rhetoric to connect with the popular mood of the times, wresting the vocabulary of freedom from the left and systematically denigrating the image of the caring state by reclothing it in the uniform of an infantilizing nanny.

The new ideology was savagely satirized in Caryl Churchill's neo-Jacobean City comedy of 1987, *Serious Money*, written at the moment of Big Bang (October 1986), which involved the deregulation of the City and the opening of its doors to outsiders who seemed to threaten to dismantle traditional hierarchies of stockbroking and to overturn entrenched class assumptions. The frenetic energy of the play, propelled by a breathless free verse erupting periodically into rhyming couplets and replete with dizzying flashbacks and forwards, conveyed the confused condition of the new financial melting pot. In the structure of the play, as in the dealings of the City, the substantial experience of existential presence is effectively erased as the hypothetical 'futures' are spun out of machines as inventive as the ambitious and upwardly mobile brains which control them. In the City itself, jobbers and stockers now mingled indiscriminately. Unearned income soared and a new breed of yuppies emerged, those young enough to survive the output of adrenalin required for dealing in the theoretical futures of the global markets which were changing second by second. If sixties' London had swung to the melodies of the Beatles and pop, then the vibrant hum of the twenty-four-hour day VDU was to provide the rhythm for the unprecedented, if short-lived, money explosion which gripped the capital like fever throughout the mid-to-late eighties. The City became the hub of a new global fiscal empire, credit promised to stop the gaps opened by lost manufacturing markets, the hypothetical became more important than the real, and London began to seem less the centre of a nation than an intersection point for a network of world markets and multinational corporations. Post-structuralist commentators could feel vindicated in their analyses of late capitalism as an economy of signs or knowledge, economists reassured of the accuracy of their predictions of an accelerated shift from a manufacturing to a service economy. And in the words of Zac in Churchill's play, one of the (*rentier*) new on whom assurance sits even more firmly than the 'silk hat' of T. S. Eliot's (cotton-manufacturing) 'Bradford millionnaire': 'The British Empire was a cartel. I England could buy whatever it wanted cheap I And make a profit on what it made to sell I The Empire's gone but the City of London keeps I On running like a cartoon cat off a cliff— bang. I That's your Big Bang. I End of the City cartel. I Swell.'

If *Destiny* and *Teeth N' Smiles* seemed to suggest that neither the counterculture nor the post-war settlement had actually constituted a watershed in British politics and society, Churchill's play *Serious Money* (though written from within the enterprise years rather than as a retrospective account of them) did assert the radical effects of the monetarist regime. Certainly as far as Mrs Thatcher was con- cerned, though the decade of the sixties had brought with it a new image of youthful independence, as *political* history it had simply represented a deepening enslavement to the dependency culture of corporate socialism or welfare consensus established in 1945. For Margaret Thatcher in 1979, the real (meaning the economic) libera- tion was yet to come. Indeed, as far as she was concerned, the economic crises, industrial conflicts, and breakdowns of law and order which disrupted the seventies simply confirmed the view that, politically and economically at least, the sixties had revolutionized nothing. It simply became more openly apparent that the fragile compromises of the post-war consensus were fragmenting. It seemed as if the possessive individualism of capitalist goals and the collectivist ideals of social welfare could not continue to be wedded in the manner of the 1945 settlement. The marriage had broken down, and, for a time at least, Margaret Thatcher's term of office was able openly to replace the goals of consensus with those of possessive individualism or enterprise.

Despite such apparent political discontinuity, however, one of the striking continuities in the literature of the period 1960–90, and one which forcibly crosses the 1976 divide, is a powerful mood of cul- tural disaffection. If writers of the sixties and early seventies reveal a profound disaffection with the inadequacies of consensus, those of the later seventies and eighties respond similarly to the brutal acquisitiveness of the Thatcher years. There was a steady drift away from social realism, itself premised on a consensus aesthetics (narratorial reliability and authority, modulation and integration of points of view, the assumption of an intrinsic and even moral organic relationship between the form and structure of the literary text and relations in the world outside it), and toward modes of fantasy, self-reflexivity, absurdism, and the grotesque, on the one hand, or a modification of social realism but in the service of a political refusal of consensus as a statement of differential identity politics by minority groups on the other. While much of the writing of the former tends to be apocalyptic or concerned with the fragmentation of value and the loss of foundation, that of the latter, particularly of feminism or post-colonial writing in the eighties, however, is sometimes much more optimistic and upbeat in mood.

In the next chapter we will turn away, at least temporarily, from the discontinuities of the period and begin to look at some of the manifestations of cultural continuity (see Appendix, summarizing changes and continuities).

2 CONTINUITIES

CULTURE AND CHANGE 1960–1990

> VLADIMIR. Now what did we do yesterday evening?
> ESTRAGON. Do?
> VLADIMIR. Try and remember.
> ESTRAGON. Do ... I suppose we blathered.
> VLADIMIR [*Controlling himself*]. About what?
> ESTRAGON. Oh ... this and that, I suppose, nothing in particu-
> lar. [*With assurance*] Yes, now I remember, yesterday we
> spent talking about nothing in particular. That's been going
> on now for half a century.
>
> (Samuel Beckett, *Waiting for Godot*)

First noted by the American critic Lionel Trilling, the insight that
the theme of all modern literature since Romanticism has been its
own quarrel with modernity seems now to be almost a commonplace
in literary criticism. Trilling observed that, in a disenchanted world,
literature expresses the 'disenchantment of our culture with itself'.[1]
Milton's Satan provided for the Romantics a powerful and fascinating image not only of an hubristic and alienated rebel, but also of the
modern condition *per se*: bereft of God and plunging into that bottomless perdition which is the non-foundational cosmos of the self.
As Romanticism was revived in the idealistic counterculture of the
sixties, in the work of Marcuse or Roszak, for example, so the dia-
bolic fears of its darker side tended to surface within literary cultures
from 1960 to 1990: thirty years when the net of Enlightened liberal
philosophies constructed to cushion the Satanic fall began to sag and
fray alarmingly. In 1974 the Marxist American critic Marshall Berman
argued that Goethe's *Faust* was the most appropriate text to sym-
bolize the driven and dangerous overreaching of the dominant and
alternative cultures of the sixties.[2] Even in Britain, varieties of

apocalypse and fundamentalist gloom continued to be a strong feature of the literary culture of the time. Thematically, crisis was pervasive; stylistically, fantasy was on the increase. By the mid-seventies a bewildering array of self-reflexive technical strategies creating effects of infinite regress would express the collapse of certain belief that political and ethical systems could be grounded in either the received wisdom of religious authority or the a priori truths of rational scepticism.

However, as indicated earlier, facile homogenizations may be useful critical strategies, but they inevitably privilege particular moods and voices over others. As we shall see in the course of this study, it has not been all gloom. In 1925 D. H. Lawrence had prophesied that 'the relation between man and woman will change for ever, and will be the new central clue to human life'.[3] In many ways 1960–90 proved Lawrence right, and gender change was a prominent theme in literature, just as literary texts, in challenging 'myths of woman', were contributory forces precipitating and sustaining such change. But gender was not the only 'problem with no name' (to use Betty Friedan's phrase of 1962) that called for linguistic redress.[4] Class, ethnic, racial, familial, sexual, and peer-group relations were similarly transformed. Indeed, fixed assumptions about human relationships as customarily defined and bound by obligation increasingly gave way to the idea of self and other as continuous processes of exchange and negotiation. Marriage was no longer the thematic mainstay of the novel, and, if romance plots flourished, it was usually in ironic or inverted forms. After the liberationist movements of the sixties, feminism in the seventies, and the continuing steady demise of the economically functionalist model of the traditional nuclear family, those writers who persisted in penning unreconstructed nineteenth-century domesticated romance-quest plots began to look decidedly dated.

That a crisis in social relations was under way seemed incontrovertible, but crises may represent loss, fear, or nostalgia for one group or individual, and undreamt-of possibility and liberation for others. As modernist writers like James Joyce had recognized some fifty years earlier in the formal play with concepts such as parallax (in *Ulysses*, 1922), perspectival seeing is determinative of what is to be seen. In Chapter 6 we will see why some of the most optimistic writing of the period has been by women, and in particular feminists, whose relation to the loosening of the consensual centre was hardly likely to be coloured primarily by a bereft mood of nostalgia. As feminist historians have persuasively demonstrated, since women had continued to be positioned on the domestic and private side of the liberal public–private split of modernity, they were unlikely to share in the nostalgia over its fragmentation. Joyce's Molly challenged assumptions about correct marital behaviour for women, but she remains embedded (and in her bed) in the sphere of domesticity and sexuality throughout *Ulysses* and is not even allowed the public persona of Baudelairean *flâneur* accorded to her husband Leopold. Post-colonialists, like feminists, would come to challenge the validity and construction of such notions of the public and private and to attempt to imagine new social identities and roles. Post-Leavisites railed against the deleterious effects of television, but dramatists such as David Mercer, Dennis Potter, and Trevor Griffiths enthusiastically explored its capacity to combine the private readerly experience of intimacy with the visually panoramic and global potential of film. Though many writers certainly expressed disaffection, they also drew on the potential of literature to be what Octavio Paz has called 'the other voice' of (secular, rationalized) modernity, to express, like many of the popular subcultural movements of the time, utopian or heterotopian alternatives to it.

Cultures of Disaffection

Even if one accepts the validity of the above argument, however, it still remains true to say that the dominant mood of literature from 1960 to 1990 was indeed one of disaffection if not outright apocalypticism. The nature of this disaffection shifted during the period and the rest of this book will explore its various expressions, but this section will concentrate on the poetry of Philip Larkin, Martin Amis's novel *Money* (1984), and David Lodge's *Nice Work* (1988). Although written from both sides of 1976, these literary works suggest a continuing writerly preoccupation across the entire period with the contradictions of a liberal capitalist culture uneasily suspended between the competing claims of individualistic desire and a more communitarian vision of the collective good. Each work seems to illustrate very well Trilling's point that modern literature has been carved out of the quarrel with modernity.

What gradually passed away in the sixties to release a variegated surge of subcultural expressions of disaffection was a dominant political culture of deference. The Director-General of the BBC stated his desire to 'open the windows and dissipate the ivory tower stuffiness' of that public institution and, on schedule, there appeared a sudden and remarkable resurgence of mordant political satire.[5] Television programmes such as *That Was the Week that Was* and magazines such as *Private Eye* (from 1962) seemed an astonishingly progressive questioning and loosening of authority, a democratization of that refusal of deference initiated in the mid-fifties by existentialism, the Angry Young Men, the New Left, and the subcultures of teenage rebellion, but much more shocking when viewed on publically accountable service broadcasting. Television satire helped to launch a whole series of damning anatomies of Great Britain and, in particular, assaults on the aristocratic ineffectuality of Harold Macmillan, presiding over a stagnant and declining nation. Satire in the sixties paved the way for later and even more outspoken critiques of political authority, though again, its impact must be assessed in specifically historical terms. What seemed unequivocally progressive and democratic in 1962 may appear less so in the mid-nineties. If *That Was the Week that Was* helped to create a climate of political free discussion, it also initiated a trend which would be confirmed in the eighties and nineties by such television programmes as *Spitting Image* and popular youth-appeal satiric magazines such as *Viz*. It is less clear that the viz. of these later offerings delivered constructive criticism of state authority than that it exerted a potentially disabling effect on effective citizenship. Matters of state were often indiscriminately reduced to caricature in a culture which increasingly witnessed a continuous *ad hoc* conversion of political principles and vital social issues into jokes or absurdities for humorous dismissal and throwaway consumption.

All caricature makes the point that politics is performance. After 1976 politics became more performative than ever, with eventual televising of House of Commons debates, three-minute news-'bites', staged television discussion predictably presenting a balanced view, and endless opinion polls. That politics has become performance, however, does not limit the extent to which politicians, as agents of the state, increasingly penetrated into the everyday lives of citizens. *Spitting Image* effectively conveyed the absurd performance which is politics. Yet, as all became grist to the satiric-comic mill, in a culture already self-conscious and increasingly cynical, trivial and serious were so indiscriminately conflated that the possibility was insidiously eroded of a considered response to major political and ethical issues by audiences functioning as concerned citizens. The message could simply be read as 'politics is a joke, ignore it'. Resistance would thus be silently foreclosed and another contribution made to what one political commentator saw as the now 'deadly disconnection between serious policies and democracy' in a Britain where the 'gap between government and governed looms wider than ever' and where the nation was 'run by one of the most centralised and least accountable systems in the industrial world'.[6]

Disaffection seemed to be endemic to the times, yet, as this discussion suggests, expressions of it sometimes and paradoxically functioned to strengthen as much as weaken the object of disaffection. The poetry of Philip Larkin is an interesting case in point. Although, in the eighties, critical opinion of Larkin's verse shifted to an emphasis on the subterranean symbolist hints of a yearning for some transfiguration of the commonplace, its earlier reception tended to stress the parochialism of a writer incapable of any self-confirmatory belief in the transcendent power of art within a planned and rationalized secular society. Critics seeking to promote a more international outlook for poetry (looking to Americans such as Berryman, Lowell, and Sexton) were particularly hostile to what they saw as the ineffectual whimperings of a defensive Little Englandism. Alvarez dismissed Movement writing such as Larkin's as 'academic-administrative verse', and Charles Tomlinson saw in the poets of the first *New Lines* anthology edited by Robert Conquest (1956), a 'failure of nerve' which removed any possibility of 'escape beyond the suburban mental ratio which they impose on experience'.[7] In a later and even more damning critique in Boris Ford's Leavisite *Pelican Guide to English Literature* (1973), Tomlinson argued that the tenderly nursed and defeatist disaffection of Larkin's poetry was indeed the perfect expression of post-war Englishness. Readers could recognize 'their own abysmal urban landscapes, skilfully caught with just a whiff of English films circa 1950'. Tomlinson regarded Larkin's poetry as a confirmation of predictable national vices: the 'stepped-down version of human possibilities' and the 'joke that hesitates just on this side of nihilism'.

Larkin published two volumes of verse in the sixties and seventies, *The Whitsun Weddings* (1964) and *High Windows* (1974). What is immediately evident in both is Larkin's concern to express a disaffection with cultural inadequacies which had ironically already been seen as characteristics of Larkin's own poetic style. His poems castigate the culture for its mood of 'lowered expectations', while critics castigated Larkin's poetry for similar effects arising out of his 'less-deceived' mentality. As T. S. Eliot had later recognized after the publication of *The Waste Land*, the mood might be more a projection of the poet's mental condition onto the culture than a meditation on the culture outside his mental condition. Yet it seems just as likely that Larkin's defeatism was the expression of a proto-postmodern recognition of the inevitable complicity of any sustained cultural critique with its focus of discontent: that is, with the ethos of a (welfare) capitalist world which, as post-modern theorists would later argue, had already invaded the entire culture of the West. If this assumption resulted in a curbing of transcendent impulse in Larkin's poetry and a suspicion of Romantic and modernist myth-creation as of popular countercultural idealism, it also produced a version of late Romantic irony which would become a pervasive feature of much of the literature of the period. The earlier and later poems, with their double negatives, reductive modifiers, and vulgar vernacularisms, showed a continuing concern with the diminished possibilities and the unavailability of beauty in a planned world where customary practice is either ignored or has become a tawdry or empty ritual: poetry itself cannot avoid contamination.

The foundation, which 'will naturally bear your expenses' (even as it converts you into an 'academic-administrative' statistic), and the tranquil abundance of the 'cool empty store' have been planned to service all needs. Any impulse toward a Platonic 'essential beauty' is spuriously beguiled by consumer gratifications which provide a temporary natureless ecstacy (in 'Here'), one of the varieties of ersatz but convenient forgetfulness provided as distraction from the thoughts of 'all they might have done had they been loved' ('Faith Healing'). The neat urban 'postal districts' of *The Whitsun Weddings* are 'packed like squares of wheat', however: organic community invoked in an apparent *analogia entis* which actually calls up that sense of vacuity peculiar to urbanized pastoral. For this planned world is premissed on the assumption that in the gratification of the requirements of the body is fulfilled the entire rationale and justification for human existence. Larkin sees that the planners have abolished spirit and reduced need to material want. But the secularized world of institutionalized welfarism supposedly founded on a less-deceived mentality actually rests upon one of self-deception: the enigma of the confessional now irreligiously inhabits the closed NHS ambulances, with their blank and indifferent windows, efficiently removing the spectacle of human suffering and screening out the 'solving emptiness | That lies just under all we do'; death is lying 'unreachable inside a room'; love, hardly plenitude, is at best, and contradictorily, 'this unique distance from isolation'. Life is an oppressively enclosed space which yet inserts vistas of mental and imaginative distance between self and other, though it offers, as in 'High Windows', only momentary and imaginary glimpses of 'unfenced existence' beyond (and, even then, beyond words and beyond other people too).

Words cannot save us, but they may protect us, and Larkin's voices, his mimicry, vernacular, parody, protect the self from the terrifying exposure to the tragic emotions of pity and fear: risk of the loss of self in sympathy and identification, terror of the loss of the other in detachment and disconnection. Talk and chat oppose authentic 'being' but remove ultimate dread. The poems themselves move between conversational tones of complicity, moments of symbolist luminosity, and the mimicry of strained as well as urbane and polite distance. There may be sympathy for the effects of those forces pushing the young and hopeful always to the edges of their lives, but it is limited by Larkin's need for an imaginative distance

on their plight which expresses both his own sense of class difference and the fear that all difference has already been sacrificed anyway
to the democratizing dullness of a welfare culture ('Here', 'After-
noons'). The 'importance of elsewhere' must never be forgotten.
The fragile 'travelling coincidence' which is life appears through
both volumes in the flashes and glimpses which move momentarily
into the lens of what seems to be an ever itinerant observer. Sometimes it is a zoom lens, occasionally wide-angle, but always 'swerv-
ing' away and into a 'loneliness' which 'clarifies' ('Here'). Snapshots
are preferred, for the 'long perspectives' serve only to connect us
with loss, with the locked room of decorum and customary grace
which is a cherished (though probably inaccurate) image of the past
('Show Saturday', 'Aubade'). Larkin's people are shut into rooms:
even ageing and dying is an experience of 'having lighted rooms |
Inside your head' ('The Old Fools'). Larkin himself is caught help-
lessly between a dread of the claustrophobia of collective imprison-
ment and a fear of the agoraphobic dizziness induced by the impulse
to reach what is outside, 'the thought of high windows': and, beyond
the frame and the screens, what, terrifyingly perhaps, 'shows | Noth-
ing, and is nowhere, and is endless'.

Larkin's disaffection is with the spiritual vacuity of the welfare
world of material needs and wants, but his protective 'less-deceived'
pose is complicit with what is condemned and forestalls the expression of any alternative to it. He presents a world reduced simply
to an empty materialism, on the one hand, or a 'vast moth-eaten
musical brocade | Created to pretend we never die', on the other.
Custom is invoked and rites of passage marked, but their sacramental
force is 'going, going', brought out on special occasions only, a
'Show Saturday' awaiting dismantlement, with its mimetic fallacy
of 'long immobile strainings that end in unbalance'. Consensus was
the secular myth designed to displace the religious one. Both are
equally fraudulent and fragmenting, though religion at least seduced
with beauty. Larkin presents the promise of 1945, the optimistic
projection of national unity into a peacetime world of justice and
abundance, as simply a temporary refuge from something which is
actually 'nearly at an end' ('Ambulances'). Life remains 'first

boredom and then fear', class divisions are as great as ever ('Mr Bleaney', 'Dockery and Son'), industrial decline spills onto the land-scape ('acres of dismantled cars'), and paradise is a half-clad model on a poster of 'Sunny Prestatyn'. Neither nostalgically evoked custom nor the new permissiveness can confer meaning: mastery of world and self, of feeling, risk, hope, and the fear of dying, must be all. If giving and sympathizing are sometimes recommended, they are subordinate always to control. The tone of Larkin's disaffection was curiously in harmony with the planned world he found so alien.

Larkin's was hardly a lone voice of dissent from the Welfare State world of the sixties and seventies or from its permissive and con-sumerist subcultures. That a new world of tawdry desire had begun (like his version of sexual intercourse in 1963) to eat into the cus-tomary fabric of tradition was an opinion reiterated not only by politicians and self-appointed moral vigilantes such as Mary Whitehouse, but also by the popular and conservative quality press. Each attempted to relocate present disaffection in some convenient and absolute source in the past, a variety of the 'if only . . .' men-tality characteristic of individuals and even nations caught between worlds which can neither quite die nor yet be reborn. This sort of critique was to find intellectual rejuvenation, particularly in the eighties, in the 'cultural-heritage' romantic conservatism of the al-most self-parodic *Salisbury Review*, with its image of a lost England of country squires, pastoral bishoprics, and patriarchal family ritual. While the New Right blamed the sixties for loss of the work ethic and the decay of moral fibre, the ex-Peterhouse College members of the revamped old right censured the decade as responsible for the current swing to commercial values and the loss of traditional reli-gious authority. Economic self-interest was not in itself ruled to be a source of evil, so long as it was framed by a religious sanction legitimating a fundamental (and Powellite) 'consciousness of nation-hood' as the highest of cultural ideals.

In the eighties, however, it was not simply conservatives who attacked the sixties. From a position well to the left of Salisbury Tory revivalism, in one of the most coruscating literary critiques of monetarism, Martin Amis suggested in *Money* (1984) how the six-ties had exposed the spiritual void at the heart of secularized liberal culture and thus precipitated the invasion and occupation of the new evangelizing faith of pure monetarist economics. Like T. S. Eliot, who had used the same argument in *The Idea of a Christian Society* (1939) to account for the rise of Fascism, Amis condemned the moral laxity and complacency of liberal culture as much as the heartlessness of commercial enterprise and showed how the inadequacies of the former had led to the triumphs of the latter. His protagonist, John Self, is a child of the sixties, 'an obedient, unsmiling, no-comment product of the sixties' who has become an enterprise Peter Pan of the eighties, commanding large advances for the production of pornographic videos and television commercials (portrayed as more or less interchangeable commodities). He wakes each morning in an alcohol, drug, and nicotine world whose diversions are masturbation, sexual voyeurism, and taxi-travel across globally reiterated dirty cityscapes. He feels continuously 'invaded, duped, fucked around . . . violated', sensing an England 'scalded by tumult and mutiny, by social crack-up in the torched slums'. He would like to unlock the door of this prison. But money keeps him there. It pays for his chemical and sexual addictions and is itself the ultimate addiction, for there can never be enough of it and the more he acquires, as in Zeno's paradox, the further recedes satisfaction. The market is seen to depend on the stimulation of feelings of personal inadequacy in consumers who then pursue its chimerical material satisfactions, believing that in the disease itself may be discovered its homeopathic cure.

Amis shows that in a society where the predictable rituals of traditional life (transcendent religious value and committed relationships of love and obligation) have largely disappeared, money is pursued as an unholy grail, seducing with its own compensatory structures of reverse value: ritual, worship, commitment (to making more). But, like all addictions, that which promises autonomy and freedom comes to be the very prison which destroys the possibility of their realization. John Self yearns for escape, buying himself ever more of the distractions which keep him in the lotus-eating land turned sour from which he longs to sail. Moments of self-consciousness must be narcotized or painful perceptions rationalized away (often comically and contradictorily):

I realise when I can bear to think about it, that all my hobbies are porno-graphic in tendency. The element of lone gratification is bluntly stressed. Fast food, sex shows, space games, slot machines, video nasties, nude mags, drink, pubs, fighting, television, handjobs. I've got a hunch about these handjobs, or about their exhausting frequency. I need the human touch.

In a world of privatization, the self literally becomes an island, though one supplied by luxury goods: videos, fast cars, expensive junk food, executive hotel bedroom suites, designer drugs, electronic music. The world is both an extension of the body in its chaotic impulses towards pleasurable sensation, and a substitute for mind as the requirement of reasonable feeling becomes redundant:

that's what I'm letting you into, my private culture. Look at the state of it. It really isn't very nice in here. And that is why I long to burst out of the world of money and into—into what? Into the world of thought and fasci-nation. How do I get there? Tell me please. I'll never make it by myself. I just don't know the way.

Self enters a chemically induced fantasy tunnel of sex, drugs, and celluloid, but, though he hits bottom, it is to discover that the plot was never his own anyway and never can be: there is no actual escape from the world of money. He discovers only its other side, the underworld of bottomless perdition of London's destitute and homeless. The novel can be read as a twentieth-century gloss on the Satanic recognition that hell is inescapably oneself, but given the inflection of late capitalist possessive individualism. From slick urban operator to pavement down-and-out, John Self is still 'inner city' and adrift in a world where goods control lives. His London sits beneath a Dickensian chemical fog even thicker than that of *Bleak House* but without the glimmer of a self-sacrificial Esther Summerson to redeem it.

What is interesting about the example of disaffection voiced first in Larkin and then in Amis's work is that the style of each is argu-ably complicit with its object of critique. Larkin derides the less-deceived mentality born of Welfare State lowered expectation, yet his poetry has been criticized for its own deflation of transcendent impulse. Amis's satire of nihilistic commercialism and the culture of style and surface is developed in novels which eschew psychological depth and actually espouse the slick style of the urban operator (owing much to the stylistic complicity of American black-humour writers such as Kurt Vonnegut). Although, as we shall see, there was a stronger tendency in the earlier part of the period to believe in the possibility of a redeeming space outside rationalized or commercialized culture, a sense of the inescapable complicity of art in a debased consumer culture began to develop from the sixties. It was made fully explicit in those post-modern theories of the eighties which posited not only a breakdown of distinctions between critical and functionalist knowledge and therefore of belief in the transcendence or autonomy of art but also the universal invasion of capitalism, the inescapably social construction of all thought, the contestation of boundaries between high and mass culture, and the end of the idea that there are grand narratives of truth and freedom which can provide absolutely foundationalist or consensually binding legitimation for universal ethical and political systems.

Indeed, just as the 1890s had been the era of the 'New' (the New Woman, the New Age, the New Drama, the New Spirit, the New Unionism), the 1990s was the era of belatedness, of a generalized 'post'-condition, as history, Europe, Marxism, colonialism, modernism, Christianity, feminism, industrialism were claimed to be at an end or in a transitional or belated state. A number of novels of the eighties reflected this mood: Martin Amis's *London Fields* (1989) as well as *Money*; Ian McEwan's indictment of familial repression and disconnected object-relations as the ground of the Fascist politics of the patriarchal state in *The Child in Time* (1987); William Golding's vision of an ambiguous second coming in *Darkness Visible* (1979) and his excursion into the roots of British imperialism in *Rites of Passage* (1980); Margaret Drabble's analysis of fraying liberalism, marriage, and law and order in *The Radiant Way* (1987). All expressed varieties of profound disaffection with the entrepreneurial spirit of the eighties, though each seemed equally uncertain as to where to locate the blame. David Caute published a more focused and Disraelian critique of Thatcherism entitled *Veronica or the Two Nations* (1989). An interesting historical analysis of the uses of nostalgia to support forms of authoritarian populism was provided by Kazuo Ishiguro's *The Remains of the Day* (1989). This novel fictionalized a social psychological thesis (reaching back to the writings of Karl Jung and developed in the work of the Frankfurt school of critical theory) which suggested that the rise of National Socialism was in part facilitated by a conformist urgency to fill the vacuum left in the twenties by the demise of the authoritarian Victorian father. Ostensibly, the novel is simply the pastoralized tale of an obsessively conformist butler's subserviently blind and unwittingly self-destructive loyalty to an impeccable gentleman, his master, whose hierarchical amateur nationalism has led him into collaboration with National Socialism. Through the antiquated syntax and clipped precision of the butler's evasive and self-deceptive narration, the reader is brought to recognize the connections between emotional repression and political oppression: each is dependent on exclusive discourses where the limits of language foreclose the possibility of subversion or oppositional articulation. In this Hegelian parable of master–slave relations, Ishiguro constructed a fiction which examined the Fascistic implications of the moral and political uses of a traditional code of honour in modern and technologized societies. His parable is clearly relevant both to the hierarchical class politics of Britain and to those of expansionist imperialist Japan.

The social and cultural fragmentation of the eighties seemed to prompt a return of that mid-nineteenth-century genre, the industrial or 'condition-of-England' novel, though economists now referred routinely to a post-industrial world of 'flexible-accumulation' and '-rostering', where the consumer targeting of the wants of specific social lifestyle niches had transformed mass or Fordist industrial production. A wryly self-conscious intertextual condition-of-England novel of 1988 was David Lodge's *Nice Work*, which managed to integrate features of the campus novel of the post-sixties' student generation with reworked motifs from the nineteenth-century industrial novel as practised by Mrs Gaskell, Charlotte Brontë, Benjamin Disraeli, and Charles Dickens. Lodge's novel is prefaced with a quotation from Disraeli announcing the continued existence of 'Two nations, between whom there is no intercourse and no sympathy'. The representative of the modern academy, itself struggling to survive the onslaught of post-structuralist semiotics on the one hand and Thatcherite contraction and vocationalization of learning on the other, is a feminist English literature lecturer, Robyn Penrose, who specializes in the nineteenth-century industrial novel. She is sent once a week on a government 'shadow scheme' (designed to encourage connection of the circulating signs of cultural with those of industrial capital) to an engineering factory in the manufacturing conurbation of the West Midlands. The shadow is managing director Victor Wilcox, whose lessons in what Charlotte Brontë in *Shirley* referred to as 'something real, cool and solid' are, however, subverted by a growing romantic attachment to Robyn, whose own pedagogic certainties are equally challenged by what she encounters in the harsh industrial world of the West Midlands in 1986.

Impinging painfully on both these worlds of modernity, however, is the new post-industrial and post-Enlightenment realm of hypothetical 'futures' finance: the Big Bang world of the city inhabited by Robyn's brother Basil. Here, neither the academic text nor the machine part is an end-product of the work process, for all transactions and commodities exist only in the realm of pure signification. Even the class distinctions of an earlier modernity are being replaced by those of a new and brutal plutocracy. As knowledge itself becomes the most powerful if least stable commodity, the modern and tangibly productive worlds of Robyn and Vic are shown indeed to be shadows of each other: two sides of a modern political economy which is itself now paradigmatically under threat. If their encounter is brief, it is at least, and unlike those of the city, still humanly face to face. As Robyn learns the value of workaday metonymy and is forced to situate her idealized signifiers in an emphatically non-textual world of industrial production, so Vic begins to see in his newly defamiliarized factory an extended metaphor for the expression of a sense of disaffection which he now recognizes to be more than simply material. However, resolution at the level of character is given no macro-structural equivalent: Britian remains not only divided but even fragmenting. An academic theoretical critique which claims to have wiped out character (and authors too) is shown to be dangerously complicit with the dehumanizing drift of a monetarist economics which promises to be even more brutal than what it supplants. The novel's use of the present tense does not allow for final teleological certainty and the mood is one of transition. Yet its comic confrontations and uncertainties express a benevolent Horatian satire, and its plea for humane tolerance a resonant, if quiet, liberal *cri de cœur* in troubled times.

We have seen that there was no sudden literary watershed corresponding to the political shift in the mid-seventies from the compromise collectivism of welfare capitalism to the monetarist individualism of the New Right. Literary expressions of disaffection were prominent from 1960 to 1990, and it is evident even from literary texts of the time that the ideals of welfare capitalism were always far from the practice. The compromise was riven with internal strains even before the arrival of monetarism. In the eighties the newly emergent and almost dizzying diversity of literary voices did reflect the weakening of consensus politics, but also arose out of social and cultural trends gathering from much earlier. The rest of this chapter will begin of indicate some of these trends and the variety of literary responses to them.

Life as Literature

Andy Warhol announced in 1959 that ' "everything" can be art and art can be "everything" '.[8] Arnoldian cultural theory had always regarded art as a criticism of life and necessarily, therefore, set apart from it. We have already seen, however, how the concept of complicity began to creep into aesthetics from the sixties. In the influential title essay of *Against Interpretation* (1966), Susan Sontag argued that art must now be regarded as the extension of life and that 'interpretation is the revenge of the intellect upon art'. She saw art's capacity for sensory renewal rather than moral vigilance as vital to a culture dessicated by bureaucratic rationalization. Both Sontag and Warhol were influenced by Marshall McLuhan's argument that history is a succession of technological revolutions which extend the capacities of human beings for self-expression. Accordingly, she argued that it was pointless to withdraw into a pessimistic cultural conservatism about the new technological mass media, and more valuable to recognize that film, television, computer graphics, for example, had already aestheticized the raw material of 'high art' (that is to say, life) and that this recognition must now be embodied self-consciously in works of literature. Sontag was one of the first to argue that the particular form taken by earlier distinctions between mass or popular and high art might now be obsolete and a new criticism was needed to respond to a new art practice.

Similarly, John Fowles proclaimed, in what was probably the first 'historiographic metafiction', *The French Lieutenant's Woman* (1969), that 'fictionality is woven into all; I find this new reality or unreality more interesting'. He was only one of many writers who saw that, if literature still reflected a world, its mimeticism was a perverse one, for the world reflected was already thoroughly fictionalized, 'socially constructed' (Berger and Luckmann), and imbued with stories and narratives (Hayden White, Erving Goffman), so that any fact was already likely to exist as the projection of a theoretical construct.[9] Beckett's Unnameable had pondered thus upon the situation: 'The fact would seem to be, if in my situation one may speak of facts, not only that I shall have to speak of things of which I cannot speak, but also, which is even more interesting, but also that I, which is if possible even more interesting, that I shall have to, I forget, no matter.' He is caught between a sense of the exhaustion of positivism ('no matter') and the human limitations of rationalism ('I forget'), whilst recognizing the force of Wittgenstein's insight that 'whereof one cannot speak, thereof one must remain silent'. Even within a discourse of negativity, however, to speak is in some sense to be. Beckett's characters continued through the sixties to engage in their minimalist but obsessively repetitious discourses, addictively imposing on an increasingly entropic and unpredictable reality absurdly comi-tragic rituals which might provide, if not some measure of meaning, then at least the illusion of control. In a detraditionalized world, the self had become a reflexive narrative project requiring the continuous revision of biographical narratives.

While sociologists described modern culture in terms of a continuous disembedding from traditional structures and a concomitant reliance on expert discourses which not only make sense of, but actually construct, social reality, literature also took a markedly self-reflexive turn throughout the period. Poetry became linguistically self-conscious. Novels explored the tension between the desire to recover a realm of pure aesthetic experience and the unavoidable recognition that, in a secular age, fictions may degenerate into myths with frightening political consequences. Later writing explored the shift from an early sixties' faith in the possibility of liberating an essential self or ground of history, to the post-modern social constructivism which claimed that there could be no such essence and that history was a plurality of 'islands of discourse', a series of metaphors which could not be detached from the various institutionally produced languages brought to bear on it.

Just to prove that history too was now to be contemplated as a work of art and understood through the recognition of generic convention, the twentieth-century narrator of *The French Lieutenant's Woman* famously and flamboyantly transgressed ontological boundaries and entered the nineteenth-century world of history. Once straddled across the boundaries normally separating omniscient narrators from the worlds of their fictions, he proceeded to conduct conversations with the characters, even discussing their textuality through the lens of structuralist thinkers such as Roland Barthes or existentialist philosophers such as Sartre. (Indeed, from the vantage-point of reading this text in the mid-nineties, and as the structuralist moment has itself been brought to a close, another fascinatingly complex hermeneutic layer is added to its interpretative possibilities.) In B. S. Johnson's *Albert Angelo* (1964), the author even proclaimed a disgust with the inescapability of the condition of fictionality by exploding into the text with expletives of the order of 'fuck all this lying'. Malcolm Bradbury's *The History Man* (1975), focusing on the clouding of the ideals of the 1963 Robbins report on the expansion of higher education, portrayed a sixties' radical sociologist who opportunistically exploits the new democratic educational ethos and, in particular, the rhetoric of utopian redemptiveness in the popular Marxism of the time, but in order (and hypocritically) to deny in action both the contingency of experience and the validity of all but his own historical plots. A self-consciously presented nineteenth-century character, Miss Callendar, attempts through liberal humanist literary criticism to remind Howard of the openness of the text to multiple interpretation and of the importance of equality as well as liberty to social justice. Her very liberal tolerance, however (presented, as in Bradbury's earlier novel *Stepping Westward*, 1965, as confident in what it is opposed to but confused and unclear as to what it stands for), is the Achilles' heel which brings him victory. English Literature, English liberalism, and Miss Callendar herself are simultaneously and symbolically (and sexually) conquered.

While Bradbury's *The History Man* exposed the dangerous effects of unscrupulous Marxist historicizing, John Berger's *G* (1972) was a more positive affirmation of the humanist version of Marx's theory of history. Under the influence of the French *nouveau roman* and Brechtian theories of *Verfremdungseffekt*, however, Berger too abandoned the ordered Hegelianism prominent in the nineteenth-century European realist novel. History is explored as a narrative, and metafictional disruption reminds the reader that there are always alternative ways of writing it. Berger's novel, like that earlier example of metafiction, *Tristram Shandy*, incorporated extensive essayistic digression into its fictional universe, a literary tendency which would become even more marked in the eighties. Indeed, one of the most noticeable aspects of the relation between literature and criticism between 1960 and 1990 is that, as academic critics turned away from an interest in contemporary writing (particularly after the mid-seventies) and toward the theoretical projection and creation of their own imaginary worlds, so creative writers increasingly began to incorporate self-reflexive critical commentary into *their* fictional universes. The obvious intellectual precedent for this shift was in those post-Wittgenstein and anti-foundationalist philosophies which argued that all truth-claims are only ever truth-effects which are clearly fictions when viewed within the frame of a different language game. One of the consequences of this is that the distinction between aesthetic world-creating discourses and critical problem-solving ones begins to break down, and indeed this paved the way for that crisis in the legitimation of knowledge announced in Jean-François Lyotard's influential book of 1979, *The Postmodern Condition*, an intellectual position taken up with much urgency in the social and cultural theory of the mid- to late eighties.

However, there are other ways of viewing the implications of such tendencies within the literary sphere. From 1960 all academic discourses became more specialized and institutions of higher education were professionalized in order to house an increasingly enclosed guild of experts. Literary criticism was no exception. Some writers welcomed the critical indifference to contemporary literary writing which arose contemporaneously with the British critical 'theoretical revolution' of the mid- to late seventies. A. S. Byatt, for example, in a *New Review* Symposium on the state of fiction in 1971, argued that if 'criticism is getting feebler and less inventive' it was a positive blessing for creative writers. If criticism became less inventive in traditional areas, however, it aspired to be more radically improvisational in others: determined, in a non-deferential age, to create hypothetical worlds of its own rather than compliantly to service those of others. The 'theoretical revolution' had actually begun with a professionalized assertion of the objectivity of criticism, its status as a science, in an academy where, increasingly and *pace* C. P. Snow, only the hard sciences were accorded the status of knowledge. In the formalist–structuralist critical years of the sixties and seventies, criticism as science was set off from literature as art, but already (as we shall see in Chapter 4) critiques of method were radically unloosening assumptions of objectivity even in the sphere of science itself. The textuality released by structuralist theory further subverted its own distinctions between truth and rhetoric: critics and imaginative writers alike began to question authenticity at its very linguistic source. Perhaps, in the circumstances, literary critics felt that the past represented a more seductively unmapped territory, and they tended to carry their deconstructive tools off in this direction rather than turning them on the literary texts of the present. What ensued was a turbulent decade (the eighties) of challenges, extensions to and explosions of the settled assumptions about the definition and constitution of 'canonical' literature.

The effect has been to revolutionize the reading of earlier literary texts, but to withdraw academic interest from contemporary writing. Not that contemporary writers have, in any case, been particularly well disposed to academic critics. Estragon's ultimate ritual insult of his more rationalizing intellectual partner Vladimir in *Waiting for Godot* (1956), was 'Crritic . . . !' Beckett, like many other writers, articulates through his character a not uncommon attitude of ambivalence toward the inescapability of rational commentary in an age of information, and with this a suspicion of the arrogance of the critic in assuming that she or he can convey, through the crisp prose of analytic commentary, thoughts which do lie too deep even for the compacted and resonant words of the poet.

However, there are evidently negative effects of this withdrawal of critical interest. In an increasingly commercially driven publishing world, the absence of intervention from academic criticism (with the exception of feminist writing) has tended to result in a diminution of the influence of criticism on the formation of new literary movements and the development of schools of writing. Indeed, by the late eighties even the term post-modernism tended to be used less to describe formal aesthetic strategies such as irony, fragmentation, parataxis, and parody (as in the early seventies) which seemed to move beyond modernist experiment, than to indicate a situation of cultural fragmentation and collapse of value where the only driving force was money and where there could be no uncompromised critical position. As academic critics busied themselves learning to pronounce and to apply the new vocabulary of theory and thence to extend and reorganize the traditional canon, the evaluation and cartographic organization of the contemporary literary scene was largely taken over by professional journalists and newspaper reviewers, or organized around success in literary competitions such as the Booker Prize, which would guarantee fame, fortune, and consumer interest. Although many writers viewed the withdrawal of academic critical interest as something of a mixed blessing, one of its effects was certainly to implicate literature even further in an instantly assimilable 'sound-bite' culture where the reception and dissemination of all contemporary cultural artefacts passed increasingly to professional journalists whose medium is that of a necessarily brief and newsworthy copy.

The Society of the Spectacle

We have seen in the last section how generally after 1960 literature came to reflect a growing self-reflexivity within British culture. Of course, literary self-consciousness is hardly a new phenomenon. The idea of the world as a stage and related metaphors of theatricality have been deployed since Elizabethan times to explore modern tensions between appearance and reality. In the period 1960–90, however, this opposition was both intensified and deconstructed. If the twentieth-century spirit of the age before 1960 had seemed to be one of loss, nostalgia, and reparational desire for recovery, by 1970 it could be more accurately described as a fear of the loss of depth itself. What if there was nothing to recover, but only surfaces to inhabit? Or nothing beneath the appearance except more appearances? Fastened to an insatiable yearning toward plenitude, the literature of 1960–90 reflected the powerfully 'desiring' nature of the times: haunted by a nostalgia for wholeness yet increasingly and self-defensively scep-tical of its attainment. If writers in the sixties and seventies explored plot as an individually constructed and potentially liberatory script, many also recognized that the other side of such narcissism must be a paranoid fear of being trapped in other people's plots. Beckett's Krapp, the 'wearish old man' and central character of *Krapp's Last Tape* (1959), expressed the new mood in unmistakable Beckettian terms as the more assertive voice of his 39-year-old self speaks to him out of the tape machine and into the darkness of auditorium and time future: 'With all this darkness round me I feel less alone. [*pause*] In a way. [*pause*] I love to get up and move about in it, then back here to . . . [*hesitates*] . . . me. [*pause*] Krapp.' The sense of being trapped within an outworn machine with no possibility of redemp-tion, or in a script which has become a less-than-heroic substitute for destiny, entered sociology and literature in the late fifties, reiterating the themes of continental existential philosophy and emerging power-fully not only in the imaginary worlds of writers such as Samuel Beckett but also in the sociological analysis of intellectuals such as Erving Goffman.

Such ideas were ludically and parodistically explored in Tom Stoppard's *Rosencrantz and Guildenstern are Dead*, which first brought its author to critical attention in 1967 by reimagining *Hamlet* as the drama of two minor characters who play their parts comi-tragically aware that the script has condemned them to an ignominious end. In many respects, the play was reminiscent too of Beckett's *Waiting for Godot* (1956), where the two tramps Vladimir and Estragon attempt to liberate themselves from a script premised on what appears to be the Augustinian uncertainty and absurdity of 'Do

not despair; one of the thieves was saved. Do not presume; one of
the thieves was damned.' The intertextual relation of Stoppard's to
Shakespeare's and Beckett's dramatic meditations on identity, time,
and destiny, however, was limited to an echolalic pastiche which
seemed to preclude engagement with serious metaphysical specula-
tion. Stoppard is best understood, perhaps, as a late modern dandy,
another author driven to the artistic appropriation of what he finds
morally reprehensible, using the mode of camp and pastiche to achieve
his effects. Susan Sontag had written an influential essay on camp
in 1966 suggesting that the essence of camp is to dethrone the serious, to annihilate hierarchies of judgement by developing a 'good
taste of bad taste' which establishes a connoisseurship of the awful
and the vulgar. Inventive extemporization with the metaphoric potential of 'theatricality' provided exhilarating aesthetic spectacle in
Stoppard's drama, but was morally condemned as duplicitous obfus-
cation through its ideological message.

Although *Jumpers* (1972) and *Travesties* (1974) seemed to present
a superficially anarchic display of moral and mental gymnastics,
metatheatrical effects were always in the service of a mildly romantic conservative belief in an ultimately simple truth only ever *obscured*
by language, ideas, political philosophies, and ethical schemes. In
Travesties, for example, Lenin is exposed as a hypocrite; Henry Carr
(the narrator and biographer) as hopelessly at the mercy of delusions
of grandeur; Tristan Tzara as an infantilized nihilist and practical
joker. James Joyce remains a mystery, presented through the animus
of Carr's memoir as a tight-fisted mendacious hypocrite and outside
of it as both a stage Irishman and a baroque and ironic wordsmith
armoured by a love affair with language and an addiction to chop
logic. As a character in Stoppard's play, he is also, and paradoxically,
the personal embodiment of his own impersonal theory of art: anxious
to destroy the Romantic theory of art as personal expression, but
effectively reconfirming it in the unmistakable signature of his
pyrotechnic stylistic mannerisms. Stoppard meanwhile reserves for
himself, at least by implication, the dubiously acquired virtue of
honesty: because he does not claim to tell the truth, his alone is the
most veridical account, conveyed through the self-proclaimed
fictitiousness of his endless Byzantine pastiche. Truth itself must

remain outside verbal play and beyond aesthetic manifesto and ethical system.

Indeed, *Professional Foul* (1978) contained an explicit denunciation of all non-correspondence theories of language, even as its entertainment was provided out of their exuberant articulation and repudiation: 'The importance of language is overrated . . . it is very useful for communicating detail—but the important truths are simple and monolithic. The essentials of a given situation speak for themselves.' The manner of the plays was post-modern, but the avowed ethos ran counter to post-modernism. As audiences were pleasantly diverted by Stoppard's own linguistic bagatelles, the declared theme was that linguistic diversion is the vice of those incapable of connection with the pure bedrock of truth. Stoppard gave his bourgeois audiences the dandyish wit he assumed they wanted and then denounced them for being duped by it. His characters were treated in similar fashion. Moral philosophers (George in *Jumpers*) were seen to play the same dangerous games as totalitarian dictators (Lenin in *Travesties*): all suffer from an egotistical failure of the imagination with destructive moral consequences. Stoppard's dandyish anti-intellectual intellectualism can be seen as yet another example of the contradictory disaffectedness and self-reflexivity of the time.

A more directly savage if still self-reflexively expressed disaffection was to be found in the plays of Joe Orton. Here is a typical dramatic exchange from *What the Butler Saw* (1969):

DR RANCE [*with a bray of laughter*]. You're in a madhouse. Unusual behaviour is the order of the day.
MATCH. Only for patients.
RANCE. We've no privileged class here. Its democratic lunacy we practise.

The 'madhouse' is both the literal setting of the play and a reference to Orton's theatre itself, but most of all it is a metaphor for that English bourgeois liberal society which Orton regarded as the ultimate embodiment of insanity. Here was another writer who self-reflexively used what he found to be repugnant as the vehicle through which to articulate that sense of disgust: in Wildean fashion, farce was to be both the expression of cultural anarchy and its antidote. Orton's spectacularly mannered and self-consciously theatrical farces were constructed out of the deceptions of that unacknowledged theatre which is everyday middle-class existence. Martin Esslin could not prise the manner from the matter and saw him as the literary equivalent of a football hooligan. In Osborne's *The Entertainer* (1957), post-Suez Britain had been presented as a superannuated musical hall propped up by a seedy comedian. In Orton, the metaphor took a savage turn and Britain was to appear as a lunatic asylum manipulated by fraudulent consultants and libidinally insane directors. His vision of middle-class society was a brutally amoral one: polite behaviour is never more than a mask of brittle social convention concealing a truth which is the voraciousness of human greed and the material reality of that rotting corpse which is its house. Morality is viewed nihilistically as the ultimate form of a bourgeois will to power which can only be undone, if at all, by a flamboyantly aesthetic exposure of its own artifice. If Stoppard used metatheatrical devices to assert the existence of truths outside of theatre, Orton's self-reflexivity exposed an infinite regress of screens and surfaces which implied that artifice is all. Theatre as a self-reflexive, superficial, and therefore honest game would reveal life to be a dishonest one. If existence is nasty, brutish, and short (and Orton's could be described this way), then his plays would expose life's nastinesses by stylistically outbrutalizing it. The last lines of *Loot* (1966), actually the first commandment in the world of theatre, were presented as the axiomatic credo of the bourgeois citizen too: 'People would talk. We must keep up appearances.' Theatricality is used in a 'bootstrapping' fashion: as a moral gesture to show the impossibility of morality. Antinomian surface is all, depth a theatrical projection providing spurious legitimation for what is in reality the nasty brutishness of human nature.

The image of life as theatre is an ancient one, hardly requiring post-structuralist gloss. Yet when earlier dramatists explored the interpenetration of play-acting and life through the metaphor of theatrical performance, they could not have imagined the extent to which their tropes would be literalized on the stage of late twentieth-century history. Theatrical experiences were once special occasions, framed and clearly demarcated from everyday life, even if dramatists were fascinated (like Orton later) by the imaginative potential of the stage as a metaphor for the world. By 1960, however, television would change all this. If in 1950 only 4.3 per cent of homes had television sets, by 1964 the figure had soared to over 90 per cent. As the playwright David Mercer pointed out, in such a situation theatre 'becomes a consumer object for a restricted audience—whereas in television fifteen million people can, at least, switch on for free, and if they want they can switch off. You couldn't get more democratic than that.'[10] Anxiety about the culturally corrosive effects of television resounded through the sixties, most noticeably perhaps in Denys Thompson's 1964 collection of essays *Discrimination and Popular Culture*, which carried a strongly Leavisite fear of the negative influence of the American mass media on British cultural standards. The concern was understandable: by the seventies, television broadcasting was by far the most influential specific source of cultural information and opinion in the British Isles.

Television encouraged that sense of the globalization, segmentation, and aestheticization of experience mentioned earlier and prominent in arguments that Britain, like all Western societies, had entered a new post-modern cultural condition. Everyday life was now endlessly and pervasively recycled through the generic conventions of soap opera, documentary drama, and situation comedy. Unlike theatre, television mingled with domesticity, and, for millions of viewers, life became segmented by the technological flow of stylistically and epistemologically distinct worlds which were continuously and almost osmotically assimilated into those of everyday experience. This prompted the French social theorist Jean Baudrillard to describe as hyperreal a cultural condition where the boundaries between artificial fantasy and empirical reality had collapsed altogether, producing a conformist silent majority which Martin Amis would later describe as the 'moronic inferno'. Unlike Americans such as Thomas Pynchon or Robert Coover, however, few British writers took as their subject the televisualization of experience, though a number reflected the growing preoccupation with and influence of media publicity.

John Berger had sensed the trend in 1972 in *Ways of Seeing*, noting that publicity never operates in the present tense, for consumer capitalism thrives out of deferral, that desire which is always oriented to a future place: 'the truthfulness of publicity is judged, not by the real fulfilment of its promises, but by the relevance of its fantasies to those of the spectator-buyer. Its essential application is not to reality but to daydreams.'[11] Muriel Spark was one writer whose fascination with the fallen desires of consumer society was reflected in sparse and elegant novels which wittily explored the dangerous effects of taking one's desire for one's reality in a world where that Supreme Fiction which is God has been utterly forgotten. The plots of many of her novels of the sixties and seventies were structured through an idiosyncratic prolepsis where the ending of the novel was deliberately revealed at its beginning. The technique, which flaunted the position of the novelist as an all-knowing God-substitute, was used to raise questions about the ethical implications of usurping divine authority through the projection of fictions in art or in life.

Her 1971 novel *Not to Disturb* examined the pervasive effects of publicity in its portrayal of the moral collapse of an aristocratic middle-European family whose media-wise and entrepreneurial servants are busy in the background recording the decadent spectacle for profitable sale to various mass media organizations. In a remarkably uncanny projection into the future, the plot would come to bear a curious resemblance to the real-life dramas of the British Royal family some twenty years later: rudely expelled from a world in which subdued theatre was acknowledged to be an essential part of the constitutional machinery of state and into the celebrity world of a publicity culture where glamour had almost entirely replaced the religious mystery of divine right. Spark's view of Western culture as caught between a decadent aristocracy and a rising and barbarian new entrepreneurial class, however, also looked back to Matthew Arnold's late-Victorian and class-obsessed vision of imminent cultural anarchy.

Her enterprising butler Lister, future yuppie but also a modern representative of the ancient 'clever servant', sees that as the 'popular glossy magazines have replaced the servants' hall in modern society', the new media world of truth-effect will bring the old class barriers crashing down: 'the career of the domestic servant is the thing of the future'. As the aristocrats sink further into their narcissistic web of sexual intrigue and emotional obsession, the servants are left with the perfect free space from which to exploit the media potential of this high class *Grand Guignol*. Lister prophesies wisely, for the imperial Austro-Hungarian lifestyle of such as the Klopstock family was already in 1971 little more than an image on the screens of sensationalist Hollywood cinema and a blank space in the Communist history books. Spark's upwardly mobile and declassed plutocrats speak in the future tense of high technology, play on the opportunities thrown out by the decadent narcissisms of a dying European high culture, and celebrate the dawn of a new democratizing era of Americanized mass media.

Spark was not the only writer to recognize the role of publicity and the media in the economic and cultural invasion of Europe by America which gathered force throughout the period. By 1972 over 80 per cent of the top advertising agencies in Britain were American-owned, American films occupied more than half of the entire world's screen time, and even as early as 1957 Richard Hoggart was decrying the collapse of an authentic British working-class culture into the tawdry candy-floss world of the imported juke-box and the milk bar. F. R. Leavis heightened his campaign against all things transatlantic, proclaiming that 'we are rapidly heading for the hopelessness of America'.[12] Cultural conservatives such as Daniel Bell, writing in 1976 (in *The Cultural Contradictions of Capitalism*), saw American popular culture promulgating a cult of hedonism and sensation, a 'porno-pop culture', where affluence had simply unleashed people's most primitive and destructive instincts. Christopher Lasch added his voice to this in 1978 (in *The Culture of Narcissism*), seeing in the global effects of American culture a collapse of the moral self into primitive pleasure-seeking mechanisms. A long tradition of British writers including George Orwell and Evelyn Waugh had indicted America for its cultural barbarism, though fewer of them after 1960 sought inspiration in its contemporary writing: Hughes, Gunn, Tomlinson, Dunn, among the poets; J. G. Ballard and Martin Amis, with his style of morally insouciant urban radical chic, of the novelists. American media culture and popular music had significant effects on British youth subcultures throughout the period (on jazz, Teddy boys, reggae, punk, for example), but literary culture in Britain tended to remain aloof.

The Trial of Lady Chatterley *and the Trials of Salman Rushdie*

The influence of the mass media and of the new world of publicity on that of literature was to be found less in Britain in the form and content of literary texts than in their reception and status. A fast-growing genre from the late seventies was the literary biography, and high culture as much as mass succumbed to the obsession with fame and celebrity. It is difficult to assess whether public fascination with the personal lives of poets such as Larkin or Plath was an extension of interest in their verse, or merely bound up with voyeuristic gratifications far removed from those of purely literary appreciation. As publicity became an ever-more pervasive aspect of everyday life in Britain, it entered increasingly into debates and issues about the legitimation of literary value. Indeed, the literary history of the period under survey opened with the *Lady Chatterley* trial and drew to a close with the Salman Rushdie affair. Both involving issues of publicity, cultural value, and free speech, they are convenient literary frames through which we might gain a purview of the continuing cultural preoccupations of the period, but also of the cultural distance separating 1960 from 1990.

The first was fought inside the privacy of a British court with a broadly unanimous agreement by defence and prosecution alike as to what should constitute good and offensive literature. The Obscene Publications Act of 1959, pioneered by Roy Jenkins, had effectively ratified the liberal Romantic view that art is ultimately beyond good and evil. Each side in the *Chatterley* trial thereby concurred that the sexual scenes in the novel were justifiable, providing their aesthetic presentation honoured the moral requirement that sex be portrayed as a form of spiritually symbolic communion. The defence proceeded essentially by offering lessons in practical criticism. Indeed, the trial demonstrated the claim which Perry Anderson was to make in 1966 (in an essay entitled 'Components of a National Culture') that English literary criticism had always functioned as the moral and intellectual arbiter at the heart of a national culture with an impoverished tradition of analytic and abstract social thought. The trial revealed that the axiomatic values of English culture in 1960 were still those of traditional liberal individualism: honesty, conscience, choice, fulfilment, commitment, dignity, and freedom. Firmly within the ethos of Leavis's Scrutineers, 'the English intellectual tries to explain his ideas or to interpret those of others by resituating them in his literature'.[13] So long as there was unanimity that Lady Chatterley's sexual activities with the gamekeeper Mellors were presented as sacraments rather than pleasures, there could be no disagreement about the merits and high seriousness of the book. Literary critics and writers such as Graham Hough, Helen Gardner, Rebecca West, and Richard Hoggart were brought in to defend Lawrence on ethical grounds as an essentially puritan writer concerned with an 'intense sense of responsibility' for his conscience.[14]

Such a quasi-religious terminology was, however, the moral vocabulary of a broadly consensual liberal culture (though Mary Whitehouse was never to forgive the Bishop of Woolwich for likening Lawrence's descriptions of sexual intercourse to acts of Holy Communion). Turning to the Rushdie affair, however, one is confronted with a global media event, fought not within the privacy of a courtroom or even the national press, but staged internationally before millions of newspaper readers and television viewers and involving a confrontation of the incommensurable values of Western secular liberalism with an Islamic fundamentalism still medieval in its canons of blasphemy and heresy. If a liberal consensus could prevail over the trial of *Lady Chatterley's Lover*, it was powerless to reconcile the multicultural contradictions of the case of *The Satanic Verses*. In each arena, important struggles over cultural value took place, but in the second case publicity had transformed the author into an international celebrity. If most of the members of the prosecution in 1960 were willing to accept lessons in literary appreciation, most of those of 1989 had not even read the book. Since most of the defence had not read it either, it was likely to be one of those unedifying tutorials where participants merely reiterate existing convictions or prejudices rather than attempt to arrive at a newly formulated condition of understanding.

Martin Kettle has argued that in an information culture people prefer to read about books rather than to read books, and 'in a bizarre way, Rushdie's novels, which are ostensibly the reason for his situation in life, are almost irrelevant to his public standing. *The Satanic Verses* was famously unread by those who burned it.'[15] One of the ironies of the Rushdie affair is that the political fictionalization of history which had been the basic method of *Midnight's Children* (1981) and *Shame* (1983) was suddenly turned against Rushdie himself in the events proceeding from the publication of *The Satanic Verses* (1988). The author appeared to have become the grotesque victim of one of his own fictional plots, as the lurid glare of world publicity created its own metafictional scenario of life imitating fiction. Another irony was that historical events after the publication of the later novel provided purgatorial resolution of that authorial post-colonial guilt about writing which had been expressed repeatedly in Rushdie's earlier work. One of the pivotal conceits of *Midnight's Children*, for example, is that the narrator Saleem (one of the magical children of history born at the moment of Indian partition on 15 August 1947), whose body somatizes the splits, schisms, and conflicts of the new Independence, is gifted with a telepathic power which makes him a determining agent in the unfolding of India's later history. Rushdie deploys significant shifts of narrative voice to convey his own investment in this plot device. Saleem suddenly refers to himself in the third person when he condemns the possible squandering of his telepathic powers.

Despite the many vital uses to which his abilities could have been put by his impoverished, underdeveloped country, he chose to conceal his talents, frittering them away on inconsequential voyeurism . . . the direct result of a confusion in his mind, which invariably muddled up morality—the desire to do what is right—and popularity—the rather more dubious desire to do what is approved of.

Moral transgression produces guilt, but in a society where public approval counts for more than private virtue, shame becomes the more powerful emotional weapon. That Saleem's suspension between both emotions is also his author's, however, becomes apparent as soon as he reverts to the first person to provide the reassurance for his readers that 'I can be quite tough in my self-judgements when I choose'.

Saleem's telepathy is Rushdie's expression of the political implications of the capacity of the aesthetic imagination to manufacture other and alternative worlds. The metafictional message of the novel is that fiction can determine history. Saleem is captured and tortured by government forces for the threat posed to repressive regimes by his imagination. Each of Rushdie's novels dramatizes the situation of artistic outsiders brought to the centre of history through the subversive power of their (Romantic) imaginations. Although Rushdie was required to make an apology to Mrs Ghandhi after the publication of *Midnight's Children, Shame* was even more direct in its statement of the political uses and abuses of the imagination: nations are shown to be palimpsests, each layer written over previous imaginary worlds. In order

to build Pakistan it was necessary to cover up Indian history . . . It is the true desire of every artist to impose his or her vision on the world; and Pakistan, the peeling, fragmenting palimpsest, increasingly at war with itself, may be described as a failure of the dreaming mind . . . As for me: I, too, like all migrants, am a fantasist. I build imaginary countries and try to impose them on the ones which exist . . .

If Rushdie feels some need to justify the decision to write, he is anxious to demonstrate that his fictions will provide alternative political models to those adopted by the monologic visions of fundamentalist nationalism. Like the earlier novels, *The Satanic Verses* continued to articulate the strains of its own author's situation as a British citizen of Indian origins, writing in English and aware of the condition of migrancy as an attempt to formulate in positive terms a personally experienced post-colonial sense of linguistic absence. Rushdie is always caught: between nations, languages, ethnicities, value-systems; between fiction and history; posing the questions: 'What are the consequences, both spiritual and practical, of refusing to make any concessions to Western ideas and practices? What are the consequences of embracing these practices?' Saleem writes uneasily under an *anglepoise* lamp, but for Rushdie its beam was also calculated to produce a chiaroscuro which could illumine political truths whilst casting them under the protective penumbra of imaginary fictions.

   He had assumed that Islamic fundamentalism could be safely addressed and criticized through the rhetorical conventions of Western liberal fiction (in its most Shandyesque mode). Of course, it is impossible now to read *The Satanic Verses* as on first publication in September 1988, for this historiographic metafiction has become part of the subsequent history of its time. The fictionally enacted irreconcilability of East and West spilled outside the covers of the book to be spectacularly confirmed in the events which followed its publication. Western liberalism and, in particular, the British Labour Party and the Anglican Church found themselves caught between the incompatible claims of a libertarian demand for the primacy of freedom of speech versus an egalitarian plea for a commitment to respect and uphold the beliefs and values of all social groups. Liberalism found itself in confusion when challenged by an ethnic group for whom freedom of speech was anathema to its creed of sacred revelation of the one and only Word. The fatwa issued against Rushdie signified an absolute reverence for revealed religious truth which did not even acknowledge the Western concept of imaginative fiction as anything other than heresy in the first place. When the 'fiction' also contained the portrayal of a 'character' Mahound (evidently Muhammad) partaking in classical deity style of the sensory delights of the flesh, it was difficult for Muslims to regard the novel as anything other than the most heinous blasphemy. Rushdie's concern to expose political abuses of the sacred simply appeared to many Muslims living in Britain to be a profanation of their own deepest sense of identity and only source of security and dignity in a migrant condition more vulnerable and less privileged than Rushdie's own.

The Rushdie affair demonstrated the extent to which the *sensus communis* in Britain had fractured since 1960. Even his post-modern self-conscious games with the idea of the author playing God in the fictional universe of the book (a common trope in fiction since the sixties) had quite different resonances within Islam. From a Muslim perspective, even to write fiction which made no such theocratic claims would be a blasphemy, in that such an act arrogates to the human what can only be claimed by the Divine: the creation of worlds *ex nihilo*. Ironically, of course, it was actually the outraged response of Muslims to the novel which vindicated Rushdie's assertion of the seriousness of art within a liberal culture in which it appeared to have been trivialized or marginalized. Throughout the twentieth century Western writers have struggled with the desire to protect the freedom of the artist by arguing for the autonomy and transcendence of art, but have recognized that the price for such freedom may be its social and political marginalization. These were the issues at the heart of the *Lady Chatterley* trial. In placing the death sentence upon Western art, the Ayatollah conferred upon it a cultural significance which even its own practitioners had come to doubt in the thirty years since that trial.

A major theme of *The Satanic Verses* is the impossibility of wholeness, the necessary condition of perspectivism. In its reception, this post-modern perspectivism was reversed and revealed in its Western contradictoriness to itself through the lens of Islamic absolutism. For Muslims, the Koran is the exact word of God and to doubt this is to call into question the validity of Muhammad's mission and to undermine the very foundations of the Islamic faith. Rushdie introduced doubt by having one of his actor-protagonists dream the Satanic Verses (regarded within Islam as heretical lines planted by Satan in the mind of Gabriel, who gives the Koran to Muhammad) whilst suffering from the delusion that he is Muhammad. For Muslims, philosophical quibbles about the ontological status of dreams or delusions within literary fictions were, however, entirely irrelevant: *The Satanic Verses* was an assault on the absolute veracity of the Koran. Indeed, there was even a liberal defence of this reading available for any who were familiar with Tzvetan Todorov's argument that 'if certain events of a book's universe account for themselves as imaginary, they thereby contest the imaginary nature of the rest of the book. If a certain apparition is only the fault of an overexcited imagination, then everything around is real.'[16] If Gibreel's dream is the real fantasy, then the ostensibly fictional world outside it effectively becomes reality *par excellence* and, thus transformed, can no longer function as a safe fantastic hideout sheltering its author under the shadow of his anglepoise lamp.

Defending the novel, Rushdie mustered an earlier theme of his fiction, the notion of hybridity as a challenge to national, ethnic, or religious purity:

The Satanic Verses celebrates hybridity, impurity, intermingling, the transformation that comes of new and unexpected combinations of human beings, cultures, ideas, politics, movies, songs. It rejoices in mongrelisation and fears the absolutism of the Pure. Melange, hotchpotch, a bit of this and a bit of that is how newness enters the world. It is the great possibility that mass migration gives the world, and I have tried to embrace it. *The Satanic Verses* is for change-by-fusion, change-by-conjoining. It is a love-song to our mongrel selves.[17]

Rushdie's optimistic multiculturalism, however, wilfully ignored the inevitable strains and conflicts in such a situation. The breaking-down of national sovereignty and the new globalization of the West was accompanied during the eighties by a strengthening of fundamental ethnic identities in the Middle East and, with the collapse of Soviet Communism after 1989, a resurgence of ethnic nationalisms and arguments for purity in Eastern Europe. Even the Thatcherite revival of Little Englandism could be viewed as a reaction of tradition against what Rushdie calls translation. More dramatically, Islamic fundamentalism was rejuvenated in Iran as a response to the Shah's attempted Westernization in the seventies. In Eastern Europe, too, fundamentalist nationalism followed upon the collapse of Communism. In each of these cases, fundamentalism operated as a powerful form of counter-identification for peoples traditionally regarded as non-'First World' and thus excluded from the supposed global benefits of capitalist affluence or the universal and inevitable spread of liberal democracy. Comparing the Rushdie affair with the *Lady Chatterley* trial reveals how far this new dialectic of what has been called the local and the global has disrupted the insularities of British liberal culture since 1960. If the British liberal intelligentsia of 1960 could still regard themselves as the true moral arbiters of the nation, in 1990 their foundational secularisms, such as freedom of speech and the inevitability of modernization, were shown to be fraught with contradiction once exposed to a more international or multicultural situation. Furthermore, the local counter-identification of British Muslims found itself elevated by politicians, journalists, world religious leaders, and heads of state onto a global media stage which again dramatized the extent to which the container of British liberal culture by 1989 had sprung a multitude of alarming leaks.

For optimistic multiculturalists, such tendencies are necessary to the emergence of a more just and equal society. For pessimists, however, the continuing pluralization of culture was seen as a grave threat to the forms of representative democracy inherited from the eighteenth-century Enlightenment: for the pessimist, liberal culture was seen to be under threat from above, in the form of right-wing popular authoritarianism and its brutal materialism, and from below, with the fragmentation of opposition to such government into separate subcultures focused on their own internecine disagreements. Within this perspective, the fragmentation of literary discourse into heterogeneous voices, each of which merely articulates the specific experiences of a particular social group, must entail a worrying sacrifice of that ideal of universality which was assumed to reside in the infinite iterability of great literature: its power to speak representatively for all of us, or its potential for endless reinterpretations which allow an infinite variety of voices to make their own experiences heard through a single text and to learn to listen to those of others. This position was argued vociferously at the beginning of the period in C. S. Lewis's *An Experiment in Criticism* (1961), where he urged that we should not go to literature as a mirror to confirm a pre-established identity, but to recognize that one of the delights of art is to 'remove our gaze from that mirrored face, to deliver us from solitude': a Christian humanist position not incompatible with traditional liberalism.[18]

Despite the apparent affirmation of liberal humanist value which emerged from the *Chatterley* trial, fears about the collapse of liberal culture were gathering steadily from the early sixties. In 1967 John Osborne argued that

we live in a society of such lurching flexibility that it is no longer possible to construct a dramatic method based on a shared social and ethical system. The inexorable process of fragmentation is inimical to all public assumptions, indeed ultimately to anything shared at all . . . A dramatist can no longer expect to draw many common references, be they social, sexual or emotional. He can't generalise in the old way. He must be specific to himself and his own particular, concrete experience.[19]

Indeed, fears of cultural fragmentation were expressed across the political and literary spectrum and throughout the entire period 1960–

90. In a series of articles written for *New Society*, for example, at the end of the next decade, the Marxist historian E. P. Thompson similarly announced:

We are approaching a state of anarchy, or arbitrary and unaccountable rule, in which the constitution, or political culture of the nation is being surreptitiously destroyed and where the British traditions of middle class and working class dissent have collapsed into local squabbles and fragmented identity politics.[20]

For Thompson, the ideal of a democratic common culture seemed to have been replaced with the reality of arbitrary despotism and individualistic greed. In the next chapter we will begin to examine how some of the literature of the period reflects and responds to this sense of a crisis in values.

3 KEEPING OUR METAPHYSICS WARM

SACRED IMPULSES IN A SECULAR AGE

> A man can still be capable of great moral resolution even after
> he has plumbed the depths of knowledge.
>
> (Thomas Mann, *Death in Venice*)

Throughout the period, but particularly in the sixties, whilst intellectuals bemoaned the failures of rational planning and counterculturalists sought a new heaven on earth through a liberation of the instincts, many writers were increasingly preoccupied with the interrelationship between the human propensity for violence, on the one hand, and the yearning for transcendent significance, on the other. Ethological studies of aggression were popular, the work of Konrad Lorenz and Desmond Morris, for example, suggesting that human beings were still more beast than angel and, indeed, in their territorial instincts to fight to the death, more bestial even than the beasts. Lorenz saw the human and creative desire for order being perverted by a technomorphic expert culture. Accustomed to overcontrol in fragmented specialisms, this culture had lost the capacity for imaginative empathy or the ability to feel humility in relation to all that reason cannot know. Although heralded as the efflorescence of the rational Enlightenment, strains and absences were now to be detected in the Welfare State, as indeed in its philosophical foundations. Moreover, since the industrial revolution, literature had functioned as the 'other' voice of a scientifically rationalized culture, an oppositional voice of intuition, imagination, and feeling. In the technocratic sixties, writers became intensely self-conscious of the responsibilities attached to this legacy. The progressivist dream that reason could disenchant human beings and establish a universal republic of social equality and individual justice would be more thoroughly and pervasively challenged within literary cultures than at any time since the Romantic period.

Enlightenment thinkers had promised the dawn of a new age where all would be freed from servitude to irrational forces within (the passions) and without (superstition, political tyranny). The great leveller would be reason, working on the shared data of sense-experience, bringing liberation from the tortured pre-Enlightenment self-division of a human identity caught somewhere between beast and angel. The planners of the second half of the twentieth century were the inheritors of an Enlightenment belief in the possibility of realizing a rationally planned society which would accomplish a general and progressive liberation of humankind from the confused realm of prejudice and irrational need. Harold Wilson invoked technology in a renewal of vows of commitment to such an ethos of universal welfare provision. New totally planned towns were built; institutions of higher education increased and expanded; legislation was passed to deal with the troubled areas of race, gender, sexuality, and the increasingly complex confrontations of capital and labour. There were other far-reaching though less prominent changes, like those listed by Christopher Booker, for example, in his study of the sixties, *The Neophiliacs* (1969):

The pulling down of old buildings to make way for new developments or motorways, the transformation of the appearance and character of the countryside under the impact of the new methods of farming, the modernisation of almost everything and anything from *The Times* newspaper and the telephone to the traditional liturgy of the Churches, the introduction of a whole series of reforms affecting the familiar machinery of life, such as the decision to adopt decimal coinage and the metric system.[1]

By 1967, however, none of this could divert an explosion of prejudice and passion which did not at all fit the rational blueprint: a fast-rising crime rate, football hooliganism, severe industrial unrest, continuous crises in the pound, race riots, political scandals, and a general sense of national enervation and loss of purpose. The planned society seemed to be founded on a base of real material decline and moral and spiritual vacuum. Religion had once provided an overarching order of value, Enlightenment had promised redemption on earth. Both were now fragmenting into relativist orders of competing and contradictory value-claims. Enlightened reason seemed to have narrowed into a technocratic instrumentalism which, for commentators such as Herbert Marcuse, was the very cause of the human malaise it was intended to alleviate. Politicians could no longer even draw on the fund of readily available post-war communitarian feeling which had sustained social and moral vision immediately after 1945. Older forms of community based on deference and shared social experience and obligation were fast disappearing. The new intellectual ideas had relativized earlier notions of truth and justice. Everywhere there was testimony to a trend of privatization which would make it increasingly difficult to sustain any collectivist ethos.

Literature both challenged and fed off such trends, often returning after the anti-modernist temper of the fifties to a modernist propensity to seek meaning in the deeper recesses of individual experience. Considerably weaker, however, was the underlying modernist faith in an impersonal tradition of high culture which could embody and ratify universal aesthetic and ethical value. The intellectual influence of existentialism from the late fifties was again one which put the highest premium on the absolutely present moment of personal choice: the requirement of authenticity that we wrest our individual freedom from the bad faith of social conformity and easy subservience to traditionally sanctioned schemes of salvation. Popular versions of the philosophy had obvious appeal for the newly rebellious and socially mobile young. Adorno's 'no poetry after Auschwitz' had suggested to many that the destructiveness of the new era required a new ethics as well as a new art. In 1962 A. Alvarez made his famous attack on the redundant gentility of English poetry, suggesting that the Holocaust, like depth psychology, had exposed such reserves of genocidal aggression that Larkinesque 'awkward reverence' with the bicycle clips was now quaintly obsolete both as a subject and an appropriate tone for poetry.

Faith in planning as the contemporary form of Enlightenment rationalism had been fundamentally eroded by memories of totalitarian atrocity. W. H. Auden, in an essay 'The Poet and the City', published in *The Dyer's Hand* in 1963, argued that more than ever, in the 'managed' society, poetry exists to remind us that the managed have faces. He too noted the dangerous analogy of art and life in planned mass society: a society aesthetically and economically organized like a poem 'would be a nightmare of horror for, given the historical reality of actual men, such a society could only come into being through selective breeding, extermination of the physically and mentally unfit, absolute obedience to its Director'.[2] A rapidly emergent view was that the Enlightenment had produced the violences of the modern world by closing off and perverting the human impulse toward the sacred. Justifying his Shamanistic relation to poetry after the publication of *Crow* (1970), Ted Hughes argued that poetry must redress the balance of those 'Forces of the Universe' disturbed by the rationalistic arrogance of modern technological thinking.[3] Enlightenment thinkers had recognized that need begins with lack, recommending the redistribution of material resources as the goal of social justice. For a number of writers in the sixties and seventies, however, the legacy thus bequeathed to the Welfare State was a materialist vision which underestimated the human need for spiritual as well as material nourishment.

Traditionally, spiritual nourishment has been provided by religion. By the end of the sixties, however, the erosion of social deference toward authority, the privatization of values, and the various intellectual relativisms of the period suggest some reasons why orthodox religion seemed, to younger writers and intellectuals at any rate, no longer viable as a source of absolute value and spiritual sustenance. Evelyn Waugh had lamented the loss in *Unconditional Surrender* (1961), but within the frame of an ultra-conservative portrayal of a Christendom dismembered by homosexuals, communists, and in particular the insurgent lower orders. Yet, although fewer writers explicitly proclaimed themselves to be Christian, many more voiced a need to address the forms that spirit could take in a society which had largely abandoned the idea of a transcendent supernatural authority. In the sphere of literary criticism, for example, the New Critics promised to reconcile science and religion. For, if their methodology consisted of a scientific respect for the poem as an object-in-itself, it was always in the service of a vision of the literary work as a mystically irreducible experience of plenitudinous meaning in a world desacralized by commerce and dissected by technology.

In departments of literature, the modernist text was rediscovered and celebrated as a fragmentary contingent surface invisibly anchored to a more profound and symbolically resonant depth. Somewhat paradoxically, revelation simply waited on the skilled excavations of what one New Critic had referred to as the newly professionalized 'Criticism Inc.': the growing band of academic experts skilled in stylistic analysis and textual exegesis.[4]

Writing in 1963, Stephen Spender (in *The Struggle of the Modern*) distinguished the secular rationalist contemporaries happily negotiating the new technocratic world from the more tortured moderns who must seek their human significance elsewhere. Looking back, there seem to have been more moderns around and, as we shall see in later chapters, it would not be long before they were joined by the so-called post-modernists for whom significance might be more a matter of construction and rhetorical persuasion than buried depth or latent resonance. Either way, however, these late moderns rarely looked up or talked of transcendence but, in tune to this extent with the times, usually preferred to seek their orders of significance buried deeper in the personal life. The newly discovered appeal of modernist texts such as Eliot's *The Waste Land* or the novels of Woolf or Lawrence in the sixties was in their perceived concern to relocate spiritual significance after 'The Death of God' in a subterranean rather than supernatural sphere: in the hidden depths of the individual psyche or the private life rather than in an impersonal and divine order. A more profound realization of the self was promised as an antidote to the fear of cosmic groundlessness. In the realm of popular psychoanalysis and therapy, science was appropriated as the excavatory tool which might reach and unlock the hidden casket of the modern soul. Some traditional Christian writers of the period pilloried this latest turn in the ethos of liberal individualism: Muriel Spark, for example, with her parodies of the contemporary technologized cult of the therapist or William Golding with his fallen solipsists or mediumistic cabbalists. Other broadly 'religious' writers, such as Iris Murdoch, however, made their comedy out of the excesses and complacencies of the therapy ethos, but still shared the general turn to the sphere of personal relations as the primary source of value in the late-modern world.

This chapter will largely concentrate on writing of the sixties and seventies concerned with the loss of or the search to rediscover spiritual significance. During this period a number of important writers clearly felt compelled to supply the spiritual absences in a democratically conceived but largely materialist welfare ethos. By the eighties the vaunted and in any case glaring material inequalities and injustices of monetarism, and the moral outrage of the Thatcherite appropriation of religious vocabularies, tended to stimulate a more savagely absurdist and fantastic writing and a retreat from the pure pursuit of spirit or the anatomy of elemental violence. We will examine these trends later in the book but suffice it to say here that in the novel, for example, a more directly *social* moral voice would be heard in a revival of the condition-of-England genre and an ironic and often fantastic post-modernism which signalled the demise of all forms of universality, secular or religious, and the need to address the moral and political implications of such a condition: some novels, such as Martin Amis's *London Fields* (1989), for example, managed to combine both modes. At the beginning of the eighties Blake Morrison and Andrew Motion signalled the shift in their *Contemporary British Poetry* (1982), the most significant anthology since Alvarez's collection and, like his, and Robert Conquest's 1956 *New Lines* before that, an attempt to define the mood of the times through a sense of emergent poetic movements. A more ironic, whimsically fantastic, and sceptical anatomy of everyday life tended to dominate, recalling from earlier in the seventies the tone of Ian Hamilton's *New Review* or the reasonable detachment of 'the Group'. Above all was the desire to repudiate the validity of Alvarez's poetry of extremes and to return to a more familiar historical terrain through the defamiliarizing inventiveness of the poetic imagination.

The human imagination now appeared more emphatically as a ludic force of potential renewal than a dark energy of the avenging gods or soberly detached and rational assessor of experience. Quoted with approval by Motion and Morrison was James Fenton's reductively tripping repudiation of Alvarez's oversimplistic conflation of value in poetry with extremes of feeling: 'He tells you, in the sombrest notes, | If poets want to get their oats | The first step is to slit their throats. | The way to divide | The sheep of poetry from the goats | Is suicide.' Poets such as Heaney, Harrison, and Dunn were seen to bring their verbal imaginations to bear on a responsible transfiguration of pressing political and social concerns: class or the Troubles in Northern Ireland, for example, whilst 'Martians' such as Craig Raine or the new narrative poets were regarded as reflecting a desire for renewal through the exploration of excentric or dislocated perspectives on familiar rather than pathologically extreme experience. In drama, the shift had begun as early as 1968 with the first stirrings of the political theatre movement and would be augmented in the eighties by a new generation of feminist dramatists. From the mid-seventies sixties' elementalism would begin to be displaced too by the multiculturalist and post-modernist turn in art and politics.

What remained consistent across the entire period 1960–90 was a fairly widespread intellectual retreat from belief in a transcendent deity. In some ways, this was surprising. In a period where the only viable political alternative to a stressed and failing welfare capitalism seemed to be a brutally individualistic *laissez-faire* monetarism, one might have expected writers to turn to the spiritual message and anti-materialistic values of the Christian Gospels. Yet, although it is evident that ours has not been, in any sense, an orthodoxly religious age, there is much evidence, literary at least, of a constant yearning for spirit. The Anglican Church made a number of attempts to read this sign of the times and certainly signalled its contempt for the possessive individualism of the enterprise culture with counterblasts such as 'Faith in the Cities' in 1985. One or two prominent intellectuals made well-publicized conversions, like the former Marxist art historian Peter Fuller, who declared in 1988 that

the aesthetic confusion of our times must be seen as part of a more widespread collapse of ethical, cultural and religious response. Aesthetic life cannot thrive given the disintegration of the 'shared symbolic order' of a kind which religion provides; it becomes especially vulnerable when laudable ideas derived from political democracy are extended in such a way as to outlaw discrimination within the cultural field, and to undermine the evaluative dimension in human response.[5]

Probably the most controversial Anglican document of the time, however, was *Honest to God* (1963) by the Bishop of Woolwich,

John Robinson, which again seemed intent on relocating the sacred in the sphere of personal relations. Thus reinvested, the realm of intersubjectivity would seem again to offer the promise of stability and security as well as fulfilment. Most writers, however, were more concerned to explore the gap between the increasing weight of expectation built onto this interpersonal sphere and the irrecoverable loss of those traditional obligations which, in the past, had ensured some measure of stability and predictability in such human relations. Characters in novels and plays by Harold Pinter, David Storey, Iris Murdoch, and John Fowles, for example, might be depicted as heroic in their struggle to renegotiate familial expectations, marital ties, or social duties, but such freedom also raised new and often threatening questions about personal responsibility and existential meaning. As relationships became more risky, insecurities and misunderstandings thrived and much of the dark comedy of writers such as Pinter or Murdoch was premissed on an exposure of a widespread and profound existential anxiety and confusion about the location or derivation of personal significance and the disappearance of earlier teleologies.

John Robinson's book, however, which caused a furore after its publication in 1963 and had sold 300,000 copies by 1965, promised salvation by suggesting that God was to be realized not 'out there' but inside, through a commitment to relationships of love between individual human beings. He offended orthodox Anglicans by suggesting that the time had come to reconceptualize God in metaphors of depth or ground rather than those of transcendence. The tropic shift was actually a familiar secular transposition, evident earlier in the century—for example, in the aesthetics of Bloomsbury and the ethics of G. E. Moore and later in the writings of existentialists and phenomenologists: spiritual significance is now discoverable only in the profound depths of the self in its relations with other selves. However, Robinson took this further: God is now love as the ultimacy of personal relationships. Not surprisingly, he was accused by traditionalists of wanting his religious cake but eating it at secular feasts. Equally understandable was his laudability in the eyes of counter-culturalists for whom erotic experience was the 'polymorphously perverse' expression of the divinity in the flesh. Most of Robinson's argument was actually derived from broadly existential modern theologians such as Bonhoeffer, Bultmann, and Tillich, who had expressed a Heideggerian sense of the Divine as the ground of Being: not a projection 'out there', but a divinity manifest in every particular 'thou' encountered through love, 'the unconditional element in all our relationships, and supremely in our relationships with other persons'.[6]

Whatever Robinson's intentions, however, few of his readers had even heard of the German philosopher Martin Heidegger, and it seems likely that, if anything, and certainly at a popular level, his arguments further weakened the claims of religion to transcendent meaning. If even Anglicans were substituting metaphors of depth and immanence for those of heaven and transcendence, it is hardly surprising that so many of the non-Christian middle classes would express their own need for depth through a conversion to the compelling personal religion of psychoanalysis, barely fifty years old. Karl Marx had provided for the early twentieth century an alternative vision of redemption on earth through the workings of dialectical materialism. As Marxism fell into disrepute after the Soviet invasion of Hungary in 1956, however, psychoanalysis was gradually rejuvenated in redemptive and individualistic mode.

The therapy era and the psychoanalytic movement took off in the sixties. As religion was undermined and the collectivist idealism underpinning the welfare ethos became increasingly meagre, the nourishment each had failed to provide was sought in the sphere of personal relations, which became correspondingly more intense and anxiety-provoking. Any political or ethical system of thought (as feminism in the seventies would claim with its slogan of 'the personal is the political') which did not prioritize the emotional aspects of personal life came to be regarded as inadequate. Psychoanalysis, in the ameliorative therapy mode which became pervasive in the West in this period, seemed to gratify both an Enlightenment desire for rational control and to carry the seductive offer of a return to the intensities of faith, myth, and passionate commitment.

Throughout the twentieth century, and particularly in its later decades, writers have been driven to depict modern secular life as one of inner void or the emptied-out self. There has been a proliferation of minimalist, solipsistic interiors, and impersonalized external land-scapes of commercial exchange. Often the intellectual challenge for the author or reader of such texts is to discover latently or invent performatively some morality which can connect these spheres. Even in an atmosphere of welfare ameliorism and social determinism, literature has shown that neither is the self sufficient to itself nor is it simply a reflexive epiphenomenon of circulating and competing language games and social forces. None of the heroes of modern literature has felt what he or she is supposed to feel; many of those after 1960 were presented as ignorant of what they were supposed to feel: the writers who captured such confusion also caught critical attention. As nature was tamed, the self grew wild, for, although a fence could be placed around a forest or a bridge built over a can-yon, the inner life refused to offer itself so easily for safe contain-ment. Psychoanalysis seemed thus able to provide for this world what religion had provided in the past: a means of charting and making safe its unknown terrain in existential and universal terms. It provided a means to dismantle the hell which was now oneself and other people, and thereby supplied a faith arrived at authentically through struggle and doubt with its own initiation rites, sacraments, consciously held doctrines, and unconsciously lived-out rituals and practices.

Appropriated by the therapy movement, psychoanalysis seemed the new fundamentalist religion of the individualistic West. It came complete with an ineffability thesis to satisfy rational sceptics (for the unconscious, like God, is in the end unknowable) and an inner sanctum of high priests with divinely appointed access to the ulti-mate mystery. Their hierophantic powers were exercised in the lit-urgy of emotionally heightened free association called the therapy session, where the mystery would be called up and appeased with doctrinal talk of castration complexes, patricide, and ancient inces-tuous impulses only to be laid to rest through an immolatory submis-sion to Our Father whose Name is Freud. The pervasiveness of therapy in the period 1960–90 (three-hundred-plus varieties of it on the official register) seems a testament to what David Riesman has referred to as the loneliness (and concomitant narcissism) of the late-modern self, the breakdown of community in the West, and the moral and spiritual starvation amongst the plenty of a rationalized, affluent, but unequal society.[7] Though Freud never intended it, his tragic liberal vision of the non-recuperability of the past, the absolute gulf between our desire and the real, and the nonconformity of history with our material and psychic schemes was tamed in order to provide an individualistic version of the satisfactions of religion within the frame of rational, progressivist post-Enlightenment thought.

In a world of moral and spiritual uncertainty, there will always be a temptation to embrace false gods or to project onto others personal desires dressed up in the impersonal languages of systematic thought. Those who create self-consciously artificial worlds of words are ideally situated to explore the way in which buried theories of who we are shape what we do, but writers too have been caught up in the general permeation of Freudianism: seduced by the attractions of its heroic vision whilst repudiating the facile textbook therapist as engineer of the inner life. Even before the therapeutic explosion, W. H. Auden had noted in 'In Memory of Sigmund Freud': 'To us he is no more a person | Now but a whole climate of opinion | Under whom we conduct our differing lives.' The insight was treated ironically in Iris Murdoch's *The Black Prince* (1973), where various critical commentaries, including an overblown and clearly inadequate literal Freudian interpretation of events, are appended to the novel as a wry reflection on the twentieth-century assumption that hell is other people and Freud the divinity who will harrow it and save us. Murdoch knows that Freud had announced: 'Before the problem of the creative artist analysis must, alas, lay down its arms,' but she can also see that Freud's theory of art as compensation leads ultimately to a view of it as 'the egotistically motivated production of maimed pseudo-objects which are licences for the private concluding processes of personal fantasy': literature as advanced pornographic release for the diseased psyche.[8]

Even as she relentlessly exposed its more inauthentic popular formulations, however, Murdoch's own writing espoused a view of art as magic in a revisionist Platonism after Freud. The motivations for most of her plots relied on loosely Freudian psychological insights into power and desire for their coherence and narrative impetus of curiosity: only a return to buried structures of the past might unlock the symptomatology of the present. Indeed, the same could be said of most writers of the period who attempted to recover a metaphysical dimension to human experience: the language of psychoanalysis not only pervaded the everyday but in a manner finally and compellingly heroic. Yet it was a language as accommodatingly modern as ancient tragic and religious discourses seemed increasingly and unaccommodatingly remote. Whatever their avowed intentions, from the sixties on, writers who evoke a psychic hinterland or reach toward some sense of the sacred have been unable to avoid at least critical interpretation through the lens of Freudianism. Harold Pinter, for example, in an interview in *Paris Review* in the early sixties, exploded against critics looking for such meanings in his plays, arguing: 'I'm just a writer; and I think that I've been overblown tremendously because there's a dearth of really fine writing, and people tend to make too much of a meal.'[9] But a dramatist who requires that actors attend special rehearsals on conveying the difference between a pause, three dots, and a silence in his scripts must desire that some psychological meal be made of his presentation of human interaction and know that in a post-Freudian age it is impossible to recover a pre-Freudian innocence.

That writers, like all of us, are drawn most toward and fascinated by what they abhor or fear is itself a Freudian insight with particular relevance to the subject-matter of this chapter. Many, even avowedly Christian, writers during this period revealed as much of a fascination with what was found to be deplorable—fantasy, power, violence, trickster figures, and dangerous myth-makers—as with discovering remedies for its control, transcendence, or containment. The false gods and violences of the demonized sacred in writers as various as Murdoch, Hughes, Golding, or Pinter were often presented as compellingly glamorous compared to the mundane good of everyday liberal moralities. The profane charisma of Muriel Spark's Mussolini-mimicking Jean Brodie or that of the devilish enchanter Mischa Fox in Murdoch's *The Flight from the Enchanter* (1956) has a self-declarative Nietzschean aristocratic vitality which may seem more attractive than the pettily destructive self-delusions and dishonesties of liberal bourgeois existence. These writers reveal how, in the absence of the sacred, the inverse realm of the profane may seem to supply what is lost, even if in grotesquely parodic form. As religion once organized the realm of the sacred, so psychoanalysis has been brought in to domesticate that of the profane. But as sin is replaced with medicalized sickness or pathology, the issue of personal responsibility and the possibility of a viable ethics becomes problematic. Most of the writers to be discussed in this chapter have been accused of complicity with what they reveal to be destructive in its effects: power, violence, the irrational, desire. Many are self-professed liberal humanists, yet their work is often a savage indictment of late liberalism for its moral dishonesty and exclusions and its spiritual failings. In exposing such absences, however, they open themselves to the dizzying experience of cutting away the ground on which they stand, the soil of what Auden called 'this island now', the loam of liberal England.

One way of understanding the drift of much of the literature of 1960–90 is to see in it a record of the confusions of a liberalism forced to reassess its very foundations. The official markers of liberal 'progress' in the period have also been precisely those developments (in science and technology) which have most clearly signalled the inadequacies of its inherited liberal ethics. The bomb, technologically created unemployment, genetic engineering, iatrogenic diseases, surrogate motherhood, *in vitro* fertilization: these are just a few of the consequences of developments in scientific knowledge which now confound the established ethical frameworks of liberal individualism. Indeed, throughout the sixties and seventies there were a series of 'Death of Literature', 'Death of the Author', and 'End of Liberal Culture' debates, where writers expressed their sense that it was no longer possible to write coherent causally determined plots or to present rounded characters whose behaviour corresponded to some ultimately fathomable core of individual personality. Postmodernism was born with a series of manifestos largely imported from America or the Continent: John Barth's essays on the literature of exhaustion and replenishment, Jean-François Lyotard's announcement of the end of the legitimacy of all those grand narratives (religious and historical teleologies of redemption or progress) which had sustained cultures in the past, Kurt Vonnegut's sense that there are no longer characters because people are the playthings of such enormous impersonal forces they defy representation within the conventions of traditional liberal bourgeois fiction.

In consequence, even the British novel, viewed by Bernard Bergonzi in 1970 as still parochial and non-experimental, subsequently went off into non-realist Shandyesque frolic in the pages of writers such as Julian Barnes or Salman Rushdie, or into *nouveau-roman*-esque in those of Christine Brooke-Rose or A. S. Byatt, or Gothic fantastic in those of Alisdair Gray or Angela Carter. Most writers, however, recognized that, amidst the crisis in the liberal legacy, one consistent element in human beings seemed to be the need to find and create orders of meaning. The self-reflexive formalism of writers such as Christine Brooke-Rose or the parodistic absurdity in the work of self-declared liberals such as Angus Wilson suggested an impulse less to hold the mirror up to nature than to place old conventions under the microscope of critical scepticism in order to test the continuing viability of their sense of order. As Western societies began to move out of that economic phase of industrial and productive capitalism which gave rise to the earliest liberal politics and ethics, and into an electronic, knowledge- and consumer-driven economy, literature seemed thrown into its own condition of crisis. It had become evident that Enlightenment reason could neither explain away human desire nor efficiently contain the human impulse toward transcendent meaning: more than ever from the sixties, it seemed imperative that literature address such absences.

Fictions of the Sacred and Profane

Throughout the sixties and seventies a number of writers concerned to retrieve the sacred or to express the profane often attempted to reconcile them with a tormented humanism. A novel which seemed to gather controversially and intensely into itself both the apocalyptic violence and the fantastic self-consciousness of the preceding decades was D. M. Thomas's *The White Hotel*, a bestseller and Booker Prize contender of 1981. To admirers, the novel represented a virtuoso and responsibly honest fictional exposé of the depths of the human soul, but for critics it was the worst sort of amoral and sensationalist voyeurism.

By way of prefatory comment, the novel opened with the admonitory lines from Yeats's 'Meditations in Time of Civil War': 'We had fed the heart on fantasies, | The heart's grown brutal from the fare; | More substance in our enmities than in our love . . .'. The quotation established an interpretative frame for the treatment of Thomas's ethically tricky subject-matter: the experiences and suffering of Jews during the Holocaust, and in particular the Babi Yar massacre. Defenders would bracket him with other writers who aesthetically revisited the Holocaust (such as Sylvia Plath, Ted Hughes, Geoffrey Hill, and Martin Amis, for example), as they argued for the cultural requirement that the atrocities of the concentration camps be kept imaginatively alive. However, no other non-Jewish writer appropriated an actual eyewitness account of a survivor, nor drew on the erotic and thanetic preoccupations of psychoanalysis in order to place the unique horror of the Holocaust in a poetically conceived and mythically legitimated pattern of loss, reparation, and redemption.

Further ethical issues arose in the plagiarism debate which followed publication, for it was realized that the description of the massacre included a more or less verbatim reproduction of four pages from a documentary eyewitness account by a survivor Dina Pronicheva. Thomas claimed in 1982 that the four pages were aesthetically and therefore morally justifiable as marking the need to signal at this point in the narrative a departure from fiction and a step into the brutality of history. However, from the initial inclusion of Freud's correspondence and throughout, the novel conflates fiction and fact in order that they be subsumed into the rhythm of what is presented as a final and historically transcendent mythopoeic truth about human desire. The historical specificity of the outrage which was Babi Yar is preserved by the inclusion of the eyewitness account, but then cancelled by an aesthetic strategy morally justified by an appeal to Freud's theory of the drives: all human experience is seen to be propelled by the universal instincts of sex and violence. Only in art can they be satisfactorily sublimated and so, at the end of the novel, all is redeemed in the aestheticized life hereafter which brings it to a close. In a travesty of humanism, Thomas lets Nazism utterly off the hook by claiming to have exposed the Nazi in each one of us. He updates the religious and pre-modern concept of original sin in the modern and post-Enlightenment language of psychoanalysis, presenting as a sickness without cure a condition in which we are both victim and victimizer, awaiting the final reckoning when all will be made well.

Events are presented through seven sections which include letters of Freud, a poem, a prose elaboration of the poem, a Freudian case history, a third-person historical narrative, and a final vision of life after death. From the beginning, however, a basic pattern of correspondence is set up between the events and narratives of a single life and those of revolution-, genocide-, and war-torn Europe between 1917 and 1939. Not only is the heroine Lisa (or Frau Anna G in Freud's casebook version) connected to the upheavals in middle and Eastern Europe by birth and complicated marriages; she is analysed by Freud in a case history and writes her own fantastic version of the neurosis and its analysis. The narrative logic and poetic imagery used to convey her illness and its Freudian interpretation is repeated in the account given in the later third-person sections of the novel: the belatedly emergent twentieth-century history of middle Europe up to the point of the Babi Yar massacre. The main protagonist of the book is as much Freud as Lisa, for he too is caught up in international history and is as self-divided as she: on the one hand, a progressive liberal scientist of the Enlightenment and, on the other, a poetic child of its dark side. Propelled toward myth and cosmic theories of destruction, Freud's limpid scientist's prose is endlessly tripped up by his blindness to his own condition of psychic repression. To read the novel is necessarily to identify with Freud, for only as psychoanalyst/detectives can readers themselves make sense of events. Freud's own reading of Anna's psychosomatic responses to childhood familial traumas (as symptoms of repressed homosexual impulses) is initially persuasive, but, as the story moves forward to 1930, reinterpretation is required. History is seen anamnesically and darkly to materialize the fantastically personal narrative of Lisa's earlier poem and journal. Lisa is found to be suffering not from the effects of a personally traumatized past but from a racially murdered future.

Her physical symptoms mimic the violence to be done to her in the abyss at Babi Yar. It is Freud's inability to face the racial question himself, as much as his adherence to a deterministic scientific logic, which produces the misdiagnosis. Yet this disavowal poetically and paradoxically vindicates his own theory that we most absolutely bury that which is the key to our condition. It is the absolute no-win clause of psychoanalysis. The historical exposure through the fictional plot of the repressed racial identity of Lisa as a Jew leads to the sexualized violence of her death: suffocation under corpses as she is speared on a soldier's bayonet. In appending to the novel an imaginary restorative afterlife, however, Thomas doubly connects the main narrative to Lisa's initial and poetically proleptic writing. The imaginary White Hotel is a totem of absolute desire: the lost wholeness of the Freudian body of the mother, recovered only in art and realized through the poem in an orgy of sucking which verges on the pornographic, and in oral imagery of mingling and merging where all is healed and nothing any longer hurts. Psychoanalysis is seen to be less a science than a mythic recognition of the spiritually and sensually redemptive powers of art which yet arise from the same psychic source as murderous aggression and cannibalistic lust.

Thomas's mythic vision, however, thereby denies the specific suffering of the Jews who were murdered in the Holocaust. Nazism itself fed off precisely those myths invoked by Thomas to justify his narrative: the Fascistic invocation of art to redeem politics in a seductive vision of reparative return to the pure and the whole. If this seems a harsh judgement, it can be supported by responsible historical accounts of the Holocaust and by the unrecontextualized words of its survivors. What emerges most arrestingly from these accounts is precisely the recognition that atrocities of this order leave surviving victims utterly unable to construct those comforting narratives through which the rest of us redeem human life by making retrospective sense of it. The survivor is condemned to rehearse again and again events which can never cohere in either formal or moral terms. The experience of the survivor wrecks all aesthetic and ethical schemes. Years earlier Walter Benjamin, a survivor himself, had conjured up the image of the Janus-faced Angel of History to attempt to convey such sense of disconnection: caught between the headwind of a receding world of religious significance and stable ultimate meaning and blown into an oncoming rush of the meaningless piles of debris of the future. Between them is a no man's land, bereft of redemption, impervious to the consolation which is art.[10]

Thomas's complicity with what is condemned in the examination of art as sympathetic magic afflicts, to some extent, all those who make this their subject. A novel on this theme which particularly caught the imagination of the mid-sixties was John Fowles's *The Magus* (1966, revised and reissued in 1977). Fowles had summed up his quasi-existential and then fashionable philosophy in the aphoristic *The Aristos* (1965): 'Mystery is unknowing, is energy. As soon as the mystery is explained it ceases to be a source of energy.' The existentialist Fowles saw the need to repudiate God as an illusory projection of human desire for comfort and certainty. Only without such illusions may we embrace the painful condition of freedom which alone confers full human responsibility. *The Aristos*, like Conchis in *The Magus*, preached a doctrine of hazard: so long as we regard our actions as reflective of some divine scheme, we can be neither free nor responsible.

Appropriately, the novel is an existential labyrinth with no final *telos* or significance, though expectations set up by its romance form tend to lead the reader into an anticipation of moral education and fabular resolution. Fowles's ethical position, however, creates aesthetic difficulties. If your message is the goodness of mystery, contingency, and the need to avoid belief in redemptive orders, it would seem inconsistent to bow to an aesthetic requirement that moral paradoxes be resolved and hermeneutic endings neatly tied up. However, the open-endedness of *The Magus* seems obfuscatory to a pointless degree. Fowles non-doctrinaire doctrine of mystery creates an aesthetic and ethical abyss: in relativizing every frame and position offered, it undermines even as it embodies the authority of its own ethics of hazard (indeed it is impossible even to unravel the contortions of its vertiginously complicated plot).

Readers are clearly meant to despise the initial pseudo-aristocratic insouciance of its rebel hero without a cause, Nicholas D'Urfe, who draws adeptly on a superficial acquaintance with existential philosophy in order to justify the conversion of others to objects for his own detached (and often sexual) pleasure. So, too, we can take in our readerly stride the book's transition from a drab social-realist delivered London bed-sitterland to the exotically Romantic and self-consciously *Tempest*-parodying Greek island of Phraxos where he takes a teaching job. As experienced readers of romance we might even accept that the shift of gear simply requires us to recognize that Nick has gone to this land of Oz not in order to teach but in order to learn: he will enter the magic kingdom of art to return sea-changed into the rich strangeness of human decency. Certainly, Conchis, the Prospero figure, takes him through his metatheatrical paces on the way to knowledge, setting up a series of eidetic images, romantic projections of desire, each to be discredited as selfish illusion. However, Conchis is even more questionable in the practice of his art than Prospero himself. An ambiguously double-faced Jungian trickster figure, most of his magic is mumbo-jumbo that conveniently allows Fowles to parody sixties' psychobabble while keeping the reader in the dark about Conchis's real motives by refusing any omniscient authorial glimpse into his inner life.

Yet, we desire him to have one. A romantic device cannot talk about the boundary situation of its own terrible moment of existential choice between betrayal or loss of human life in the midst of a war which actually happened: Conchis is more than a device but less than a character. In presenting him, Fowles manipulates the reader as much as Conchis manipulates Nick. What are the ethical implications of this? Nick does return from Conchis's Godgame (the original title of the novel) knowing he must not sacrifice others to selfishly romantic illusions: but without its romantic illusions, Fowles's novel would not be worth reading. Without some complicity in the sinister pretentiousness of Conchis's morality-through-art therapy, *The Magus* could not assert its own sense of the immorality of pretension. For Fowles is an atheist who attempts to redeem a beleaguered humanism by fastening onto it the requirement that only by existential submission to the moment of extraordinary choice may we discover a sacred sense of who we are. Much of the novel, however, wallows in the romantically projected moments it wishes to expose as inauthentic. When the boundary moment arrives, therefore, we are unable to muster an appropriately venerable response. Several critics of the time found its romanticism tedious and its assertion of moral education unconvincing: it is undoubtedly, as its author subsequently admitted, an 'adolescent novel'. More positively, however, it can now be regarded as an important attempt to address post-war anxieties about the relations between Fascism and fictionality and, adolescent or not, it did help to steer the British novel out of the complacency of a suburban realism and platitudinous Englishness.

Iris Murdoch was another writer whose work had explored such terrain since her first novel *Under the Net* (1954). While Fowles's novels pulse to an alternating rhythm of immersion in romantic fantasy and form followed by a stripping-away of illusion and a return to a modified realism, Murdoch's work attempts to see both processes as part of the same movement, much as a wave may be a particle in the new physics. She has called such impulses the 'crystalline' and the 'journalistic' and they continually break down into each other: 'to combine form with a respect for reality with all its odd contingent ways is the highest art of prose.'[11] It is one which she admits rarely to have achieved. Her rhythms are propelled by the tug of a final *telos* and a faith that art can be truth and not lies, that there is good magic and bad magic. She is concerned less to educate her readers into the recognition of an authentic moment of existential choice, and more with a pilgrim's progress toward the 'good' through the annihilation of the ego altogether. The moral lesson is a difficult one, however, for in our yearning for the good we may come to worship false gods. Moreover, in the aftermath of their eventual abandonment, we may fail to see that, because the good does not inhere in a thing or an intellectual system, this does not entail that it has no existence whatsoever.

Murdoch has quoted Simone Weil extensively in her philosophical work to support the idea that the proper goal of intellectual or aesthetic activity is that which does not exist, and that 'the good artist, the true lover, the dedicated thinker, the unselfish moral agent solving his problem: they can create the object of love'.[12] The ready-made label will not take us there. Despite good intentions, however, most of us cannot face the necessary void which must be experienced in order to arrive at such love. Her novels plot the misunderstandings, comic and tragic, which ensue from this, and present the occasional saints who get there and the devils who usually destroy them on arrival. Her first novel of the sixties, *A Severed Head* (1961), explored the chaotic violence which is unleashed in the complacent attempt to conduct human relationships according to facile intellectual systems and faith in absolute rational self-control. Its cast of academics and psychoanalysts fall into a carnivalesque maelstrom of sexual complication as the dark gods return to wreak their revenge on those who blindly believe in the magic of the analytic textbook.

In *A Fairly Honourable Defeat* (1970), the force of good as contingency and opacity, and that of evil as order and the imposition of pattern, was diametrically presented through the characters of the saint-like Tallis and the evil incarnate Julius, the latter a survivor of Belsen and morally contaminated by its bureaucratized killing. From his trivial compulsion to tidy up, to his Iago-like obsession with playing on the weaknesses of others in order to trap them in his self-aggrandizing plots, Julius is no respecter of the Murdochian virtue of acquiescence to the contingent. However, the exposure of evil through the assertion of love is no guarantor of justice either: love is simply its own reward and cannot take away pain. What is so frightening about Julius is his recognition that 'it is characteristic of this planet that the path of virtue is so unutterably depressing that it can be guaranteed to break the spirit and quench the vision of anybody who consistently attempts to tread it. Evil, on the contrary, is exciting and fascinating and alive.' His success depends upon a charismatic glamour which can be exposed through the good magic of morally responsible art, but which is more difficult to defeat in the real world of muddle, pain, and insecurity.

Although Murdoch's later work continued the concern with art and moral choice, like much of the writing of the seventies, it became more directly preoccupied with language as the medium through which we present our fictions and negotiate with the world. In an interview published in 1982 she confessed to seeing language and art as falsehood and yet still the means of redemption: 'there is a religious way, as it were, to the divine which rests in these things.'[13] Her novels since *The Black Prince* (1973) have tended to shift from a fascination with the return of the dark myths which reason has repressed to an exploration of the limits of language as we use it to construct fictions by which to live. Interestingly, almost all her central characters and particularly her first-person narrators are males, usually intellectual, egotistical wordsmiths who use language dishonestly or self-deludingly as moral evasion or rationalization even as they struggle to identify themselves as artists. Characters who are not suspicious of words even as they are drawn to them are almost always shown to be the worst and most dangerous self-deceivers. The enlightened are those who recognize that truth arrives only through void, as Loxias sees at the end of *The Black Prince*: 'All artists dream of a silence which they must enter, as some creatures return to the sea to spawn. The creator of form must suffer formlessness. Even risk dying of it.' We exist in the revelation of our acts rather than in any 'nut-shell of self-theory', reaching the distant Platonic good, as the Kantian sublime, in a level seeing of the thing in itself which involves a continuous avoidance of the consolations of self-theory.

The novel is Murdoch's ideal art form because it is seen to have precisely that 'open texture, the porous or cracked quality' through which 'life flows in and out of it'.[14] In shaping its flow into pattern, the novelist can create high consolatory forms, but also lay bare those moments when comforting illusion cannibalizes the other and becomes an egotistic obsession with power. *The Sea, the Sea* (1978) was a meditation on such themes, again contrasting a 'good' magician with a 'bad' one. Charles is a theatre director who has left the theatre as a place of false magic and is living in a remote cottage by the sea. James, his cousin, is a religious man determined to divest himself of those magical aspects of religion which facilitate narcissistic fantasy rather than moral self-abnegation. Charles fails: theatre is simply re-created in the space of the domestic in everything from exotic and eccentric cuisine to manipulative and possessive relationships. James succeeds, but only by sublimating his erotic love for Charles in an act of self-abnegatory rescue which causes his own death. For Murdoch, the good can only be achieved through a death of the self. And for her handful of saints, it is usually a literal death.

Dramas of Recognition

Why does Charles decide to leave the theatre? He believes that 'even a middling novelist can tell a lot of truth. His humble medium is on the side of truth. Whereas the theatre, even at its most "real-istic", is connected with the level at which, and the methods by which, we tell our everyday lives.' He goes on to reflect further that theatre works its magic only by casting an absolute spell, creating 'a factitious spell-binding present moment' and thereby imprisoning its spectators. This may read as a description of the ethos of total theatre or of the idea of life as a continuous drafting of dramatic scripts. We have seen how both concepts entered British theatre in the sixties and influenced the work of new directors such as Peter Brook and Peter Hall. Until then, Osborne's *Look Back in Anger* (1956) had put British theatre back on the international map. The play expressed that sense of cultural dislocation arising out of national decline and the renunciation of imperialist dreams after Suez, and also the class disaffections thrown up by social changes and the inadequacies of the Welfare State. Yet its hero's well-documented anger had always been misogynistic and unfocused and striated by a romantic nostal-gia for the old 'great causes'. Osborne's technique of rhetorical assault would be challenged by the influence of Artaud and Brecht in the sixties, but even then British theatre was rarely one of total spectacle or total alienation. It remained a theatre driven by language con-ceived as the primary mode of engagement by which people usually negotiate their relations in the world and establish bids for recogni-tion and power. In fact, if one were to look for an epithet to describe the theatre of the time, 'Theatre of Recognition' would be as good as any.

Theatre is usually a markedly social form of art (except perhaps in Beckett's dramas of the solipsistic self), presented through ex-ternal dialogic engagement in what Murdoch's narrator Charles calls a 'factitious present because it lacks the free aura of personal reflec-tion'. Until the advent of political theatre in the late sixties, the important works of British drama reflect the uncertainties and shifts of the time largely through examining their effects on the social relations between human beings. This did not, of course, preclude exploration of the metaphysical implications of social existence. Recognition is a fundamental human need, usually but not exclus-ively enacted in a social arena. To be recognized for what one takes oneself to be is to feel one's existence and one's worth confirmed:

to feel esteemed and ultimately loved. Not to be recognized is either to feel anger against the other or to feel shame or guilt that one has failed to live up to expectations: that one is somehow defective—or 'junk', as a character in Pinter's *The Caretaker* puts it. Recognition becomes problematic in societies undergoing significant change. Social codes appropriate for one group may break down in relation to another, ethical claims may become irreconcilable and incommensurable, available moral and political languages inadequate. Traditional assumptions about social place and obligation and the expectation of deference disappear.

Hence, insecurity and fear are bred. It becomes harder to read the signs of the times as they appear in the behaviour of others. Misunderstanding occurs and violence ensues. In order to attempt to force recognition of the violent injustice in Vietnam upon a diffident Britain, an actor burnt butterflies to death at the end of Peter Brook's 1966 London production of *US*. Most of the audience refused to be bludgeoned into recognition by such an explosive collapse of the boundaries of art and life and left the theatre in anger, not at the war, but at the director. When violence erupts, scapegoats are sought, usually those whom the fragile social order has deemed to be outside its limits: the Stanleys and Davieses who haunt Harold Pinter's plays, the tramps and misfits. Increasingly between 1960 and 1990 the democratic ethos encouraged by the Welfare State commitment produced new demands for recognition by increasing numbers of social groups. Equally, the media world of personality cult enhanced the desirability of recognition in its own often tawdry fashion, and so, too, the burgeoning nationalism in Scotland and Wales; the troubles in Northern Ireland; the independence demanded by former British colonies; and the new demands for gender, ethnic, and racial equality: all asked for recognition of unique identity marked by the social or political acknowledgement of difference.

Recognition is the marker of social belonging. In its megalomaniacal modes, however, it is also the impulse behind imperialism, and, when it is withheld unjustly or enigmatically, may produce anger, violence, and breakdown. Whereas the novelist can reflect discursively on this process, dramatists must show it, reveal its effects in the conversations people have with each other and in the way in which they engage with the world. The problem of recognition was foregrounded in the sixties in the linguistic evasions of Pinter's 'dramas of menace'; in the individualistic rebellious rhetoric of Osborne's Luther; in Orton's bourgeois-baiting, anarchic exposure of hypocrisy in the farces which he saw as a revenge on society; and in the fables of social aggression in the work of Bond or the dandyish intellectual wit of Tom Stoppard. Some dramatists were concerned directly with the social or political implications of recognition, others with its more metaphysical or existential aspects. Each conveyed the uncertainty of the time, like the novelists and poets, as a problem involving language: even if we could say what we thought we meant, we would still be unable to guarantee a correspondent meaning for the listener. Words are the vehicle, but continually frustrate the achievement, of our dramas of recognition.

Throughout his career, Harold Pinter made tantalizing statements about what he was not doing in his plays and, somewhat like the utterances of the Cretan liar, the only consistent line seemed to be that they were about the impossibility of verification: the truth that there is no truth. Everybody in Pinter lies all of the time. In the original programme notes to the 1960 London production of *The Room* and *The Dumb Waiter*, he informed audiences that

The desire for verification is understandable but cannot always be satisfied. There are no hard distinctions between what is true and what is false . . . A character on the stage who can present no convincing argument or information as to his past experience, his present behaviour or his aspirations, nor give a comprehensive analysis of his motives is as legitimate and as worthy of attention as one who, alarmingly, can do all of these things. The more acute the experience, the less articulate its expression.

The note could be read, somewhat paradoxically, as a justification of British stiff upper lip. Curiously, in fact, this is not so far from an accurate reflection of the Pinteresque, for his drama works not so much through direct lying as through constant evasion, unfinished sentences, absence of markers of social orientation, a continuous and dislocatory lack of fit between words and stage action.

Threats arrive indirectly through the choice of a particular resonant word or phrase: as when Mick enters *The Caretaker* (the play of 1960 which established Pinter's reputation and success) in Act 3 and, without looking at Davies, but directing the statement at him, says, 'All this junk here, it's no good to anyone.' Similarly, Davies later makes the mistake of interpreting Mick's irritation with his brother as a signal for their collusive exclusion of Aston on account of those mental deficiencies which Davies secretly fears may also be his own. Mick responds with the menacing 'You get a bit out of your depth sometimes, don't you,' following it up with the newly confident and direct 'You're a bloody imposter mate.' This is recognition parading as non-recognition which Davies, with his pathetic fiction of the self-identificatory Sidcup papers and his fearful obsession with the supposed welfare world of social security regulation, dreads most of all. Pinter's point—also an important emphasis in the existential anti-psychiatry of R. D. Laing at the time—is that to invoke depth, to stray from the surfaces of evasion, risks a dangerous exposure of vulnerability which enables the other to claim one's identity in his or her own power games. And Mick pounces upon the opportunity.

As Pinter has said,

I think we communicate only too well, in our silence, in what is unsaid, and that what takes place is continual evasion, desperate rearguard attempts to keep ourselves to ourselves. Communication is too alarming. To enter into someone else's life is too frightening, to disclose to others the poverty within us is too fearsome a possibility.[15]

Recognition in the Pinter universe is mostly from the ground of an existential and social insecurity where identity can only be realized through the negative modes of power struggle. The most trivial phatic communion is loaded with a demand for recognition which is never under rational control and is incessantly present. Not knowing who they are, seeking constant reflection through the other, the powerful in Pinter are as enslaved as the weak, and as vulnerable. His dramas of recognition are as atavistically territorial as to suggest that very little of human social intercourse is conducted according to rational criteria. Such theatre perfectly suited the climate of official welfare commitment with its pervasive underlying private unease at the failure to produce a culture of compassion or existential and material security. The plays explore the impossibility of conducting the moral life through purely rational formulas and in a world where social planning has made little inroad on fundamental social injustices or profound human fears.

Not that Pinter has ever been an overtly political playwright: rather, one who responds to the political temper of his time. His plays are devoid of idealism, for the characters seek at most that temporary containment of fear which is fleeting acceptance by another human being. They rarely find it. The later plays tended to move out of working-class environments and into the psychologically tangled webs of deceptive narrative of the bourgeoisie, but they can still be read as meditations on the need to establish secure territory in the world through the appropriation of the desire of the other. *Old Times* (1971), for example, which is a struggle between three characters over their implication in each other's version of the past, perfectly exemplified Hegel's observation that to feel secure in our identity we desire not so much the other as the desire of the other. Even in the confines of the family, people are territorial possessions to be struggled over. In *The Homecoming* (1965), the return of Teddy, Jewish working-class son made good and now an American academic, catalyses a semi-oedipal family collapse. The family line up to finalize sexual deals on the body of Teddy's wife, Ruth. Teddy, the prodigal son already castrated for daring to break the ranks of masculine and virile working-class culture, is shorn of the sexual possession which he can no longer claim as his own. As emasculated dealer in middle-class ideas, he loses the recognition of his family and his wife that he is its son and her lover. The play caused much critical controversy in Britain, where many regarded its eruption of familial sexual violence as too disturbingly pathological. In the context of the child-abuse and incest revelations of the eighties, however, perhaps it now seems rather less outlandish as a portrait of family life in Britain of the late twentieth century.

If Pinter exposed the sadism inherent in supposedly compassionate institutions, Edward Bond savagely indicted modern technocratic society for its violations of human dignity and its incapacity to care. Of all the dramas of the sixties, Bond's plays were probably closest to the Marcusean spirit of the counterculture and represented one of its most responsible literary voices. Though Bond saw himself as a supporter of reason, like the counterculturalists he also believed that a rational society cannot be produced through rational means. For Bond, human beings are made violent in a world where nurturing has become the rod of punishment, and compassion the iron arm of social regulation. His second play, *Saved* (1965), staged at the Royal Court, caused as much controversy as Pinter's *The Homecoming* in its literal enactment of Blake's aphoristic 'sooner murder an infant in its cradle than nurse unacted desires'. Though adamant that his plays constituted a critically realist 'rational theatre', Bond worked often through irrationalist means, drawing on the sacramental force of particular symbols, returning in each work, for example, to the biblical theme of the 'slaughter of the innocents' and, more disturbingly, sometimes drawing on emotionally shocking eruptions of physical violence. The plays incorporate Brechtian techniques of distance, however, so that the audience not only feels the direct emotional shock of physical assault but is made to reflect upon its own implication in and political responsibility for what happens.

Thus, the ritualized stoning of the baby before an indifferent and impotent audience in *Saved* (1965) was a shocking manifestation of Bond's belief that industrial technocratic society murders its inhabitants through emotional and spiritual denial even as it promises them material welfare. Shakespeare's social withdrawal into his walled garden in *Bingo* (1974) is presented as an enactment of what Bond regards as the enclosure of psychic repression which energizes his plays. In Bond's play, Shakespeare, the landowner, does not want to acknowledge that the physical withdrawal of land from the rural poor in the early capitalist enclosures of the Elizabethan period is an act of violence. So he writes what Bond implies may be immoral and conscience-assuaging plays about an irremediable suffering which is the essential condition of a universal human nature. Indeed, walls appear in overt or symbolic form in each of the plays, most spectacularly in *Lear* (1972), but always testifying to the erroneousness of a faith which sees security in exclusion or in mental or physical territorialism, as in Lear's misguided: 'My wall will make you free.' The wall which keeps out the enemy is always the prison which cages in the 'free citizen' in another Blakean realization that 'A

Robin Redbreast in a cage | Puts all Heaven in a Rage.' Picking up Lear's comment to Cordelia in *King Lear*, Bond shows that a caged bird cannot sing, and that it is not innate evil which breeds a Regan or a Goneril but the repressive state and its destructive morality. Workers are dying of the disease of 'wall death'—work as alienation —under a political regime which expects absolute responsibility from its citizens without showing any corresponding care for or respons- ibility toward them. Thus Cordelia, who puts protocol and abstract honour before love, is still the ethical centre of Bond's play, but as the villain who embodies the fundamental immoralism of such morality.

In *The Fool* (1976) as well as *Bingo*, the wall reappears in the shape of the rural enclosure which creates the class divisions of modern capitalism. Bond traces the political roots of violence in the contemporary world through historically situated dramas which deny audiences the comfortable security of *plus ça change* assumptions. So in *The Fool*, he suggests that an artist like the Romantic peasant poet John Clare, who was dependent for recognition of his work on the faddish sensibilities of the new early technocratic élites, was bound to fall into a state of politically induced psychic self-division. Those who granted him the status of artist were the same who had dispossessed his class and framed his talent as merely decorative and bucolic diversion from the serious and grimy business of capitalist profiteering. Depoliticizing the sources of the poetry in class conflict and explaining away its multivocal effects as the madness of artistic inspiration, the new middle classes could then enjoy his verse as a leisure pastime and neutralize its subversive relation to political authority. Like Elizabethan fools, the artist in a capitalist society is a seer whose wisdom is compromised by his dependency on pre- cisely those hypocrisies which his wit exposes. Irrational action is the product of repressed need in a world where, more terrifyingly, the threats cannot remain purely verbal because 'this is the whole dialectic of violence, I threaten you, you threaten me, and finally you have to carry out your threats, otherwise there is no credence behind them'.[16]

The plays of Bond as well as those of Pinter reflect the influ- ence of R. D. Laing upon notions of identity and social interaction throughout the sixties. Bond announced in directly Laingian terms that in an unequal and unjust society 'men . . . are driven to a kind of madness', for 'no one could quietly bear to live the sort of life we have to live now unless he'd been made morally insane and this state is brought about by our education and the erroneous pressures to conform, possess and compete that threaten us all our lives'.[17] Theories of the innateness of evil and violence are seen to be the immoral and spurious but ideologically desirable foundation of a Western bourgeois morality urgently requiring new theatrical anatomy. In the preface to *Lear*, Bond justified his inclusion of scenes of violence such as the horrendous Nazi-like torture of Gloucester:

I write about violence as Jane Austen wrote about manners. Violence shapes and obsesses our society, and if we do not stop being violent we have no future. People who do not want writers to write about violence want to stop them writing about us and our time. It would be immoral not to write about violence.

Poets and Shamans

The poetry of Ted Hughes presents the paradox that, in denying the animal inside and the gods above, we have become bestial in our violence and theomaniacal in our presumption to be lords of all that we survey. However, because the roots of the sacred are also those of the barbarous, only in extreme states or depraved conditions do we discover our full capacities. The poet Elizabeth Bartlett, like a number of Hughes's critics, demurs from this assumption in an amusing condemnation of the masculinization of poetry in the period: 'Lying awake in a provincial town | I think about poets. They are mostly | men, or Irish, turn out old yellow | photographs, may use four letter words, | stick pigs or marry twice, and edit | most of the books and magazines.' Her poem, entitled 'Stretch Marks, from The Czar is Dead', is an entertaining conundrum which teases the reader to infer from each epithet the identity of the poet to whom it seems to belong. More seriously, it can be read as a comment too on the predominant versions of male egotistical sublime which seem to inform the definitive poetics of the sixties and seventies. In more conventional critical discourse, Hughes's style is indeed often described in terms such as 'muscularity of diction' or 'impacted masculine energy' or as the Dionysian *animus* to Plath's *anima*.

Tom Paulin has called Hughes the poet as 'masculine hunter-gatherer' (the primitive tribesman most likely to 'stick pigs'?). Sometimes, though, he may be cropper of the moors or hillfarmer who must kill to be kind, as in the *Moortown* (1979) description of a half-neonatal lamb, slaughtered to save its mother. The lamb is 'hooked in a loop' which pulls tighter around its neck with each birth contraction of the unknowingly complicitous maternal body until its torso arrives in 'a smoking slither of oils' separated from the shockingly 'hacked-off head'. Hughes, however, has always preferred to see his own tribal role as one of Shaman, less a gatherer of food than one of spiritual energy. It is still a decidedly masculine function, that of priestly communicant: 'The dog's god is a scrap dropped from the table, | The mouse's saviour is a ripe wheat grain. | Hearing the Messiah cry | My mouth widens in adoration' ('Gog').

Hughes set out to reinvent himself as mythic Rainman in a demythologized world where Nietzsche had claimed that human beings 'grub about' in the broken traces of the past to reinvoke lost magic. In an interview in *London Magazine* in 1971, the function of poetry is asserted now to be 'the record of just how the forces of the Universe try to redress some balance disturbed by human error'. If his earlier writing had shown a Shamanistic identification with the coiled evolutionary purposefulness of an animal world free of the dissipating burden of consciousness, by *Wodwo* (1967) and *Crow* (1970) he is more concerned with that instinctual return of the perverted repressed in the form of the dark gods come to scourge over-rationalized Western humankind. Liberal niceties have no place in what Anthony Thwaite has called the 'portentous grimness' of this world. The avenging furies return in a variety of shapes: with bubbling mouths as the 'Ghost Crabs' in *Wodwo*, 'their eyes | In a slow mineral fury | Press through our nothingness', or they fasten on an unsupecting Anglican clergyman in the Joycean Nighttown of the 'defrocked inner world' of *Gaudete* (1977). Earlier images of caged jaguar and exhibitionistic strutting parrots functioned to suggest that our compulsion to colonize nature outside is a defence against recognition of the caged and contaminated nature of our own internal primitive energies, now that 'convulsion in the roots of blood' which boils to be free. The hawk, apotheosis of all that is most predatory and therefore supreme survivor whose 'manners are tearing off heads', has no naturally self-selective use for compassion and announces menacingly 'I am going to keep things like this' ('Hawk Roosting', *Lupercal*, 1960). The short monosyllabic sentences dispense with the hesitations of consciousness as with any other evolutionary handicap. This is a world of pounce, stab, bounce, drill, spring, coil, of impacted verbal as well as semantic energy. Hughes condemns the violences we perpetrate on each other under cover of consideration and yet celebrates and admires the Lawrentian vitalism of a natural world untramelled by liberal ditherings. Despite his vision of human life as a numb and shut-down travesty of evolutionary survival after Auschwitz, however, Hughes comes perilously close in his poetry to the affirmation of a religion of the blood. The creativity of the artist, as that of the devouring pike, is seen as a universal will to power foolishly and aberrantly dressed up in those liberal moral platitudes whose fraudulence the poet must expose. Nature is beyond good and evil and yet an other within ourselves. Denying the power of this realm of amoral energy, of the 'bang of blood in the brain deaf the ear', we simply perpetrate a greater violence upon the world through our complacent and arrogant rationalisms.

Depravity, confusion, and nihilism reign. Barren landscapes are sterile mindscapes. Humans are whipped by apocalyptic avenging horses, thistles metamorphose into Viking warriors 'stiff with weapons', and God as *logos*, mistaken and consolatory projection of human desire, is overcome by the destruction spawned from the greater primordial chaos of his mother's belly. At the 'exact centre', the humanoid Wodwo cannot find its place or emerge from 'roots roots roots roots . . .' to know why it is here or what it is. Genesis is blasphemously revisited in the comic book Black Bible of *Crow*, whose own cartoonish mechanical vitalism has at least guaranteed survival in a world where compassion kills and nurturing breeds death. *Crow* is the absurdist slapstick laugh that laughs at itself laughing because there is no other audience left to listen: the mimic of Old Testament incantation, ancient myth, and psychobabble, the nihilistic mocker of all systems. In some essays, Hughes has argued that this violent state of affairs is consequence not cause of our suppression of the sacred energies:

The inner world, separated from the outer world is a place of demons. The outer world separated from the inner world, is a place of meaningless objects and machines. The faculty that makes the human being out of these two worlds is called divine. That is only a way of saying that it is a faculty without which humanity cannot really exist. It can be called religious or visionary.[18]

Judging by Hughes's poetry, however, the visionary can manifest itself in the contemporary human world only by the grotesque caper of the indestructable cartoon character, or in the bleak determinism of a natural order of Darwinian survival. Either way, it is an unkind world in which we live.

In his writing of the late fifties, Thom Gunn was preoccupied with violence, mechanical movement, and a potentially cynical or nihilistic philosophy of pose, all of which seemed to ally him with Hughes, though his official allegiance was, for a time, with the Movement. Certainly his work seemed to partake of a clash of rule and energy, though of a more formally disciplined kind initially crafted according to the poetics of his teacher Yvor Winters. Poems such as 'On the Move' showed concern, like those of Hughes, about the loss of human existential direction and reflected some need to induce artificial states of energized purposefulness, revving up the motorbike of the human body in attempts to emulate the instinctual 'gust of the birds | That spurts across the field'. The hum of the bikers' machines 'bulges to thunder held by calf and thigh' but the power of their physique to swell the moment into purposefulness is no more than the futile 'dull thunder of approximate words' of the preceding paragraph. The boys don their leathers and strap in doubt, presenting yet another image of over-masculinized self-sufficiency, marriage to the machine, a 'lighting'-out which is itself the purpose of the journey rather than any expectation of arrival at what might become home. This early poetry is driven by a barely disguised erotic energy, controlled through metrical discharge but dissipated by the unavailability of any appropriate erotic object. However, where Gunn departed from Hughes was in the gradual discovery, particularly by the time of *Touch* (1967), of a relational identity where the will to power is subdued by the force of love. Like a number of writers in the period, Gunn discovers, in the ability to loosen the boundaries between self and other and to acknowledge the infantile need for mergence, that sense of personal significance which seems to elude those who go smashing their way self-consciously to a more impersonal demesne of the sacred.

The violence of pose was ever an uncertain and defensive swagger, disguising the desire to discover a will which is not self-created. The later poems tended to shift away from cityscapes, and they are full of moments of delicate illumination when a wall or boundary momentarily or suddenly falls and a reciprocal nakedness unites human beings to each other or to some perceived beauty in the world. Light imagery is used throughout *Moly* (1971) to suggest, in Wordsworthian style, that only when the controlling eye of vision is suspended can the inner eye of illumination come to light the world. The sun appears suddenly as a 'Great seedbed, yellow centre of the flower' which can illumine with passionless love a circle of care and 'kindle in acceptance round your centre' all that it shines upon. Touch, of the sun's rays or another's cradled body, is a physical metaphor for connection of all kinds. In *Jack Straw's Castle* (1976) the metaphor was stretched, rather in the manner of metaphysical wit, by invoking the image of a hinge to convey a sense of the discovery of own's own identity in a mutual connectedness with the other which allows for both autonomy and at-oneness: 'And that mere contact is sufficient touch, | A hinge, it separates but not too much.' The masculine pose has been abandoned with the primacy of the gaze, the unavoidably confrontational existential demand for recognition. Now, a model of intersubjective relationality, dissolving the boundaries of ego and other, and usually associated with or defensively projected onto the feminine, is comfortably embraced.

Many of the poems, again like those of Hughes, are about the need for acceptance of the non-rational elements in human experience. For Gunn, however, it is not too late to achieve this, and in tune with the countercultural ethos, with progressive liberalism and the existential theology of the time, it is assumed that a sense of the sacred can be recovered through loving personal relations. Literal images of uniformed man, as in the poem 'Innocence' in *My Sad Captains* (1961), about the callous indifference of the militaristically trained soldier, continue to evoke the ignorant violence bred by isolationist regimes of puritanical self-discipline. *Moly* takes the ancient name of the drug in *The Odyssey* which protects the self by opening consciousness to an awareness of the body, and indeed was written after Gunn's emigration to California and the subsequent acceptance of his homosexuality and experimentation with hallucinogenic drugs. The post-holocaust survivor of 'Misanthropos' (written in the looser form of syllabics, lines of equal numbers of syllables with unequal stress patterns and in violation of Winters's own precept of the fallacy of 'imitative form') is stripped gradually of each protective layer of social convention until, entirely relinquishing control and entering a void of disgust and contempt for humanity, he comes through, no longer a 'courier of identity', to reach instinctively and without thought of self-protection towards another suffering human being. The impulse would be described again some fifteen years later in *The Man with the Night Sweats* (1992). Here, the initial reassurance of 'the stay of your secure firm dry embrace' resounds consolingly throughout the subsequent poems, but gathers on its way ironic accretions which arise from the new horror of the times: 'As if hands were enough | To hold an avalanche off.' In the era of AIDS, touch may cure one sickness to become horribly implicated in another. The poems are a tender requiem for the dwindling and stilled lives of those who are the victims of the disease.

Octavio Paz has argued that 'all poets in the moments, long or short, of poetry, if they are really poets, hear the *other* voice'.[19] It is an insistence that poetry, like the sacred life, should be a calling: you do not choose it but must simply submit if chosen. However, the assumption can produce very different kinds of poetry. Another poet who has constantly used sacramental language but without writing specifically 'religious poetry' is Charles Tomlinson, for whom the poem, after Wallace Stevens, is a Mundo: an imaginatively inspired 'Supreme Fiction'. Art creates worlds of its own which are always other than the world that is. The poet may not be a divinity, but poetry, self-consciously purveyed, can serve as some form of compensation for that promise of revealed truth which has failed to materialize: 'The artist lies | For the improvement of truth. Believe him' ('A Meditation on John Constable'). However, if poetry must substitute for heaven, a 1972 poem 'Ars Poetica' explicitly distanced its author from the *in extremis* school of verse, whether that of the forties or sixties, announcing 'No Decline of the West | full stop.' The poet may be *homo faber* after the Death of God, but he is first of all *homo sapiens*, arriving in a world which pre-exists his construction of it and surviving through co-operation as well as conquest. Rather than rail against this earth's material recalcitrance, Tomlinson enjoins a passionate humility before the 'hiddennesses' of its energetic otherness (and it is not surprising that Heideggerians have been attracted to his poetry).

While the 'pop poets' called for the dissolution of poetry into life as event, urging that the poem leave the spatial order of objects and enter an undifferentiated flow of temporality, Tomlinson insisted from the first that life and art are different and he proceeded to make it the theme of his verse. Each poem is a testimony to what James referred to as the 'solidity of specification': the attempt to convey the materiality of a visual world which the poet can neither enter nor possess through language. But he also asserts that 'Art | Is complete when it is human. | Once the looped pigments, the pin-heads of light | Securing space under their deft restrictions | Convince, as the index of a possible passion, | As the adequate gauge, both of the passion, | And its object' ('A Meditation on John Constable', *Seeing is Believing*, 1960). Language creates only in the sense of naming what must ever be other than it, but it is a 'kind of birth' and one which 'echoes in our being' ('Adam', *The Way of a World*, 1969): a revelation which is also a kind of concealment.

Like some of Gunn's, many of his poems thus advocate a Wordsworthian response of humility or subservience to the natural world with which one communes, a response which preserves a sense of the sacred in nature. Only by acceptance of your (the inclusive pronoun is well chosen) position at the edge can you intuit the centre: the edge is the gossamer which will net a universe but 'one whose centre is not you' ('At the Edge', 1981). It is a threshold. Like George Eliot's scratched pier-glass in *Middlemarch*, the image reminds us that any pattern we see exists in itself outside the light of perception which plays on it. Phenomenologically, the centre is both inside and outside the observer. His best-known statement of the theme was in a poem entitled 'Swimming Chenango Lake'. The embrace of body and water, an immersion in a 'mercilessness' that is a kind of 'mercy sustaining him', brings the swimmer to recognition of the body as an envelope of sense posted into a world which stamps its meanings wordlessly upon his epithelial surface. Again the image draws on the sacramental associations of baptism, but although naming occurs in the subsequent interpretation which is the poem itself, the poem is something new and radically different. The swimmer's experience of the body in water is an Adamic intimation of phenomenal existence: body and water 'free' beyond the possession of self or language.

Faith, the Grotesque, and the Visibility of Darkness

It is evident from the above discussion that the sacred can be variously addressed through literature quite outside the framework of orthodox belief. This is not to claim that there have not been a number of important Christian writers during the period, though it is clear that there are only a few who deal explicitly with religious belief as the overt theme of their work. Most of those who do are Catholics or ex-Catholics (Anthony Burgess, Graham Greene, David Lodge, Piers Paul Read, Muriel Spark, Seamus Heaney); even fewer have written explicitly from the Free Church tradition as the Bunyans and Wesleys of the past; some Anglicans, like Geoffrey Hill, write mainly of the painful and difficult struggle for faith or, like A. N. Wilson, of the problem of truth in literature and history, whilst others, such as Sara Maitland and Michele Roberts, attempt to connect Christian themes or icons with socialist and feminist commitment. The most famous of them, William Golding, created fictional theodicies which most directly of all confront the nature and problem of evil in human society. Like that of Burgess, however, Golding's sense of evil arose as much from his experience of the Second World War as from his theological preoccupations.

Graham Greene published several novels in the period, including *The Comedians* (1966) and *The Honorary Consul* (1973), still pursuing religious themes though often indirectly through exploration of betrayal and the redeeming capacity of human love. Typical of this apparent secularization of religious themes was *The Human Factor* (1978), where he described the situation of a secret service agent, driven into professional betrayal through a conflict between duty and a love for his wife which is seen to constitute a leak in security and the grounds for his extermination. In the Cold War atmosphere of post-war Britain, Greene suggests the extent to which all human beings are forced to become secret agents, manœuvring through deceptions and duplicitous disguise in order to survive, exposed to betrayal and annihilation if feeling is allowed to leak from the armour of control. Again evil is seen to be routinized and banalized, existing at the heart of the rationalizations of the modern state, in the automated execution of duty in the service of a questionable but never morally questioned national security. Its perpetrators are so accustomed to faceless international negotiation that the human factor which the defence services were originally set up to protect now represents that leak which is most threatening to their own self-perpetuation. The novel very well embodied Auden's fears, mentioned earlier, of the effects of the faceless political regimes of a Cold War world.

Although evil was shown to exist, residing in the modern state, in Greene's work, he also suggested how it might be redeemed through the exercise of human compassion. Anthony Burgess continually criticized Greene for (as he saw it) such misplaced Pelagian belief in the redemptive truth of human love and the possibility of moral progress. Burgess's own stated preference was for a commitment to the doctrine of original sin and the existence of grace as a mechanism arriving from outside the human sphere altogether. Like other uncompromising Augustinians, he has tended to prefer a detached and finally anti-humanist comedy as the means for exploring the implications of this more austere form of belief. In the novel *Earthly Powers* (1980), his itinerant popular writer Toomey revisits the important events of the last sixty years, including the horror of the concentration camps, in order to present his own Manichaean vision of life as a struggle of evil and good. On the way, however, he functions as a device through which Burgess can orchestrate a scathing satire of recent reforms in the Catholic Church which are viewed as a thoroughly misguided attempt to displace Augustinian severity with Pelagian temperance. Indeed, Burgess's Pope Gregory is seen to unleash actual chaos and evil on the world through his misplaced liberal reformism. The consequences are disastrous and the Pope himself is seen to be the destroyer of Christendom.

The title of David Lodge's novel of the same year, *How Far Can You Go?*, posed a question (albeit playfully) with particular resonance for modern Catholics. Largely sympathetic to the liberal argument for modernization and tolerance in the church, its author nevertheless recognized that its fundamental religious identity might be destroyed if 'you go too far'. His novel follows the lives of a group of Catholic students from the fifties to the seventies as they confront the gradual deconstruction of a metaphysical structure which has safely if sometimes suffocatingly held the boundaries of their ethics, existence, and identity. The Second Vatican Council had begun to meet in 1962 and throughout the decade the Catholic Church moved toward a greater ecumenism and an acknowledgement of institutional temporality. The Mass shifted from Latin to vernacular and a new emphasis was placed upon the role of the Church in the world, now accepted to be responsible for social as much as divine justice. In *Earthly Powers*, and in the satirical tradition of Evelyn Waugh, the subsequent confusions of these reforms end in the cannibalistic consumption of members of the Pope's family at an Africanized Mass. In Lodge's novel, however, the issues are presented through a compassionate liberal exploration of their impact on each of the character's lives with an occasional *Verfremdungseffekt* which allows the narrator to situate their personal experiences in a broader social and historical context.

Much of the novel, like his earlier *The British Museum is Falling Down* (1965), focuses on the conflict of liberal tolerance versus spiritual authority specifically through an engagement with the controversy over birth control which had arisen after the publication of the Pope's encyclical letter *Humanae Vitae* in 1968. As Lodge himself playfully acknowledged, however, in his analogous metafictional subversion of realist convention in the novel: deconstruction may be liberating but, if you go too far, there may be no mystery left, no stimulus to read on, and no identity left to defend or to be liberated from. The removal of one foundation stone may have unexpected effects on the rest of the doctrinal edifice. Lodge's narrator describes traditional Catholicism as a predictable and binarily ordered snakes-and-ladders board, a 'marvellously complex and ingenious synthesis of theology and cosmology and casuistry' which promises a ladder to heaven for the good, and the snaky path to hell for the rest. But snakes and ladders is a children's game. Though religious reform might involve some loss of the innocent excitement of play, it might also, without destroying the rules of the game entirely, facilitate an acceptance of historical pressures to grow up and to confront a world very different from that which supported the Council of Trent in the sixteenth century. And if non-Catholic readers wonder what all the fuss is about, Lodge self-reflexively reminds them that 'we all like to believe, do we not, if only in stories? People who find religious belief absurd are often upset if a novelist breaks the illusion of reality he has created.' How far, then, can he or she go? Even in the sphere of the Catholic novel in the period, foundations become uncertain.

One problem facing Christian writers (as well as their characters) in a secular society is how to negotiate the relations between, on the one hand, ethical value-systems and literary forms more accustomed to presenting human behaviour in the terms of secular and civil right and wrong, and, on the other, the call of an absolute system (call it snakes and ladders if you wish) which opposes ultimate good to ultimate evil? Indeed, for many non-Christian writers between 1960 and 1990, the events of the preceding decades seemed to expose the inadequacy of secular vocabularies and call for a return to absolute terms of moral reference. Anthony Burgess was in no doubt that 'there is a definite malevolence in the universe somewhere; and in our history this century we have seen it thoroughly manifested, not only at Auschwitz, but in the Russian labour camps, in the violence on our own streets'.[20] For some writers, such as Fowles and Murdoch examined earlier, the problem of presenting essentially religious concepts through conventionally secular forms was addressed in their attempt to transpose notions of good and evil into the vocabulary of existential, pre-Christian mythic, or modern psychoanalytic frameworks. For broadly anti-humanist Christians such as Burgess, Muriel Spark, Geoffrey Hill, or William Golding, however, all secular systems seemed to be inadequate and incapable of expressing the essential existence of evil as it has manifested itself in the twentieth century.

These writers tended therefore to retain an explicitly religious conceptual framework and to employ it as the founding moral and formal base of their writing. It is interesting that, as with most expressions of the sacred in the period, their work too has tended to focus on negation and violence as expressions of evil, and to approach any possibility of the good only through a bleak and difficult *via negativa* or a revelatory apocalypse as a last desperate assertion of eschatology. Muriel Spark's fiction has always been concerned to explore the consequences of living in a society which has forgotten God and, dangerously morally adrift, has thus fallen into evil. The novels are full of explicitly evil characters: the Iago-like Dougal Douglas in *The Bachelors* (1960) who begins to grow horns, or the narcissistic Selena for whom poise is perfection and who rescues a Schiaparelli dress rather than a human being from the conflagration which burns to the ground the women's hostel of *The Girls of Slender Means* (1963).

For such writers, as in all truly apocalyptic texts, the assumption of election lurks: redemption may only be available for those who are able finally to recognize their sinful condition and to seek atonement for it. William Golding's work revealed some of the problems in accommodating such a vision to the traditional forms of the novel. He reminds the reader in *Free Fall* (1959): 'We are the guilty. We fall down. We crawl on hands and knees. We weep and tear each other,' but is then faced with the task of conveying this vision through a literary form more attuned in his time to irony, anti-heroism, relativism, and liberal rational scepticism, and to a concept of character confused by a social constructivism or existentialism which seemed to have emptied out the self to the point where, if all of us are victims of social forces beyond our control, not one of us can clearly be said to carry a clearly definable personal responsibility for our actions. In Golding's novel, the protagonist Sammy Mountjoy has confronted in the prison camp the dark thing in himself, the condition of sin which, in Golding's eyes, makes us all guilty. He has come to feel shame about his seduction of Beatrice. Shame, however, does not entail self-sacrifice or denial and it is not until he later accepts guilt and privately recognizes the absolute requirement of the renunciation of desire that he can recover his freedom by discovering when and how it was lost.

He must acknowledge that he sacrificed Beatrice to his own egotistical desire, using her to facilitate the narcissistic path to his own self-discovery. As she catatonically pisses 'over her skirt and her legs and her shoes and my shoes', he recognizes that her destruction is his responsibility. Confronting her cataleptic madness in the psychiatric institution, Sammy learns the full meaning of the lesson earlier ignored: 'if you want something enough, you can always get it provided you are willing to make the appropriate sacrifice. Something, anything. But what you get is never quite what you thought; and sooner or later the sacrifice is always regretted.' For Golding, evil is at the root of desire, but we live in a society founded on desire where the self cannot always ascertain the sources of its promptings. Sammy comes to recognize that he chose to sacrifice Beatrice to a desire which could have been resisted. He chose evil. As the pool of urine splashes over him, he is grotesquely baptized into spiritual awareness of the full extent of his guilt, burnt by 'a flake of fire' which transmutes him.

So, Sammy is saved, but Beatrice, lamb first of all to the slaughter of Sammy's earthly desires, is now simply the sacrifice required for his celestial elevation. She remains the mute and slaughtered innocent because only thus can she function as the hinge between Golding's anti-humanist vision of evil and his humanist impulse toward reparation and redemption through knowledge of the self in recognition of the other. After the experience in the prison camp, Sammy renounces what he sees as an earlier misplaced belief in rational political systems, accepting that only a 'vital morality' can redeem him, a 'relationship of individual man to individual man'. The novel begins with Sammy's recognition that he cannot 'clap the universe into a rationalist hat' and proceeds with his search to discover the pattern of his fall elsewhere. Ultimately he sees that it lay in his emotional blindness to Beatrice's goodness, that she had always been 'simple and loving and generous and humble', qualities which 'have no political importance and do not commonly bring their owners much success'. Sammy's salvation, however, is dependent upon their destruction. Spirituality in Golding always follows upon darknesses which involve the destruction of innocents and which may be partially but never wholly redeemed by human love and compassion: his vision of the human condition remains fundamentally dark. Like that earlier Beatrice who gave new life to the poet Dante, it seems that this one too continues to remain simply the object through which the male questor realizes his own, once secular, now sacred, desires. Of course, this reading imposes secular humanist (and incipiently feminist) values on Golding's religious framework: but indeterminacy of reception is itself one more instance of the difficulties which face religious writers in a secular and pluralist age.

Yet indeterminacy of meaning as the preservation of mystery is also regarded by Golding as our only defence against a mechanical Newtonian view of the universe. Again, we see a writer for whom 'right reason' is unavailable and all human systems of knowledge or self-knowledge complicit with the corruptions of desire. In each of his novels since *Free Fall*, human motivation remains unknowable and judgement therefore must be left to heaven. In *The Spire* (1964), Jocelyn's hubris in persisting with the attempt to realize his vision of the spire may have its origins in a genuine adoration of God or in a megalomaniac identification with him, driven by diseased libidinal energies. In the context of a later post-modern awareness, one can see that Golding's work was always concerned to show how, from the human perspective, we need to recognize that history has many cunning passages; that the historicist universalism which promised salvation through a world *telos* where man plays God is precisely what has brought the suffering, the concentration camps, the penal colonies, and the variety of ethnic purgings and cleansings of the modern world. In *The Spire*, he limits omniscience and uses the religious, physical, and psychoanalytic associations of the central image to convey meaning, thus precluding judgement by reminding us of the partiality of knowledge and the ambiguity of all signs taken as wonders. As the spire collapses, so does Jocelyn's diseased spine.

As he crawls upon the ground like a snake, it is difficult not to infer a further literalization of metaphor and to perceive his desire as satanically corrupted. Jocelyn has tried to play God, has brought disaster and suffering on all around him, and is shown as impotent to create the good. The text offers itself up unapologetically for Freudian analysis, but the phallic associations of the central symbol are so trite that any simple psychoanalytic interpretation is fore-stalled by the novel itself as it travesties the reductiveness of the human impulse toward total rational formulation. Human motivation cannot be reduced to rational explanatory schemes. The spire, built in a 'trance of will', is effectively the symbol of a symbol, the objective correlative for whatever desires are projected onto it: pagan, Christian, sexual. It is the physical realization of the mystery of Jocelyn himself.

If *The Spire* flirted dangerously with the grotesque in its explora-tion of spiritual identity, Golding's *Darkness Visible* (1979) posit-ively embraced it, anatomizing the condition of England through a parable of the forces of good and evil apocalyptically mapped onto a modern fable of survival as an amoral will to power. The novel begins as the maimed child Matty walks out of the fires of the Blitz, like a latter-day Moses or Ezekiel, a monstrously deformed second coming which hovers fantastically and Chiliastically between em-pirical and historical contexts and Messianic and sacred associations. Is Matty a prophet of Apocalypse in its traditional and ultimately regenerative mode, signalling the intervention into human history of a divine world beyond? Or is he, deformed, burnt, psychotic, and only semi-articulate, no more than a sign of the end which human beings have themselves produced, apocalypse as simply the ima-gination of disastrous ending in the nuclear age? The novel displays all the features of the fantastic as a condition of suspension between two ontological conditions and employs literary devices of the gro-tesque to convey its undecidability. The grotesque may be the only available if fallen vehicle to allow for a manifestation and interven-tion of the divine into contemporary history or it may simply convey the absurdity of human desire and the collective psychosis of a world which has passed through Auschwitz, Dresden, Hiroshima, and now faces final burn-out. Such profound ambiguity is embodied in the Faustian semi-comic spirits of fundamentalism who tell Matty to throw away his Bible, in his bathetically frustrated attempts to speak with tongues, in his absurd sexual maiming by the Aborigine and subsequent baptism, and finally in the bizarre activities with the group of small-time middle-England communicants.

Matty's grotesque Messianism is matched, however, by the bizarre but Satanic designs of the twin Sophy. Just as Matty has come to understand his vocation as a second coming, his mission to introduce into post-war Britain a new spiritual understanding beyond words, Sophy has identified her vocation of evil with the law of thermodynamics, believing that Britain in the second half of the twentieth century has entered upon the final phase of an entropic running-down, a physical whimper rather than a divinely ordained bang. If Matty is the herald of spiritual apocalypse come to usher in the new Jerusalem as a blessed release from the tyranny of time's arrow, Sophy is committed as catalyst to a materialist and physical winding-down. Representing the forces of darkness as inevitable decline toward disorder and stasis, the evil which she represents may be visible only to the spiritually elect (again grotesquely represented through the absurd activities of the Spiritualist cabal as well as through the character of Matty). Indeed, Sophy's evil is as grotesque in its manifestations as Matty's good and may equally represent the sign of collective psychosis as much as Divine Revelation.

For many critics, patience ran thin when the third section of the novel failed to resolve the ambiguities of the grotesque events of parts 1 and 2, and there was much grumbling about mystification for its own sake (especially as Golding himself resolutely refused to offer clarification or explanation). But this response seems feeble. Surely we need to ask why Golding should fasten his apocalyptic vision onto an almost ridiculously comic and grotesque plot? What is the function of the grotesque in the period under survey? What has it to do with religious faith and doubt?

One way of approaching the novel is to note that in it Golding eschatalogically invokes two 'Grand Narratives' of cosmic purpose which have sat uneasily together since the nineteenth century. The first is the Christian scheme of death and redemption through rebirth into spiritual life at the end of linear time and history. The second is the classic Newtonian physical understanding of the universe as permanent and inert matter which exists independent of perception and time and offers us the consolation of a finally ordered design. In the nineteenth century both were challenged, the first by theories of evolution which seemed to confirm that survival was a random process based purely on the natural selection of the fittest and the most adaptable and having little to do with moral behaviour. Newtonian physics was also challenged by the newly discovered laws of thermo-dynamics, which suggested that although natural processes are regulated there is also an irreversible movement toward disorder in nature. The ever more complex Darwinian harnessing of energy is offset by an ever-increasing dissipation of energy which will eventually bring the physical world to a condition of undifferentiated chaos and stasis: the scene was set for a proliferation of decline-and-fall theories of history. Golding treats the religious vision of redemption in the world hereafter as a sublime and comic plot which must be set against the materially entropic and tragic picture of history inspired by nineteenth-century physics.

Matty resides problematically as bearer of the first plot, Sophy as carrier of the shaky frame of the second. If the twain shall meet, however, it can only be in the region of the grotesque. The present condition of history is a confused and liminal realm caught between hope and tragic determinism, where grand and heroic spiritual plots are continuously kept alive but simultaneously deflated and exposed as the sublimation of desires arising from the material and physical limitations of human corporeal existence. Collocations of different orders of reality have become a common feat of modern fictional engineering, from the modernist interpenetration of subjective consciousness and objective physical event in works such as Joyce's *Ulysses*, to the magic realist and post-modern reincarnations and physical materializations of dream and fantasy in the work of writers such as Marquez and Rushdie. Golding, however, does not embrace either the Joycean modern or the later post-modern condition, but situates his characters at the intersection of grand and foundationalist but ultimately incommensurable and competing plots which can offer neither the comfort of absolute faith nor a release into a blithe and celebratory nihilism. He shows that to be caught in the condition of hesitation where one can neither make a leap of faith toward God and redemption nor yet resign oneself to the materialistic determinism of scientific entropy is to exist in a condition of grotesque, yet in its own way heroic, absurdity and mystery where it may be impossible to tell the saint from the fool or the true mystic from the charlatan.

A number of writers of the period who deal with broadly religious themes (perhaps most notably Samuel Beckett) have similarly and self-consciously situated their dramas and fictions at the intersection of the grand schemes outlined above. One of the common features of these fictions is a recourse to the stylistic mode of the grotesque as a means of expressing the uncertainty of human knowledge and the vertiginous experience of being always suspended between finally unknowable redemptively comic or entropically tragic grand plots. As Beckett's tramps know, the desire for final explanation will always be a whistling in the dark, revelation indistinguishable from fantasy, reason a construction on the back of desperation. In both Beckett and Golding, intimations of the sublime, of the existence of a transcendent and redemptive order beyond common-sense experience, all too easily and continuously collapse into the amoral promptings of the entropic energies of the body (lusts and drives, stinking breath and stinking feet). Indeed, the grotesqueries of Beckett's tramps were intensified in the scientifically entropic images of disappearing bodies in the exponentially diminishing worlds after *Happy Days:* bodies speaking from urns, or from worlds after death, or reduced to the minimalist synecdoche of a mouth attempting manically to affirm itself in a physical void. Comedy as even the hint of the possibility of redemption dwindles. Still, in Beckett and in Golding (as Wilson Knight had noted about Shakespeare's *King Lear*), the grotesque functions as a stylistic mode which can express the uncertainty of suspension between a classically tragic world without redemption and one where some hint of a promise of apocalyptic salvation lingers on.

If Golding is often accused of writing in a grotesquely obscurantist style, so too is the poet Geoffrey Hill. In both writers, their dense, ambiguous, and compacted style is an attempt to probe metaphysical truth in an age where language has largely lost its sacramental force.

Also like Golding, Hill tends to explore religious themes negatively: it is uncertain whether human beings may uncover the good, but evident that they have embraced and encountered evil as a force in history. Like many writers in this chapter, Hill has tended to invoke Auschwitz to suggest that all poetry, as language itself, is contaminated and compromised: partaking of the sacred, it will inevitably, however, have its roots in the barbarous. 'There is no bloodless myth will hold', all language is impure, and art, like the saint picked out in coloured glass in the poem 'In Piam Memoriam', or the 'fatted marble' in 'Of Commerce and Society', is 'stained'. The poet, as maker of graven images, is never far from at least the condition of trickster and at worst that of Fascist. Whereas Golding uses narrative devices to create deliberate effects of spatial, temporal, and finally ethical uncertainty and ambiguity, Hill seals layers of etymological resonance into each word or runs puns trippingly through his stanzas, referring, for example, to a God who 'scatters corruption' or Christianity as a 'composed mystery'.

All human yearning toward the condition of purity is seen to be necessarily impure. The first poem of *Tenebrae* (1978), 'The Pentecost Castle', is prefaced with a quotation from Simone Weil: 'What we love in other human beings is the hoped-for satisfaction of our desire,' and one from W. B. Yeats: 'It is terrible to desire and not possess, and terrible to possess and not desire.' We can never fathom the purity of our motivation or our love. Sacrifice for a cause may simply be 'dying | to satisfy fat Caritas' and *King Log* (1968) is itself replete with gross images of feeding. Gods have ever been born and fattened from the blood of sacrifice and martyrdom. In 'September Song', Hill refers explicitly to the concentration camps, recognizing that, though writing about them is always open to the accusation of exploitation, 'I have made | an elegy for myself it | is true', nevertheless there must be some protest against the apparent mechanized inevitability of the state-authorized 'patented' extermination of a 10-year-old child. 'As estimated, you died. Things marched, | sufficient, to that end. | Just so much Zyklon and leather' is the sufficiency of a violence which has become habitual, the 'proper time' of bureaucratized evil which can no longer even recognize itself as such. The defamiliarizing glare of poetry impels collective acceptance of responsibility, but the last stanza is a reminder that poetry has changed nothing. The September of the world of nature 'fattens on vines' as the speaker partakes of a plenty which is more than enough, not measured, not estimated, but guilty, therefore, by the very ease of its pagan forgetting.

The theme of 'An Order of Service' is the potential for egotistical satisfaction which lurks in martyrdom or self-sacrifice, the vulnerability of the self to dazzlement by 'renunciation's glare', for there is (again punningly) 'no end to that sublime appeal'. In 'Annunciations', the Word is back from its travels with an ambiguously 'tanned look', whilst, unambiguously, 'cleansing has become killing'. Because we desire gods, we invent them; history is a 'vacuous | ceremony of possession'; and art itself always ethically compromised by implication in such impure composition. Hill seems to say that art cannot redeem, language exposes but also covers over the bloodlettings of history, the Wars of the Roses, the Holocaust, the Great War: sacrifice is ever suspect, authority corrupt. Language itself is a manifestation of empirical guilt. So, although a 'religious' poet, Hill is also curiously post-modern, undermining every ethical gesture, exposing the corrupt etymology of each uttered word.

To harsh critics, his writing is a melange of kitsch feudalism, historical voyeurism, and mannered insularity parasitic upon the aesthetic imagination of T. S. Eliot. Certainly the learning is not worn lightly and there is little concern for the common touch. His audience is largely academic, for the esoteric allusions make for a time-consuming read and the poetry tends to remain opaque if they are not understood or recognized. If his theme is the struggle for understanding, he makes certain that his reader will have a hard time of it too. If humanitarian compassion seems lacking in Hill's verse, he might justify it thus: 'the grasp of true religious experience is a privilege reserved for the very few . . . one is trying to make lyrical poetry out of a much more common situation—the sense of *not* being able to grasp true religious experience.'[21] Here is yet another statement of *via negativa* as the only remaining authentic aesthetic mode for the religious writer. It is hardly surprising that the apocalyptic, rather than the redemptive, seems the characteristic mood of the times.

4 PLANNERS, POLITICS, AND POETS

INTELLECTUAL CULTURE AND THE LIMITS OF REASON AFTER 1960

> Out at the far-off edge I hear
> Colliding voices, drifted, yes
> To find me through the slowly opening leads.
> Tomorrow I'll try the rafted ice.
> Have I not been trying to use the obstacle
> Of language well? It freezes round us all.
>
> W. S. Graham, 'Malcolm Mooney's Land'

If the search for spiritual significance seemed as often as not to lead to a preoccupation with the nature of the self, then meditations on Spirit and Self were also likely to end as reflections upon the nature of language. Indeed, it could be argued that most literary manifestations of the urge to transcendence since 1960, whether of a Romantic or a religious variety, have tended to reflect an ironic awareness that the limits of my language may mean the limits of my world, my self, and even my Divinity. For rationalists too in the period 1960–90, the problem of truth could not be separated from the issue of representation and questions about representation would also inevitably lead to the problem of language.

The words of W. S. Graham, quoted above, express a familiar paradox in contemporary literature: the pressure to connect with a world beyond language, to recover some plenitudinous state of being, but the simultaneous recognition not only that language inevitably interposes its constructions, but that it is also the very vehicle of connection. Language 'freezes round us all', like a cryosurgeon destroying in order to heal the wound. Malcolm Mooney's land is both the frozen wastes of the explorer and the intertextual game with words which is poetry. But what or whose are the dimly heard 'Colliding voices' drifting to find the speaker through 'the slowly opening leads'? In another poem in the same collection (1970), Graham attempts to glimpse the 'beast that lives on silence'. His voices seem to replay the strangulated whispers of T. S. Eliot's earlier Waste Landers, self-imprisoned in a 'closed car' and thus armoured against intrusion from 'the other side':

> Shut up. Shut up. There's nobody here.
> If you think you hear somebody knocking
> On the other side of the words, pay
> No attention. It will be only
> The great creature that thumps its tail
> On silence on the other side.

'The Beast in the Space'

The strategic placing of the word 'only' after the future imperative and with the heavy stress on the penultimate syllable of the line emphatically conveys the sense of exclusivity, uniqueness, of this and nothing else. However, its run-on deflationary juxtaposition with 'The great creature', mythic beast or phobic infantile imago, has an almost oxymoronic force. The combined effect is to recommend resignation. We assume that we name and thus control the world, but sometimes need to 'Shut up', for our 'only' control over 'the other side', mortality, that which lies beyond the words of rational discourse, is an imaginative acceptance of its unknowability and absolute inevitability.

Graham's technique of ontological transgression through linguistic self-referentiality, reminding us of the poem's status as a world of words in order to recall us to a sense of the limitations of the word and of the absolute mystery of worlds beyond its grasp, is one example of what has become a powerful tendency in contemporary literature. As the corporate planners mapped out their new and orderly worlds, many and not necessarily religious writers of literature increasingly manifested a concern either with that which is excluded by rationality or with the limitations of rational discourse. The cry of 'O reason not the need' and the assertion of aesthetic experience as an antidote to social planning were heard throughout the sixties in a Romantic revivalism which entered literature, the counterculture, and the writing of the New Left. It was buoyant in literary criticism in a persisting Leavisite commitment to 'felt life', in the post-Coleridgean organicism of the New Criticism, and in the turn to myth and psychoanalysis examined in the previous chapter and which located significance outside consciousness altogether. The tendency accelerated as it became evident that not only had the Welfare State planners failed to take account of the needs of spirit, but also their promises of universal salvation from material deprivation were not to be honoured. By the late sixties there had been a retreat from the principle of a free health service; it was evident that expansion of education had failed to erode class difference or to bring about true equality of opportunity; race riots had intensified since Notting Hill in 1958, and in 1961 the Parker Morris report on planning had fallen on deaf ears when it called for architects and planners to listen to the needs of actual people and expressed concern at the disappearance of traditional communities.

The previous chapter explored the way in which writers of the sixties and seventies responded to a sense of the spiritual vacuum at the heart of late modernity. This chapter will concentrate on literary and cultural manifestations of the urge to expand or to find non-religious alternatives to the rationality of the planners and will examine the role of language in the construction of new subjectivities. Examples abound of the attempt to extend language beyond its functionalist and instrumental uses. In Samuel Beckett's dramatic work from the sixties, in *Happy Days* (1963) and *Play* (1964), for example, habit was presented as a vacuous substitute for liturgical ritual, now reduced to a purposefulness without purpose, a solitary and temporary displacement of dread rather than an act of communal worship. The 'dead voices' of these later plays circle endlessly and revise obsessively in an emotional prisonhouse which is also a Dantesque purgatory with no promise of release. Both plays reflected a sense of those corporeal limits to rational optimism which seemed to have been ignored in the blueprints of the social engineers as in the utopianism of the counterculturalists. In each was conveyed an awareness of the need for but the diminishing force of a sacramental dimension to language in a secular culture. In the previous chapter, we saw how such themes also appeared in the incantatory battles of Harold Pinter's characters, whose struggles for tribal recognition infused contemporary absurdist language games with the fierce impetus of ancient warrior honour. A number of linguistic studies too showed a related interest in the potential absurdism of language (R. D. Laing's *Knots*, for example) or in a reinvigorated approach to metaphor which emphasized its capacity to convey a sense of the unknown through the known, to create the new (within a Romantic aesthetic) or to reveal a more profound depth (in the terms of a classical one). Such studies revealed how, seeking that which cannot be named, and in what Mercia Eliade has referred to as a 'desacrilised' culture, aesthetic language becomes a vital means of conveying a sense of mystery or of alternative conditions of being.[1]

Indeed, we have already examined the work of a number of writers who sought to push language to its polysemantic limits in order to convey a sense of the silence beyond: Thom Gunn created a contemporary style of metaphysical wit with ingenious extended metaphors, teasing out and yoking together the superficially heterogeneous, striving after some sense of a more profound underlying correspondence between the patterns of the desiring imagination and the material world beyond; Basil Bunting's *Briggflatts* (1965) traversed space and time by compressing dispersed etymologies and regional dialectal variations into single words; so too the compacted, stressed diction of Geoffrey Hill's *King Log* (1968) punningly conveyed layers of etymology connecting past to present in an ambivalent search for an original purity of the word beyond those ethnic and nationalistic violences of a post-Holocaust world where, however, 'cleansing has become killing'. We have seen too that a sense of the profanation of the word, but of the potential significance of that which inhabits the silence 'whereof one cannot speak', induced a turn to myth and fabulation as a means of conveying what lay 'under the net' of language in the work of Iris Murdoch, Edward Bond, Ted Hughes, John Fowles, and William Golding.

Debates about the validity of adducing aesthetic experience as a form of counter-rationality had already flared up in the late fifties. The absurdist dramatist Ionesco defended himself against Kenneth Tynan's charge that absurdist theatre was nihilistic and irresponsible in its effect of undermining Enlightenment faith in rational progress.[2] Ionesco's argument was that absurdist theatre set out to destroy language as a logical medium in order to provide a more profound metaphysical understanding of the way in which the human condition determined social and political activity. The point of absurdism would be to repudiate a facile rationalist progressivism which liked to invert this fundamental causal chain and to regard the human condition as a consequence of political and social arrangements. The terms of the debate provided the dramatic centrepiece of Peter Brook's spectacular production of Peter Weiss's *Marat/Sade*, one of the high points of the RSC Theatre of Cruelty season in 1964. Brook drew on the dramaturgical methods of the supremely rationalist Marxist playwright Bertholt Brecht and on those of the advocate of sensationalist 'total theatre', Antonin Artaud. Indeed, form and content appeared to coincide, for the subject-matter of the play was the ideological debate represented by the rationalist French Revolutionary Girondiste Jean Paul Marat, and the Revolutionary libertarian individualist the marquis de Sade. In effect, and like Brecht and Artaud, they spoke respectively for the light and dark sides of the Enlightenment.

For Marat, human beings are rational creatures and human society is therefore perfectible through the application to it of that rational faculty and the elimination of irrational desire and prejudice. For de Sade, human beings are driven by an irrational desire that is both libidinal and violent as well as visionary and poetic, but by far the greatest destructiveness comes of refusing to accept the primacy of such desire. In effect, the ideological battle between these two positions had been revitalized in the sixties in the quarrel between the counterculturalists and the social planners. The play was staged as a play within a play set in a post-Revolutionary lunatic asylum bathhouse where de Sade and Marat and other Revolutionaries are played by actors playing lunatic inmates. Weiss's use of the device of the play within a play established a framework which would allow Brook to play endlessly with transgressions of ontological levels of reality and fiction, to suggest relations between theatre and politics, and to present a Laingian thesis about the tendency to define as insanity the expression of passionately held but unconventional personal convictions.

The visual impact of the play tended to emphasize desire over reason, of course, simply by virtue of casting the Revolutionaries as lunatics. It was by no means the only text in the sixties which set out to subvert, in the light of the events of modern history, the post-Enlightenment, and progressivist belief in reason. Already in *The Death of Tragedy* (1961), George Steiner had asked for recognition of the historical specificity of such beliefs in reminding the reader that 'tragic drama tells us that the spheres of reason, order and justice are terribly limited and that no progress in our science or technical resources will enlarge their relevance'. Weiss's play essentially juxtaposed the tragic consciousness of a de Sade against the more modern rationalist ameliorism of a Marat. Steiner had argued that tragedy may exist only in societies which accept that the forces shaping human lives lie outside reason or rationalized social justice. Weiss, like a number of other writers of the period, attempts to reinvoke a tragic consciousness but recognizes that it can no longer be contemplated innocently and outside the frame of a modern rationalism now grown inescapably tainted in the aftermath of Auschwitz, Belsen, and Hiroshima. In a later text, *Language and Silence* (1967), Steiner too would meditate not only upon the death of tragedy but also upon the end of meaning and upon the significance of Adorno's observation that there could be 'no poetry after Auschwitz'. As de Sade predicts in Weiss's play, so too for Steiner in this book: 'the reach of technological man, as a being susceptible to the controls of political hatred and sadistic suggestion, has lengthened formidably towards destruction.'[3] Reason has failed, and language has been struck dumb by the horrors unleashed: language too is become corrupt. Authenticity might now be no more than an acceptance of the terrible Pascalian silence of cosmic space.

For the writer in the sixties, one way in which to invoke such silence without ceasing to write was to return to the body, to the roots of drama in sacred physical ritual. The conundrums of linguistic scepticism might be circumvented by opening the self to that cosmic terror induced by a theatre of cruelty or total sensation which, like a reflex of the nervous system, might return to a sense of the tragic in bypassing reason and the word altogether. In a world where art seemed to have lost its capacity for magic, Artaud called for a release of theatre from linguistic scepticism and into a new meta-physics of sensation, involving 'shouts, groans, apparitions, surprise ... brilliant lighting, vocal, incantational beauty ... object colours, the physical rhythm of the moves whose build and fall will be wedded to the beat of moves familiar to all'.[4] In forcing audiences to con-front the cruelty of the world and the inadequacy of reason to control it, Artaud believed that such a theatre might provide an education in humility. If we could arrive at the recognition that we cannot control the world through reason, then we might come to accept the dark forces in ourselves and thus cease to perpetrate violence on others in those acts of sadism which arise as a consequence of the repres-sion of imagination and feeling.

To experience such theatre would be similar to finding oneself adrift in the materialized world of a Francis Bacon painting. Indeed, Weiss's play was brought experientially alive in such a fashion in Brook's production. Visually dramatic imagery of blue and red blood, maniacal twitterings, and the clinical paraphernalia of the lunatic bath-house provided the backdrop. Set off against it was the unfor-gettable image of the actress Glenda Jackson seductively chastising with flaying tresses the somatically driven Marat, who seeks balmful respite from an acute eczematous condition in the watery embrace of the asylum bath (whilst simultaneously denying the primacy of the body in the formation of human drives). Weiss had been influenced by Brechtian theories of alienation which urged the need to disturb easy psychological identification with characters in a play. Specta-tors might then bring to it a detached rational judgement and thus undermine the facile but functionalist bourgeois equation which expresses the view that art is simply escapist and trivial leisure, whereas work is to be regarded as the serious and legitimate oiling of the wheels of industry. Equally, however, Weiss had registered the persuasiveness of Artaud's theories of the necessity for non-rational and total theatrical immersion. Ostensibly at odds with each other, both theories in fact had in common the desire to shake ra-tional liberal complacency by questioning the agency and autonomy of a self now seen to be displaced from itself in denying the dictates of the body and decentred by the refusal to acknowledge determina-tion by forces beyond its control or comprehension. Accordingly, in

Marat/Sade itself, Brechtian detachment and Artaudian immersion, as well as the political philosophies of Marat and de Sade, are presented as a clash of dramatic styles and philosophical contradictions in the aesthetic demonstration of a continuing dualism of body and mind which cannot be resolved away either by Cartesianism itself, or by any other available form of logic.

De Sade arraigns Marat's Newtonian, technocratic political economy as a denial of the existence of the will as non-rationalizable desire. He accuses him of giving rise thereby to an automated and counter-revolutionary reign of terror. The theory explicated in the play by de Sade had been articulated by the philosopher Hannah Arendt in her description of the routinized destruction in the concentration camps as a 'banality of evil'. For de Sade, the alternative is to liberate desire through the imagination, for, even if this involves the expression of perverse lusts and violences, it also necessitates an honest acknowledgement that reason is not the antidote to desire but is actually bred out of it: to believe otherwise is to live in the greatest condition of unreason of all, and to perpetrate the greatest evil. Political revolution which ignores the lineaments of human desire which lie beneath reason and beyond material need will fail to liberate anything, for 'those cells of the inner self | are worse than the deepest stone dungeon | and as long as they are locked | all your revolution remains | only a prison mutiny'. Marat, so conspicuously, and in such perfect Freudian casebook fashion, a bodily victim of his own repressed desire, rejects de Sade's libertarian attempt to integrate mind and body, and persists in his materialist belief that 'Imagination can't break down | any real barriers'. His utopia is one of technocratically planned egalitarian efficiency, where 'electrified magnetic forces | whizz about and rub against each other', but with such precise synchrony and adaptation that, to use an epithet derived from his own corporeal condition, 'the more you scratch' no longer entails 'the more you itch'.

Countercultural Utopias

The *Marat/Sade* play is an important literary document of the sixties, for it highlighted a number of prominent tensions and themes which cut across popular, literary, and intellectual cultures of the decade.

At the centre of the play is a debate about the relations between rationality and imagination in the shaping of human lives and environments. Similar debates flourished in New Left, scientific, and countercultural movements and would begin to emerge powerfully in the feminist writing of the seventies. One of the implications of Weiss's play, however, is that a salvationary belief in imagination which entirely displaces reason may be as destructive as the vaunting of reason totally at the expense of imagination and feeling. A choice between an absolutely planned world and a world conducted according to a countercultural ethos of sensual pleasure and imaginative play might be no choice at all. In fact most literary intellectuals of the time drew back altogether from the notion that the individual could play God and plan worlds, whether through Enlightenment reason or through Romantic imagination, moulding lives and creating out of chaos universal orders with which to frame all of human experience. Muriel Spark, for example, in a 1961 interview about her conversion to Catholicism, talked of the need for artists to see themselves as minor public servants and for intellectuals to be more humble in their assertions and to recognize the fictionality of the truths they project onto the world:

Fiction to me is a kind of parable. You have to make up your mind it's not true. Some kind of truth emerges from it, but it's not fact. One of the things which interested me particularly about the church was its acceptance of matter. So much of our world rejects it. We're not happy with things. We want machines to handle them.[5]

(Accordingly, the shadow of the four last things was consistently cast across her ostentatiously fictional worlds of fallen creatures, characters whose profane desires condemn them to a purgatory of solipsistic language games where a greater script might fearfully or painfully be glimpsed, but never be encompassed.)

Humility, however, was hardly a generally favoured virtue in the sixties, and the investment of the counterculturalists in the power of the human imagination was sometimes as Faustian as the belief of the planners in human reason. The roots of the sixties' counterculture in Britain were actually in an earlier romantic critique of industrialization: Blake and Shelley were its newly revived heroes, though a long tradition of conservative thought had always opposed social planning. The movement had nowhere near the impact here that it had in America (where it fed into powerful student protest against the excesses of the military response to the guerrilla tactics of the Korean and Vietnam wars), but it did contribute another thread to the burgeoning dissatisfaction with the limitations of social rationalization. However, by the end of the decade its combination of naïve sublimity and easy commercial appropriation tended to result in a general intellectual shift toward the recommendation of a more temperate approach to the critique of reason. E. P. Thompson castigated Theodor Roszak's *The Making of a Counterculture* (1970) as a dangerously erroneous conflation of reason with the 'total ethos of the bomb': an allusion to Marcuse's notion of a 'logic of domination' which is seen to empower modern societies in every political and social arena, from the destruction of nature in the search for profit, to the planning of welfare states and to the technological exploitation of science in the development of a terrifying modern weaponry of war.[6] The poet Alan Brownjohn was typical of the retreat from the countercultural critique when, in 1972, he repudiated emotional extremism in art, arguing that, as we 'move daily deeper into a complex and alarming kind of a technical, late capitalist civilisation where the surfaces get smoother and the realities ever more violent, irrational and ruthless', it is more important than ever to assert a 'rational, sceptical temperament which will calmly and wisely dismantle the machinery of horror'.[7]

By 1970 it was evident that the wholesale rejection of rationality was always likely to play into the hands of the capitalist entrepreneurs and subsequently into those of the authoritarian right. Many of the student counterculturalists, often relatively affluent, chose to view as the coercion of the managerial state a consensus which they regarded as crippling to the imagination and a dispossession of their true soulfood. The Marxist historian E. P. Thompson regarded such arguments as the dangerous slogans of an imaginary 'revolutionary psycho-drama' which allowed its participants to continue with a comfortable bourgeois lifestyle conveniently untouched by their radical political assertions. This mood was later recaptured in David Edgar's play *Maydays* (1983), where a working-class Communist and 'left culturalist', Jeremy Crowther, sees after 1968 an earlier ideal of a noble and common culture betrayed by what he regards as the self-indulgent trivialities of middle-class and affluent disaffected youth. As yet another radical impulse is 'dissipated in a sit-in, or a sleep-in or a be-in, at the university', Jeremy thinks to himself, 'oh, come on . . . this isn't what you meant at all'. By the late eighties a number of liberal and leftish political historians were to take an even harsher line on the counterculturalism of the sixties. By this time, it was possible to view its anarchy and erosion of deference as strategies which actually played into the hands of reaction. Student disruption and rebellion provided media-friendly images of the destructive seeds sown by sixties' libertarianism and the state could justify its desire to return to authority by playing the role of Victorian patriarch to a confused family in need of 'child guidance' and clear boundaries. Indeed, each Conservative government would exploit the well-publicized spectacle of vociferously disaffected but relatively economically privileged student revolt in order to inculpate the university as a place of self-indulgent ineffectuality.

In other ways, of course, the counterculturalist critique of state planning was on the whole closer to a prominent tradition of conservative thought than it was compatible with the tenets of modern state socialism. Prior to the writings of Roszak and Marcuse, the most vociferous twentieth-century critiques of rational planning had emerged from the sort of cultural conservatism expressed in T. S. Eliot's *Notes toward the Definition of Culture* (1948). Eliot's polemic was directed against the entire post-war welfare settlement, and in particular Butler's democratization of education, which he presented as the political arm of a dangerous new technocratic managerialism (termed 'technologico-Benthamism' by F. R. Leavis). Eliot regarded state planning as a harnessing of the forces of mass society in order to destroy the hierarchies and embodied practices, the rooted and customary religious and familial values, of traditional culture and society. His perspective of conservative *noblesse oblige* entailed a repudiation of state-planned redistribution of incomes and resources. In fact, although the countercultural critique was in the name of a Romantic freedom, rather than Eliot's austere classicism, and is usually regarded as an expression of left thinking compared to his feudal conservatism, it could be argued that both impulses fed into conservative political thinking in the next two decades. Radical conservatism of the eighties attempted to emphasize the importance of individual freedom along with the necessity for political authority. The attempt to combine them prompted a full-blown moral lambast against the evils of a welfare state seen to deprive the individual of a theologically sanctioned freedom to choose as the basis of all ethical conduct.

Eliot's critique of the material and technocratic emphasis of social engineering suggested that the most barbaric episodes in twentieth-century history were a direct consequence of the fallacious commitment to instrumental rational planning as the executive machinery of political utopianism in an age of mass society. The same theme appeared in Roszak's (leftist) countercultural manifesto. Roszak argued in his 1970 book that, although the popular image of Nazism was of a vulgarized Romanticism, an irrational idealization of the blood,

without utterly dispassionate, utterly rational technicians and administrative automatons like Adolf Eichmann, it is impossible to imagine the Nazi state lasting a year . . . The new order was . . . as thorough a technocracy as any that survives today . . . If the movement dealt in the hot passions of the masses, its success lay in organising those passions into a disciplined machinery of state.[8]

Though both attacked the state rationalization of society, Eliot's counterblast to technocratic planning was cultural tradition, while Roszak's was the individual imagination. Both positions were reflected, as we shall see, in the literature of the time, but many writers (and not simply beneficiaries from the working classes) expressed a more tempered criticism of the Welfare State, concerned less to argue for its abolition than to highlight its inadequacies and limitations. Indeed, by the early seventies it was apparent (in Britain at least) that the growth of the counterculture had largely been prompted and facilitated by the liberalizing reforms of the post-war state. Reforms such as the Wolfendon report on homosexuality (1967), the end of Capital Punishment (1965), the Abortion Act (1967), the Obscene Publications Act (1959), and the abolition of theatre censorship (1968), though products of the technocratic state, laid down the soil on which the counterculture would flourish and seek to extend its arguments for universal rights to individual expression and social recognition.

For many contemporary writers and intellectuals such as E. P. Thompson, Muriel Spark, Iris Murdoch, and the emergent New Left, however, the counterculture simply provided a reverse image of the worst aspects of state planning: as the planners and technocrats played God through the instrumental rationalization of society, the counter-culturalists believed they could invent and establish new worlds through the imagination. Those who created literary fictional worlds for a living tended to be more cautious than the aesthetic manipulators of modern life—the therapists, managers, and planners—about the moral implications of acts which are analogous to Divine Creation. As John Fowles proclaimed in *The French Lieutenant's Woman*:

The novelist is still a god, since he creates (and not even the most aleatory avant-garde modern novel has managed to extirpate its author completely); what has changed is that we are no longer the gods of the Victorian image, omniscient and decreeing; but in the new theological image, with freedom our first principle, not authority.

Accordingly, few literary intellectuals of the time shared whole-heartedly the headily vitalistic belief in creating a new heaven on earth through the revolutionary destruction of the repressive tolerance of the technocratic state. While Mick Jagger called for the Dionysian unleashing of youth desire in the erotic delivery of 'I can't get no satisfaction', the writers mentioned above revealed a self-conscious concern with the dangers both of unlimited aestheticism and the unbridled assertion of individualistic desire.

A number of these writers, including Spark, Murdoch, Golding, and Fowles, who reached maturity in the sixties, had grown up during the Second World War. Particularly after Nazism, it seemed evident to them that the projection of Promethean desire beyond the controlled realm of art had, as often as not, realized a hell of violence rather than a heaven of peace. Indeed, in his 1965 book *Shakespeare our Contemporary*, the Polish Shakespearian critic Jan Kott transformed Shakespeare's Macbeth into a post-Holocaust, fascistic, and death-infected absurdist 'steeped in blood so far' that the killing cannot stop. There can be no catharsis, Macbeth feels no guilt, and 'all he can do before he dies is to drag with him into nothingness as many living beings as possible'.[9] Kott and writers such as Iris Murdoch, William Golding, and John Fowles seemed to suggest that in a non-traditional and 'desacrilised' society, and after Nazism, aesthetic vision may seem liberating but in fact may represent a potentially and powerfully destructive and dangerous force. So, too, the counterculture, with its popular situationist slogan of taking one's desires for one's reality, even more than the technocratic state, could be seen to invest in a potentially destructive aestheticization of experience. It is not surprising that so many literary creators of the period showed an intense concern self-consciously to differentiate between the identifiable and intentional fictions of the artistic imagination and those epistemologically distinct orders in the world beyond art.

The preoccupations of writers such as Golding and Murdoch by the sixties reflect a recognition that the projection of a non-ironic Promethean desire which had given us Romantic poetry within the sphere of art had also informed the idealisms which which had given rise to the reigns of terror, pogroms, purges, and holocausts, outside that sphere. In each of these historical instances, an attempt was made to impose aesthetic blueprints on existing societies: to play God in the world of history. As a corrective, Faustian desire, embodied in literary characters—in Golding's tortured visionaries, Bond's political utopianists, or Murdoch's Magus figures, for example—is contained and subverted by the ironic frames and metacommentaries of the self-conscious author. Art is used to contain rather than to exist itself as magic: artists become obsessed with the perils of enchantment. The temper of such aesthetic self-consciousness was often deflationary, from the 'pratfalls' in the absurdist drama of Beckett to the metaphysical grotesque of Golding, or from the exaggeratedly flat and demotic prose of Bond's *Lear* (1972) to the cartoon antics of Hughes's sinister *Crow* (1970). Pessimistic critics have viewed this as a straightforward loss of artistic grandeur, the literary effect of a cynical and fragmented culture. A more positive reponse might be to see writers exploring ways to retain art's magic but without capitulation to a dangerous enchantment. Scepticism may be seen as both a virtue and a vice: 'at-one-ment', in Geoffrey Hill's hyphenated and ironically interrupted version, may be the nearest we can safely come toward plenitude.

Indeed, it may be that art could no longer be tragic when history itself had played out the rhythms of tragedy in the politicized aesthetic impulses of European modernity itself: those patterns of hubris, destruction, recognition come too late, which had been apparent in each of the revolutions and reigns of terror since 1789. Writers in the sixties seemed suddenly to recognize that the ancient grand plots of literature had been dangerously appropriated by existential desires outside the traditional boundaries of art. It was almost as if the literati found themselves increasingly cast in the role of chorus to the main dramatic action taking place on the stage of the world. It was in the sixties that the full account of the atrocities of the forties and fifties, and then of the later Korean and Vietnam wars, seeped into the collective consciousness of the newly technological and affluent culture of the British Isles. As in the American jazz age of the roaring twenties, the dark side of the so-called swinging sixties emerged through the glass of its literature. Novels like Spark's *The Prime of Miss Jean Brodie* (1961) and Murdoch's *A Severed Head*, though ostensibly about trivial love affairs in a girls' school and the adulterous deceptions of the high bourgeois intelligentsia respectively, were actually studies of the psychological and myth-making imperatives of power politics and Fascism. A number of writers were highly conscious that the realm of the sacred in a largely secularized and urbanized culture might also turn out to be that of torture and genocide. Any romanticism in the literature of the period tends therefore to be ironically expressed: aesthetic virtues were made out of moral necessities.

The New Left and New Subjectivities

From the sixties onwards, in fact, there was a growing intellectual rejection of the extreme countercultural abandonment of rationality and a concomitant concern to find ways to redefine reason in noninstrumental or in other than narrowly functionalist ways. Within the philosophy of science, we shall see that a revolt against positivism and a number of critiques of method appeared after 1960. Similar changes were occurring in the intellectual thought of the British left. The image of Soviet-style state communism had been damaged by the Soviet invasion of Budapest (1956) and by the revelations of the Stalinist purges (7,000 members had left the British Communist Party after 1956). The subsequent reorganization of the left in Britain was to result in a new concern with subjectivity and culture as equally important as hard political theory. This turn was influenced by the early work of Raymond Williams, by Richard Hoggart's 1957 sociological study of working-class Leeds, *The Uses of Literacy* (written in the language, and using techniques such as interior focus, of imaginative fiction), and by E. P. Thompson's attempt to wrest the adjective 'humanist' away from its assumed collocation with 'liberal' and toward a firmer partnership with 'socialist'.

In the pages of the New Left journal *New Left Review* (from 1960), the separation of culture from politics was presented by writers such as E. P. Thompson as a conservative liberal strategy for dissociating feeling or sensibility from reason or consciousness in order to disarm the aesthetic as a force for political and social change in the democratic enhancement of human life. In the absence of a fully-fledged British sociological tradition, literary culture had played an enormous role in defining national identities. For writers such as Raymond Williams, it was now time to argue for a more comprehensive notion of a 'common culture' and to find new ways of articulating the relations between subjective meanings and objective social structures so that culture could be recognized as both a way of life and a 'way of struggle'. E. P. Thompson's essay 'Outside the Whale' (1960) indicted what he saw as the dominant English tradition of 'Natopolitan Apathy' (identified as a current evident in Wordsworthian quietism through Eliot's conservative Anglicanism to the elemental pessimism of a William Golding or the insular complacencies of Amis, Osborne, and Wain). Instead he called for writers and intellectuals to refuse to retreat into reactionary humanisms which dressed up versions of original sin in the garments of a liberal pessimism. The essay appeared in a collection entitled *Out of Apathy* (1960) which marked the rise of the New Left from the merger of the *New Reasoner* with the *Universities and Left Review* (from 1957) to form *New Left Review*. This journal, with strong attachments to the anti-nuclear movement, would express a concern to develop forms of 'new reason' in left political thought: the belief that rational political analysis must proceed by taking account of subjective and culturally lived experience and that literature, though largely but not necessarily a middle-class cultural form, was an important area for the articulation and understanding of such 'structures of feeling'.

Educational reforms in the sixties, after the Robbins report on higher education and the Newsome report on secondary education, promised an expansion which would facilitate a new class mobility. Theatrical projects such as Arnold Wesker's Centre 42 and Joan Littlewood's Stratford East experiment also reflected a commitment to extend the 'long front' of 'good culture' beyond middle-class confines. By 1960 a number of writers, most notably David Storey, David Mercer, Arnold Wesker, and John Fowles (particularly in *The Collector*, 1963) were attempting to explore the subjective meanings of class transition or class antagonism. In each case, and despite Harold Wilson's optimistic forecast of the new classless society, their portrayal was of a working-class consciousness moulded out of exile, betrayal, and disfranchisement and often conveyed through an intense awareness of linguistic difference. Instead of offering the means of self-expression, language was more often than not seen to be the vehicle of class and self-dispossession.

The poetry of Douglas Dunn would not express outright self-conscious and political anger at the 'hierarchies of cuisine and literacy' until 1979 when he published the collection *Barbarians*, but, with the apppearance of the almost voyeuristic and certainly Larkinesque *Terry Street* in 1969, Dunn's early theme of the guilt-ridden ex-working-class revenant was firmly established. A socially realist evocation of a working-class street in Hull, *Terry Street* avoids metaphoric flights and uses effects of synecdoche to convey a sense of proximity, community, and also claustrophobia. However, the segments of an urban landscape are always shaped into wholes through the reflective meditations of a bookish observer. They are images filtered through the lens of a liminal recorder who must finally repudiate his own voyeuristic relationship to those who are revisited. The divided phenomenological realities of 'them' and 'us' are projected almost as a staged masque silently enacted behind the panes of numerous suburban windows. In the poem entitled 'A Window Affair', the perspectives momentarily coalesce for 'we were looking at the same thing' and even 'heard the same inweave of random noise', but the reassurance of empirical coincidence is short-lived and flirtation through glass actually preserves from a touch which could only confirm the observer's sense of his own mind paralytically, if sweetly, 'dying in cadences'. By the end of the poem, he recognizes that he must also physically leave a community in which he has already failed to uncover an emotional or psychological resting place. Even to revisit, whether in person or in poetry, may, if unintentionally, be to exploit. He is touched by them, but cannot touch their world. In the later poem, 'I am a Cameraman', in the collection *Love or Nothing* (1974), he confesses quite candidly that 'them' and 'us' can never be reconciled through verse, for 'they suffer, and I catch only the surface'.

If Dunn's poetry of the sixties and seventies asserted the intransigence of class difference and, in dramatizing the conflict of the working-class exile, exposed ramifications which persisted far beyond material boundaries, Tony Harrison's poetry in the eighties was self-consciously wrought out of what he saw in his own experience as the necessarily (and in characteristic punning fashion) 'forged music' of the class exile educated out of a community which is still, however, and for ever home. Indeed, the Leeds skinhead in himself is declared, by definition, to be outside literature, but he has an insistent way of erupting into Harrison's verse through ingenious and compacted puns. That English language which made Harrison's baker father feel 'like some dull oaf', the 'tongue that weighed like lead' (in the poem 'Marked with D'), is described in an interview with the poet as the same which has also made possible 'that literary frisson—"hypocrite lecteur, mon semblable, mon frère"' and 'will cost you so much in social awareness, in the consciousness of social gaps and divisions. . . . I'm building that potential division into the actual writing.'[10] Indeed, the 'V' casts its shadow through all his poetry and not just through the highly publicized 1985 poem of that name. It is there in the 'books, books, books' that come between himself and his father, in 'A kumquat for John Keats': 'one part's sweet and one part's tart'; in the Leeds schoolboy's recitation of poetry, 'the looms of owned language smashed apart'; as well as in the 'unending violence of US and THEM' explored through 'V', his own 'Elegy in a Country Churchyard'. In this poem it even remains to haunt his musings on the return home as he ponders the connection between the aerosoled 'UNITED' of the skinhead and his own some-times violent need for linguistic anchorage in a community. In an ironic allusion to Yeats's Platonically conceived aesthetic Byzan-tium, 'the day's last images recede' on the television screen which transmits the late-night news: 'police v. pickets at a coke-plant gate, | old violence and old disunity'. As the miners' strike rages on in the streets, the poet watches the televised scenes of conflict but draws near the warmth of the domestic coal fire and the comfort of shared human love. Yet this is no sentimentalization of the traditional fam-ily hearth, for the entire poem is a recognition that he is indeed heated as a body by the fruits of conflict and as a poet by the battle in himself between the classical wordsmith and the skinhead that might have been. Harrison's elegy is for all the undiscovered mute inglorious Miltons who might have been, and for the singing master who, in another world, might have been the destiny of the nihilistic and destructive skinhead: that other of his own strange meeting. In a discussion of his poetry before the publication of 'V', Harrison indicated another elegaic function that the poem might subsequently be seen to carry: 'When anyone says that I'm fighting a battle that's been fought long ago and that the class system doesn't exist, I know it does exist, I keep banging my head against it.'[11] This was in 1983. Looking back from the mid-nineties, the comment serves even more emphatically as an elegiac farewell to the promised classlessness proclaimed so optimistically by the politicians of the sixties.

In fact, even as early as the sixties a number of writers began to push against the limits of accepted literary taste in an attempt to begin to articulate subjectivities hitherto excluded from it, and to explore through a *via negativa* some means of giving birth to iden-tities and problems for which there was no name, either in the vo-cabularies of social planners or in the available canons of English literature. Feminist awareness began to develop by the late sixties, particularly as it became more apparent that the rhetoric of sixties' libertarianism had disguised fundamental gender inequalities and, as Germaine Greer was to point out in 1970, actually created new opportunities for the exploitation of women. In A. S. Byatt's *The Game* (1968), Julia's books are praised by another woman for portraying a problem 'nobody thinks anything ought to be done about. That is—women, intelligent women, who are suddenly plunged into being at home all day.' Betty Friedan in *The Feminine Mystique* (1963) had actually referred to the condition as the 'problem with no name' and from this gradually developed the idea of the need for a feminist politics grounded in the practice of collective consciousness-raising which would endeavour to give women a public identity by seeking to name their experiences. Formally, the Women's Liberation Movement in America began to take on a fully-fledged public identity after the demonstration at the Miss America contest of 1968, though in Britain it was not until the early seventies that the women's movement would begin to mobilize as a political force. As in America, the British movement too emphasized the importance of collective consciousness-raising as an alternative or complementary route to party politics as the means toward autonomy and self-definition for women.

Literature was an important focus for such political practice. Since the eighteenth century, aestheticians have regarded imaginative art as one of the most powerful means to express experiences for which no previous or available concepts exist within public discourses. Throughout the sixties, and before feminism, the gender frustrations of countless women had often been expressed through the literary construction of forms of negative space or through the exploration of poetic tropes which might convey a sense of embryonic emergence. Not surprisingly, therefore, writers in this (then) largely buried tradition, such as Sylvia Plath (resident in Britain in the years preceding her death and during her most important period of writing) or Anne Sexton in America, were first treated as cases of clinically pathological hysteria within the discourses of traditional literary criticism (whether of the pessimistic cultural conservative variety or the Romantic-apocalyptic mode) but later recognized by feminist critics to have been painfully attempting to give birth to new identities through their poetic writing.

In both her fictional prose and poetry, Plath clearly attempts to assault poetic convention and to press language toward the impossible and often violent recovery of some pre-nascent and pre-patriarchal identity. Sometimes this quest involves honing with knives (as in 'Cut'), unpeeling ('In Plaster'), resurrection ('Lady Lazarus'), or the tearing of veils (as in 'Purdah' or the scene in *The Bell Jar*, 1964, where Esther casts into the night sky her newly purchased and sophisticated 'feminine' clothing). Such violent imagery was often regarded as an expression of personal pathology, for it described a renunciation which seemed to entail an absolute negation of that feminine body which appears in the public gaze. Plath was not, of course, the first women writer to express ambivalence toward the female body as both the potential source of authentic identity and the object of oppressive containment. Woolf's earlier *To the Lighthouse* (1927) had offered the image of female identity as a foetal and chrysalid core of darkness from which might emerge a negative capability aesthetically able to shape identity as it pleased and ultimately to enter the public world with its chosen shape and to challenge oppressive stereotypes of femininity ('women can't write, women can't paint').

In Plath's poetry such paradoxically nihilistic utopianism (bordering at times on the negatively theological) often takes the form of an obsession with the body as waste, a surrender to abjection, entropy, and dissolution, to the meltdown of fever, the cold perfection of death, the negation of the body in purdah or perversely joyful submission to the sadistic boot of fascist or misogynist. In *The Bell Jar*, Esther's attempted suicide on the ski-slope is actually a desperate effort to dissolve into the form of the dispassionate white sun 'which shone at the summit of the sky. I wanted to hone myself on it 'till I grew saintly and thin and essential as the blade of a knife.' In positivistic terms, it is easy to medicalize such writing, much harder to enter its *via negativa* and arrive at that sublime space through and beyond negation (and gender) itself.

Literature and the Revolt against Method

Not only in literary cultures, but even in the social sciences at this time, there was a marked shift away from the positivism of vulgar economic determinisms to a new interest in how meanings are constructed in and mediated through language in ways which do not straightforwardly reflect economic categories. Literary practitioners had always known that words slip, slide, and perish, but sociologists could now supply creative writers with 'scientific' theories as to why this should be the case. Scientists too were beginning to recognize that, in a rationalized world, linguistic ambiguity and indeterminacy might prove more of a virtue than a hindrance, providing spaces in which to open up possibilities for renegotiation, vision, and unplanned process. Indeed, like the scientific-chaos theorists of the next decade, sociologists would increasingly borrow their metaphors for material change and social process from literature and drama itself (as in Erving Goffmann's analysis of self as theatrical presentation or Anthony Giddens's notion of the self as a narrative project). Human behaviour was seen to be learnt through ideologically inflected languages and lived out in the world in complex and contradictory ways (Simone de Beauvoir's *The Second Sex*, for example, translated in 1961, had shown how one is made not born a woman). Life itself was increasingly seen to be constructed and negotiated like a literary text, any event in it existing phenomenologically at an intersection of competing interpretations of realizations seen as ever-shifting 'sites of struggle'. If this was new to sociologists, it was all fairly old hat to literary critics steeped in the epistemologically relativist and linguistically sceptical Revolution of the Word which had been literary modernism. Even so, it would all have to be relearnt in the new theoretical languages of the seventies, when that next revolution of the word occurred, and when, for a time, literary theory itself seemed to steal the critical limelight from literature.

Within literary cultures, one of the most influential and popular philosophy texts of the fifties had been A. J. Ayer's *Language, Truth and Logic*, first published in 1936 but reissued in 1950. Its antimetaphysical, common-sense empiricism seemed appropriate to the sceptical and pragmatic mood of this decade and provided a perfect intellectual gloss on the temper of Movement writers such as Kingsley Amis, John Wain, Donald Davie, and Philip Larkin. Ayer's popularity waned in the sixties, however, and instead intellectuals took up the spate of anti-positivist disquisitions concerned with the repudiation of Ayer's thesis and with the critique of scientific method as the only method through which to ground truth. An important influence was Karl Popper, who saw in the ethos of rationalized planning a misguided transference of the methodologies of hard science to the demesne of human behaviour. For Popper, societies could never be planned simply because planners could never foresee the consequential effects of their own projected social blueprints on the worlds of the future.

In his social criticism and philosophy of science, Popper rejected the verificationist assumptions of Ayer and the positivists that individual sense-experiences are the foundations from which knowledge is derived through inductive procedures. In Popper's view, scientific theories begin life as imaginative conjectures or hypotheses, though the scientist must subsequently proceed by submitting these to possible falsification through empirical testing. No scientific theory is ever absolute and all are dependent upon the human ability to project hypothetical worlds: in effect to create fictions. He expressed this view in a revision of the metaphor of 'foundationalism' which would echo resoundingly in the post-modern epistemological critiques of the late seventies and eighties:

The empirical basis of objective science has thus nothing 'absolute' about it. Science does not rest upon absolute bedrock. The bold structure of its theories rises, as it were, above a swamp. It is like a building erected on piles. The piles are driven down from above into the swamp, but not down into any natural or 'given' base, and if we stop driving the piles deeper, it is not because we have reached firm ground. We simply stop when we are satisfied that the piles are firm enough to carry the structure, at least for the time being.[12]

Frank Kermode's *The Sense of an Ending* (1967) was an important study which reflected both the intellectual drift toward a new pragmatism (fictions as working hypotheses which can be abandoned when the needs of sense making change) and the renewed literary critical interest in modernist theories of the spatialization of time. Like Popper, Kermode emphasized the need to be aware of the provisionality of any fictionalized account of the world, to be conscious that aesthetic fictions projected onto human history may degenerate into dangerous myths. Kermode too stepped back from the fashionable apocalypticism of the counterculture, but explored apocalypse as a way of trying to understand the human need to order contingent experience through the projection of retrospective narrative order. Unable to know our end, we use fictions to give a compensatory sense of the concordance of beginning, middle, and end: without such narrative order life would seem meaningless. Although Popper wrote within the framework of philosophy of science and Kermode within that of literary criticism, their work in the sixties reflected a growing reaction against positivism and empiricism and a shift toward the recognition that there may be an aesthetic dimension in all knowledge (even scientific). Not quite post-modern, though certainly pragmatist rather than realist, their critiques did contribute to the erosion of the idea that knowledge is grounded absolutely either in abstract universals or in empirical sense experience or that either of these can provide foundations for the legitimation of the grand narratives of history which have organized human experience in the West since the Enlightenment.

Hans Georg Gadamer's *Truth and Method* (1960) would gradually produce a similar effect and was to make an impact on literary criticism with the development of interest in phenomenology in the seventies. In many ways echoing the preoccupations of the British philosopher Stuart Hampshire, Gadamer's book argued that all human beings exist as embodied agents in a culture. This context must shape the limits of perception, but in ways which cannot necessarily be known as a precise formulation. We can only begin to shape our knowledge of an object because we already have some preconscious understanding of it which arises from our cultural situation. Such knowledge can never be fully articulated, but the search for it propels us, through prejudice rather than scientific detachment, to seek understanding of the unknown. In encountering the unknown as openly as possible we become aware of prejudice and able to modify it. Knowledge always arrives too late, however, for the process of attempting to know changes the object of knowledge, and similarly changes the enquirer's own subjective experience of selfhood. Gadamer's contribution to the critique of positivism lay in his rejection of detachment as the ideal model of knowledge, and in his argument for the need to contextualize all attempts to know within a *sensus communis* which allows for negotiation of meaning but provides arbitration and final legitimation for any individual assertion or statement of what is true. His views, though expressed mainly in relation to scientific knowledge, were remarkably similar to T. S. Eliot's notion of tradition as a necessarily inarticulable condition of being: one can live in or embody it, but, once fully articulated, tradition ceases to be. In his famous essay of 1919, 'Tradition and the Individual Talent', as in the later cultural criticism, Eliot had attacked rationalized social planning by defending the importance of tradition in preserving a socially vital, but necessarily unconscious and tacit, cultural knowledge. This cultural knowing was most perfectly embodied (because never consciously and explicitly articulated) in great works of literature. Gadamer extended Eliot's argument from the demesne of cultural to that of scientific meaning.

A writer who struggled somewhat tragically throughout the sixties against such philosophical assaults on foundational definitions of truth was the novelist B. S. Johnson. Indeed, he committed suicide in 1973 without ever resolving a desperate frustration, expressed from the first novel *Travelling People* (1963) and throughout his subsequent writing, about the inability of fiction to be true in either some absolute Platonic or empirical sense. Johnson's entire *œuvre* was driven but limited by an obsessive desire to break out of fictionality and into a final correspondence of word with world: 'Telling stories is telling lies . . . I am not interested in telling lies in my novels.'[13] His psychological compulsions propelled two varieties of fiction, one more or less indistinguishable from autobiography, and the other ostentatiously fantastic and darkly Jacobean. Indeed, he seemed to take both of David Lodge's imagined routes (mimesis and fabulation) out of the crossroads of the contemporary novel, though in somewhat eccentrically personalized vehicles. In one mode, a convoy of confessional outpourings sought a Platonically destined idea to be discovered in a trawl through the dense and tenebrous regions of the inner soul, and in the other, darkly comic but desperate joyriding forays expressed an underlying and furious nihilism. Each mode, however, returned incessantly to the only clear point of departure: either brooding or Shandyesque, but always self-conscious, in its obsessive depiction of the figure of Johnson himself as author seated at his writing-desk and struggling ineffectually to realize private truths through the public conventions of linguistic form. The plots of the fantastic works, particularly *House Mother Normal* (1971) and *Christy Malry's Own Double-Entry* (1973), erupt into violent revenge scenarios where a psychopathic character balances the books (literally in the second instance) for imagined received wrongs in excessively punitive acts of revenge involving homicidal or grossly deviant and antisocial forms of behaviour. The autobiographical works, particularly the brooding abjection of *Trawl* (1966) and the morbidly angry *The Unfortunates* (1969) (presented looseleaf in a decorative box printed with luminously colourful images of inflated cancer cells), however, similarly presented a vision of life premissed on the random moral indifference of material being and the horror of living in a world with no guarantee of any final redemptive order. Fiction-making in each of Johnson's apparently very dissimilar modes was a psychological defence against a sickness-unto-death which could be relieved only by the desperate antic self-exposure and self-advertisement always also the self-concealment of the black comedian. Johnson was, perhaps, the Tony Hancock of the literary world of the sixties.

Strangely of his time and out of it, he castigated the formal conservatism of fellow British writers and developed innovative metafictional techniques but ever in the service of an absolutely oppositional concept of truth and fiction already regarded as retrograde by the progressive intellectual forces around him. Aside from the writing of Popper and Gadamer, Thomas Kuhn's enormously influential *The Structure of Scientific Revolutions* (1962) had also repudiated the positivist notion of a fact by arguing that truth claims are always made in relation to the norms of particular knowledge communities. The interpretation of what is regarded as a fact changes when theoretical paradigms begin to break down as tensions and contradictions arise within a community, but before new paradigms can be constructed there will be a self-conscious concern to return to and make explicit the fundamental principles of a discipline. Kuhn likened the experience of shifting from one paradigm of knowledge to another as akin to religious conversion: afterwards, nothing in the world will ever be the same again. Perhaps Johnson's problem was that he could not make the necessary leap of faith. He remained paralytically torn between the epistemes of modernity and post-modernity, wanting but unable to believe in absolute orders existing below the contingent surfaces of everyday experience, yet equally unable to embrace the post-modern condition and accept that truth is either a conventionalist arrangement manufactured from within a shared community or a solipsistic vision defiantly spun out of an acceptance of the condition of nihilism.

More radical theorists of knowledge such as Paul Feyerabend carried the critique of method much further. In *Against Method* (1975), Feyerabend argued that 'the idea of a fixed method, or of a fixed theory of rationality rests on too naïve a view of man and his social surroundings'. In the spirit of the counterculture, he called for a liberation of society from the stranglehold of an 'ideologically pet-rified science', urging that each must be free to choose his or her own form of knowledge.[14] The revival of Faust and Frankenstein myths in science and horror fiction and the popularity of disaster movies such as *The Quatermass Experiment* also reflected a growing scepticism about scientific method and the ethical implications of new technologies. One writer, in particular, gathered into her work a number of these various critiques of method and assaults on ob-jectivity, and she remained through the entire period 1960–90 one of the most important and consistently anti-rationalist literary voices. Doris Lessing's aesthetic self-reflexivity from *The Golden Notebook* (1962) traversed intellectual terrains as diverse as New Left politics, the anti-psychiatry movement, Jungian archetypes, and Sufi mysti-cism. Her writing remained dedicated to the pursuit of alternative cosmic visions, always involving the disintegration of individualist consciousness into pre-rationalist or supra-rationalist forms. Fictions which explored the descents into hell of psychic breakdown and the collapse of rationalized civil societies into primitive tribal territor-ialism also broke ontological frames in order to envisage a human psyche evolved for telepathic transmission, ESP, and intergalactic communication.

In many ways, her best-known novel, *The Golden Notebook*, was a precise chronicle of the time: its formal construction reflected an engagement with the countercultural Laingian notion of psychic breakdown as a means to break through to new psychic wholeness. Its self-reflexivity registered doubt about the possibility of authentic self-expression in a world where everything seemed to share 'the same quality of false art, caricature, parody'. Parody, pastiche, collage, and a mishmash of incongruent styles conveyed its author's anxiety about the role of art in a new mass-media world where even the politically committed writer could no longer assume a homogeneous audience. Lessing had already indicated that the left itself was showing all the signs of surrendering to a 'darkening fog of urbane authoritarianism', beguiled into bland verbal wit or virtuoso shadow boxing with imaginary opponents while the real enemies of culture invaded the land.[15] Even the sociological analysis of identity as self-conscious manipulation of contradictory roles was taken up explicitly in the novel as its protagonist Anna divided her different selves into discrete notebooks, each with its own prose style, each eventually breaking down into the creative madness of the final, golden notebook. Politically, too, the novel reflected the shift toward subjective experience in the New Left, looked forward to the renascent feminist seventies, and represented a sharp reaction against the parochialism and insularity of Britain in 1962, where, as Lessing had written in an earlier essay, 'thinking internationally means choosing a particular shade of half-envious, half-patronising emotion to feel about the United States; or collecting money for Hungary, or taking little holidays in Europe, or liking French and Italian films'.[16]

Lessing's critique of British insularity, however, encompassed the politics of the right and left, the complacencies of the entrenched middle classes, and the materialism of the new media professionals. With the success of the *Chatterley* trial behind it, *The Golden Notebook* also introduced into literature a remarkable frankness in the representation and analysis of sexual relationships. The novel was topical, but more profoundly, across the personal, social, cultural, and political arenas covered in the five notebooks, it introduced a theme which would continue to exercise Lessing in all her forthcoming work: the spiritual and moral bankruptcy of the West in its blind commitment to a narrow and instrumental concept of rationality. In the later novel *Memoirs of a Survivor* (1974), she would describe this rationalism as an intelligence which could 'make a rocket fly to the moon or weave artificial dress materials out of the by-products of petroleum', and which has created weapons of such horrifying destructive potential that 'as we sit in the ruins of this variety of intelligence it is hard to give it very much value'. Lessing's Anna in *The Golden Notebook* uses her rational and critical intelligence to divide herself up for survival, as her author uses it to anatomize the West and expose the destruction which breeds about its heart. Yet the device of the notebooks constituted almost a parody of Goffmanesque theories of the fragmentation of social roles and subjective identity and their collapse and failure can be interpreted as Lessing's indictment of such rationalistic and sociological dissections of the self. As the notebooks formally break down and collapse, with Anna herself, into the greater fluidity of the golden notebook, so Lessing repudiates scientific role theory and rationalistic self-division as inauthentic means of psychic survival. However, for an analytic and discursive writer, such rejection is not unproblematic. As Anna attempts to reconstitute her past as a member of a Communist group in apartheid-ridden South Africa, she exclaims at one point:

Heaven knows we are never allowed to forget that the 'personality' doesn't exist anymore . . . And so all this talk, this anti-humanist bullying, about the evaporation of the personality becomes meaningless for me at that point where I manufacture enough emotional energy inside myself to create in memory some human being I've known . . . Am I saying that the certainty I'm clinging to belongs to the visual arts, and not to the novel at all, which has been claimed by the disintegration or the collapse?

Until this point, Lessing had always articulated a Lukacsian conviction that only fictional realism was capable of subsuming the self-indulgence of personal obsession into collective social representation. Now, however, it seemed that realism itself had become implicated in the rationalizing discursivity which seemed to be the spirit of the age and was certainly the language of its sociologists and planners. Her fear was that the novel had lost its nineteenth-century capacity to represent and lay bare the soul of history. Yet Lessing's own fiction has sometimes been criticized for the essayistic discursivity of its style, and, in *The Golden Notebook*, the only fictional motivation for the frequent disquisitions on the state of the novel is the fact that Anna herself is a novelist with a writer's block: her writer's journal is, of course, Lessing's too. So, when Anna despairs that the novel has become 'a function of the fragmented society, the fragmented consciousness', the device allows Lessing to voice her own qualms. When Anna reflects that the reading of fiction has become another blind pursuit of information in a world too complex to encompass, and 'the novel-report is a means towards it', Lessing is able to incorporate a self-reflexive analysis of her own doubt. The inclusion of such analysis, however, is seen by Lessing to exemplify the problem. Abandoning the Anna-ventriloquism for once, she informs her reader that great art does not arise from consciousness in the fashion of a planner's report, but that 'flashes of genuine art are all out of deep, suddenly stark, undisguisable private emotion'. For Lessing in 1962, however, such emotion may be unhealthy unless 'the small personal voice' of the novelist can, once again, speak representatively for the experiences of a wider humanity. But that humanity has fragmented. How, therefore, may literature now express the complex fragmentariness of late modernity in terms which neither reduce social experience to particularized flashes of insular personal emotion, nor collapse the particular into the general in the rationalized discourse and with the facile ease of the documentarists and social scientists of the information age?

In the preface to the novel written in 1971, Lessing argued that

throughout the notebooks people have discussed, theorised, dogmatised, labelled, compartmentalised . . . But they have also reflected each other, been aspects of each other, given birth to each other's thoughts and behaviour—are each other, form wholes. In the Inner Golden Notebook things have come together, the divisions have broken down, there is formlessness with the end of fragmentation—the triumph of the second theme is that of unity.

Authenticity is associated with formlessness; unity, if it exists, with an expressive mode which has nothing to do with rational logic. In the novel, as Anna breaks down, unable to create a linguistic form which can correspond to her sense of internal and external chaos, she recognizes that sanity is preserved because of 'a certain kind of intelligence. This intelligence is dissolving and I am very frightened.' It is a rationality which comes into play whenever she is threatened by the fear of emotional intimacy or mental breakdown, but it prompts the Laingian recognition that:

The essence of neurosis is conflict. But the essence of living now, fully, not blocking off what goes on, is conflict. In fact I've reached the stage where I look at people and say—he or she, they are whole at all because they've chosen to block off at this stage or that. People stay sane by blocking off.

Rationality preserves us from one kind of madness, by keeping us inside another. So what of art? A. Alvarez was to make essentially the same point in his introduction to *The New Poetry* in 1962, where, even more directly than Lessing, he argued that in the last half-century

all our lives, even those of the most genteel and enislanded, are influenced profoundly by forces which have nothing to do with gentility, decency or politeness. Theologians would call these forces evil, psychologists, perhaps, libido. Either way, they are the forces of disintegration which destroy the old standards of civilisation. Their public faces are those of two world wars, of the concentration camps, of genocide, and the threat of nuclear war.[17]

His plea for a new poetry which would include the work of Sylvia Plath was also an attack on the rational gentility of the verse collected in Robert Conquest's first *New Lines* anthology, and of the decencies of the Movement. For Lessing, however, sympathetic to Alvarez's position but working in the traditionally more discursive medium of prose fiction, the challenge would be less to reject rationality outright, than to find some means of expanding its definition within a broadly realist fictional aesthetic: it would eventually lead her towards mystical philosophy, science fiction, and Eastern religion.

Already in *Martha Quest* (1952), in fact, Lessing had granted her heroine a vision of emancipation from the repressive political and familial structures of the African home. Glimmering over the harsh scrub and the stunted trees is a 'noble city, set foursquare and colonnaded . . . fair skinned children of the North playing hand in hand with the bronze-skinned children of the South'. The vision is curiously akin to that which shimmered before Hardy's Jude the Obscure: an imaginary Christminster of noble and democratic learning unconsciously projected from the frustration of Jude's situation within the internally exiled and culturally dispossessed English peasantry. Yet it is Jude's faith in the possibility of rational social change and his blindness to the force of the non-rational inside himself as well as in the world outside which leads to his destruction. For he discovers eventually that no amount of learning will enable him to penetrate what is discovered, in any case, to be a chimera protected by class privilege and impervious to rationalistic egalitarianism. By the end of the sixties Lessing too had turned utterly from her earlier albeit qualified faith in rational politics to bring about the new Jerusalem. In the last novel of the Martha Quest series, *The Four-Gated City* (1969), Martha comes to recognize, as Jude could not, that such visions are always projections of non-rational desire, of the hunger of inner space. For Lessing, we come to recognize the nature of this inner need not in rational analysis, but in conditions of madness or dislocation, or even as 'the reward of not-eating, not-sleeping': by depriving the body in order to escape its limitations. The visions cannot be willed and, it would seem on the evidence of Lessing's subsequent fiction, they cannot be materialized as planned political or social realities either.

The most direct statement of this theme was *The Memoirs of a Survivor* (1974), which explored not only the failure of rational political thought in the context of a post-nuclear holocaust, but also the possibility that the emotional repression required by a narrowly instrumental rationality might indirectly produce the violence which had destroyed the world in the first place. Set against the disintegrating Western political economy is a fantastic room on the 'other side' of a wall, threshold between exhausted materialism and a repressed and distorted spiritual consciousness. In the room, progress is made only by listening and by giving up control: allowing the boundaries of the egotistical self to merge into a collective condition before and beyond individuation and undreamt of in materialist socialist thought. Outside, Emily and Gerald continue to attempt to salvage some remains of civilization, but in continuing to apply the rationalistic principles of liberal political economy, fall once again into a competitive and hierarchical pecking order which cannot even recognize the existence nor the hunger of the soul. The famine outside is shown to be a product of the famine within: as Emily reaches out for

the embrace of her mother, she is rebuffed by the Victorian requirement of hygiene and discovers instead the iron grip of the rationalized Welfare State. The wild underclass spawned by this condition
of spiritual indifference turns cannibal. Human beings who cannot
give to each other eat each other.

The steady direction of Lessing's work away from realism in form
and rationalism in ethos gradually took her out of the city altogether,
first through descents into inner space or into symbolic looking-glass
worlds beyond material walls, and finally on to a cosmic journey
into the far outer space of imaginary intergalactic kingdoms. Her
perspective, however, has remained that of the outsider. The Britain
of her early novels is the nation as it appeared to a left-wing ex-
colonial anti-colonial woman writer arriving from Southern Rhode-
sia to a politically cautious Cold War London of 1949. In the later
Canopus in Argus novels, the defamiliarizing perspective persists,
but now cognitive estrangement becomes universal as the entire planet
Earth is viewed from other worlds. Such displacement of the
perspectival relations between margins and centre, however, would
become endemic in British fiction by the eighties. As we will see
later in this study, grotesque reversal and disorder, techniques previously associated with Juvenalian satire or Rabelaisian comedy,
would come to flourish once again as graphic vehicles for sceptical
moral anatomy. Lessing was one of the first writers, however, to
integrate fantastic forms into the conventions of realism and to take
fiction in the direction of that magic realism which would seem so
innovatory in the seventies.

Unreal Cities: Spaces in the Urban Mind

The city is a powerful symbol in Lessing's fiction for the alienated
and over-rationalized modern consciousness. Certainly the post-war
years had seen an enormous volume of new building and the
replanning and rationalization of urban space. Regulations concerning building structure were considerably relaxed in the sixties and
the contemporary image of the high-rise estate took shape across
Britain. The term 'megastructure' was coined to describe the new
urban conglomerate, the planned environment with its zones for

living, working, exercising, and relaxing. By the seventies, of course, many of the hastily erected prefabricated buildings were uninhabitable (some had indeed spectacularly collapsed), their materials rotting and their structures an open invitation to vandals. The new estates were the battlegrounds for race and urban riots, and a number of social reports suggested that children were failing to thrive, women were depressed, and drug cultures flourishing.

The failures of urban planning were laid out in Roy Fisher's series of poems and prose-poems *City* written in 1968 just as planners were beginning, somewhat reluctantly, to recognize the existence of a human need for conservation and continuity as well as for innovation and change (though one new town, Milton Keynes, was planned at this time). It is instructive to compare the mood of this poem with a later and much more vitriolic condemnation of the urban wasteland of contemporary 'Junk Britain', Peter Reading's *Ukelele Music* (1985). Fisher's Vorticist nightmare world of disused and corroded industrial machinery, blank walls, shut factories, and somnambulant semi-humans is reminiscent both of Eliot's Waste Land and of Williams's Paterson. However, its goods yards, gasworks, and sulphur tanks, where 'the imaginary comes' with 'as much force as the real', are clearly recognizable as part of the landscape of northern industrial England declining into that post-industrial inertia which would grip large areas of the British Isles by the early eighties. The surreal effect of *City*, however (and the last poem is entitled 'Chirico'), is partly created by the transference of attributes between human and machine, for, while the people seem of metal made, the heart of the great hulking engines still throbs dully in the smashed environment, enervated but ready to be reconditioned out of the Brunellian remains. The city landscape has fallen and been razed and will continue to rise again, after a fashion. Yet, like Eliot's urban pastoral, it is also a mindscape of drift, anomie, and paralysis. 'The gaping office block of night | Shudders into the deep sky overhead' and half-built towers 'Show mouths that will soon speak no more'; 'the suburb lies like a hand tonight | A man's thick hand' and, under the asphalt, in the grave of history, men and women could be 'rolled out like sleeping maggots'. Through it all roams the disaffected *flâneur*–poet, studying it, writing about it, yet outside it, unable to reach or know it, for everything that he does is 'prisoned in its act' and he 'afraid of becoming | A cemetery of performance'. He can look upon and 'consider without scorn or envy' the neat suburbia rising out of the ashes of industrial ruin because he is outside. But it is no more comfortable on the outside than the inside: to be outside without the metaphysical anchorage for which he longs is to feel stretched and fragmented across the sedimented layers of history and time, knowing only that 'I want to believe in a single world'.

If there is some vitality in Fisher's city, even that of a persisting low base life, Reading's post-enterprise vision of city life is further testimony to the pervasive spread of a dull and pernicious 'banality of evil': a casual, brutal hooliganism becomes the national pastime, child abuse seems more a social diversion than a disease, and the authorities simply respond to the automated violations of human dignity with technocratic blindness or Little England complacency. The nineteenth-century 'Capting's Tale' of Britain's seafaring imperial victories registers an astygmatic gaze so fixated on the myths of the past that the horrors of the present barely enter its frame. Unlike Fisher, Reading has renounced belief even in the redemptive and unifying power of art, though he will still try to use it to lift the veil of dullness and to make his readers see. As much at ease mimicking classical form as provincial demotic, walrus-whiskered colonels as urban bovver boys, tabloid dailies as letters to the editor, he presents an urban England irretrievably in fragments. The poet's pen cannot compete to hold this centre with the texts of a brutal authoritarian state inscribed even in the iron-tipped boot of the dispossessed young. Where none can purify the dialect of this tribe, the poet must be content to recycle a tradition and mimic a demotic both now terminally infected with a disease of urban blight which has brought even poetry to a condition of scrap, debased pastiche, and low mimicry: 'What do they think they're playing at, then, these Poetry Wallahs? | Grub St reviewing its own lame valedictory bunk'.

By the late sixties, in fact, it had become apparent that people could not be conveniently slotted into the zones of the planners, nor their lives rationalized according to a Taylorist or Fordist industrial time-and-motion efficiency plan. Jonathan Raban published an account of London in the seventies entitled *Soft City* (1974) which, unlike Reading's detraditionalized urban jungle, expressed some optimism about the aesthetic possibilities of modern city life. Raban's text, of course, written in 1974, coincided with the industrial crisis of the mid-seventies which saw the Heath Government almost under siege from the miner's strike, a record trade deficit and inflation, the oil crisis, severe problems in Northern Ireland, and a growing mood of confrontation and suppressed violence. Raban's book also appeared as faith in Fabian planning and Keynesian economics was at its lowest ebb and before the rise of radical monetarism which would gather force toward the end of the decade. The title itself signified a shift away from the ethos of hard planning with its view of the city as a rationalized metropolis of controlled mass production to one of labyrinthine, shifting consumption and entrepreneurialism, with cells of widely diverse activity independent of centralized regulation. Indeed, Raban argued

that living in the city is an art, and we need the vocabulary of art, of style, to describe the peculiar relation between man and material that lives in the continual creative play of urban living. The city as we imagine it, the soft city of illusion, myth, aspiration, nightmare, is as real, maybe more real, than the hard city one can locate in maps and statistics, in monographs on urban sociology and demography and architecture.[18]

Raban sees an aesthetically motivated protest in all city-dwellers against the concept of the urban environment as a 'machine for living', and one which has taken artistic impulses out of a minority culture and into a truly democratic arena. His optimistic postmodern vision regards city life as a continuous process of construction, negotiation, fabrication, and invention. Like any work of art, the planner's textual blueprint is fleshed out with the projected dreams and fantasies of those who build from it their own worlds. Cities are not simply places in the material world, but spaces in the imagination. The more they are planned expressions of a rationalized urban environment, the more their inhabitants will seek to reformulate those spaces in the terms of myth and fantasy or imaginatively transform it through textiles, materials, music, or words. Raban's city-dwellers self-consciously manipulate the mythic elements in modern life to create spaces of freedom for themselves. But few writers of the sixties and seventies shared his optimism. Those who did not present lives curtailed and cramped by urban squalor tended to explore the darker side of Raban's perception: that, even in the planned city, life is driven as much by unconsciously displaced desire as by consciously articulated reason.

Freud famously observed that 'a happy person never fantasises, only an unsatisfied one. The motive forces of fantasies are unsatisfied wishes, and every single fantasy is the fulfilment of a wish, a correction of unsatisfying reality.'[19] Raban's imaginary city is a mental pleasure dome built on the quicksand of metropolitan desire. However, most writers exploring urban life in the period, far from discovering *Heimat* in the fantastic hinterland of the rationalized structures of the modern urban world, revealed instead a realm of the darkly Gothic or even perverted. In his study of experimental art and suicide, *The Savage God* (1971), A. Alvarez noted that many writers who set out to explore what reason and realism exclude are vulnerable to mental breakdown. Material dredged from the psyche is not relived within the contained abreaction of psychotherapy, but within that of an intense and sustained internalization: marks on the page reflect torture chambers of the mind. We shall see that many of the fantastic worlds released out of the critique of reason in the period 1960–90 were demesnes of sickness, violence, and pathology.

In Muriel Spark's portrait of city life in the sixties, *The Driver's Seat* (1968), her central character Lise takes a holiday from the repressiveness of her rigidly organized northern urban life and plunges into the insanity of a southern European metropolis. Lise can at last release the hysteria bred of years of time-and-motion planned routine into the greater glittering madness of the consumer-oriented proto-post-modern soft city. There, like any romantic heroine, she will search for her man and look for the time of her life (as she puts it), seeking in the release of death by homicide an end to the unbearable emptiness of a routinized existence which can be summed up in the Heideggerian notion of *Unheimlichkeit*. In this world of rootless and disturbed individuals, *Heimat* resides only in the metaphoricity of desire. In another of Spark's typical inversions, urban life is so artifically planned that the already perverted natural can enter only by way of similes which are a continuous reminder of its fallen condition: the frenetic movements of a disco-dancer, for example, are hardly described as those of Dionysian release, but are likened to the death throes of a beheaded chicken. And there is no escape from the logic of this world. Even the attempted flight of one city-dweller into the peace of Zen Buddhism is represented as a manically obsessive binarization of existence into Yin and Yang which resembles nothing more than a double-entry accounting system. Modern urban existence is seen to rest on a see-saw of chaotic desire and over-compensatory organization whose rationalized structures are designed to protect 'from the indecent exposure of fear and pity, pity and fear', from that catharsis which arises from acceptance of the pain of being human.

The prose descriptions of its heroine, 'neither goodlooking nor badlooking', and her lifestyle, working in an office with 'five girls under her and two men. Over her are two women and five men', echo the equivocation of Shakespeare's *Macbeth* and reiterate its vision of hell. For beneath the overcontrol (lips: 'the ruled line of a balance sheet'; designed interiors: 'swaying tall pines . . . subdued into silence and into obedient hulks'; nature: an avid bargain-hunter like a stag sniffing the breeze) is a festering collective hysteria where the only real control over one's mortal destiny comes too late, for it is the power to end it. Lise, with all the overcontrol of the hysteric, and in a parody of boy-meets-girl romance, pursues a violent sex offender in search of her own ending. Her fictional hypothesis, rationally plotted out of the irrationality of urban-induced emotional denial, is brought to pass, though against her expressed wishes for she is raped before she is murdered. She is not ultimately in 'the driver's seat', therefore, being neither God nor author, nor even under her own self-control. Yet in the verbal tense of the novel and in its unnerving proleptic descriptions of her demise is reflected a measure of all the agency we have as fictional projection brings the future into the present. Thus do Spark's fictional devices convey the modern city-dweller's perverted desires.

Much of Spark's work in the sixties and seventies revealed the *pathological* aesthetic thrust of that frustrated desire born out of a repressive rationality unable to acknowledge a higher world of spirit. Pop art, famously recycling soup cans or cartoon characters or the urban junk of Richard Hamilton's 'Every Home should have One', initiated aesthetic post-modernism in recognizing the extent to which such desires were bound up with the stimulations of consumer culture. Many of the writers (such as Murdoch and Golding) examined in the last chapter recognized the dangers of an art unanchored in reason. But on the whole, and even if self-consciousness and irony were becoming endemic, there was still a strong belief in art as a counter-force to an instrumental 'iron cage of reason', the reductive logic of modern urban life. Planners themselves recognized the importance of art. New theatres were built in a number of regions, the National Theatre and the Royal Shakespeare Company were founded in the early sixties, poetry readings were more popular than ever, and the British novel began to lose much of its earlier parochialism and to achieve a more international profile.

Intellectual debates about the desirability or otherwise of social planning and the role of reason in human life were fuelled by the various political and economic crises of the sixties and seventies. Throughout the sixties, and particularly after the Cuban Missile crisis, there were widespread fears concerning the potential for world destruction in the unholy alliance of advanced technological knowledge and the manœuvrings of the Cold War. Anthony Burgess's *A Clockwork Orange* (1962), visually materialized in Stanley Kubrick's film, has become one of those images of the sixties integral to its mythic constructions. In the novel, violence is presented as a necessary evil which is closed to social amelioration or rational planning. In many ways, this represented a not untypical contemporary response to the limits of consciousness, but Burgess approached the subject from a theological position which synthesized a Pelagian commitment to the doctrine of free will with an Augustinian conviction of original sin. As far as he was concerned, evil, as original sin, resides within the soul of the individual and may be removed only through the destruction of his or her humanity. Outside religion, the idea had reappeared in Freudian psychoanalysis, with original sin replaced by an unconscious equally resistant to conscious or rational intervention. However, the focus of Burgess's critique was partly the sinister notion of operant conditioning developed by the behavioural psychologist B. F. Skinner, and partly the ethos of the Welfare State appropriation of adaptive ego psychology developed from Anna Freud's work and then reimported to Britain from America in the fifties. Attractive to the social engineers, this emphasized adaptation and independent ego-functioning rather than the intractable irrationality of the Freudian unconscious. Lionel Trilling had celebrated Freud's concept of the unconscious as a bit of biology which, in lying outside the reach of culture, was therefore absolutely free of its influences. Within ego psychology, however, there exists a core ego which moulds the available conceptions of self into a personal identity, and any lapse in efficiency can be remedied through welfare intervention. For Burgess, such beliefs represented a serious assault on human freedom and a dangerous denial of decent ethical limits upon social engineering.

Burgess's objection was on religious and not liberal grounds. When his hero Alex, chief 'droog' of *A Clockwork Orange*, is reclaimed and rehabilitated through behaviourist science, his freedom to choose evil is removed and the issue of personal responsibility confused as causality and agency are located in society and not the self. Even more provocatively in the context of the socially ameliorist early sixties, Burgess had his hero commit his acts of pornographic violence to the accompaniment of the sublime music of Beethoven. The removal of Alex's violent instincts simultaneously erases his capacity to respond to art. For Burgess, at least at this time, art had absolutely nothing to do with ethics, and their separation was imperative if art was not to become another therapy nourishing the arrogant instrumentalism of the social engineers. There were several problems, however, with his account. First, in order to castigate the arrogance of what he was to refer to in a later novel *1985* as the 'cacotopic' state (a place where all is evil), he must make Alex and therefore evil sympathetic. Perhaps like Milton, he succeeds too well, and Alex, with his vital language, quirky love of art, and native intelligence is a latter-day romantically rebellious Satan: evil as glamour, and also as youth, rebel in the age of Elvis Presley, James Dean, and Mick Jagger. Moreover, Alex and his partners in crime inhabit a technologized landscape of unrelieved urban decay, manipulated by a sinister authoritarian state regime, so that violence is presented, with drugs and television, as a sort of necessary and continuous adolescent vacation. The central question posed by the novel is whether it is better to be free to choose evil rather than have good imposed upon one, and the answer given is that, yes, one must be free to fall. But the second problem of the novel is that, despite his theological frame, in presenting such a ferocious Orwellian image of society as a sinister technocracy, Burgess makes it difficult not to read the sympathetically presented Alex as simply a product of social conditioning and therefore amenable to reconditioning. However, if such an interpretation seems to contradict the belief in innate evil and actually to bolster the argument for social intervention, then, paradoxically, *A Clockwork Orange* could be read as a novel about the failures of a particular variety of social planning rather than as a religious study of the definitive wrongness of all such social intervention.

If Burgess's novel struck a chord of apocalypticism in the sixties, a writer whose entire work has been a presentiment of the end is J. G. Ballard. From his second novel *The Drowned World* (1962) and throughout the seventies, Ballard was writing fictions which explored many of the ideas about evolutionary degeneration associated with philosophers such as Nietzsche and historical pessimists such as Spengler. The religiously apocalyptic note in his writing is supplied by the fascination with the idea of genocide or racial suicide as the necessary prelude to rebirth. Only then might the human imagination be affirmed in a world overrun by the deadly automation of the machine in a final and collective act of self-sacrifice before the adaptive mutation into a new form of species altogether. Neo-Darwinism had been a flourishing branch of science throughout the period, but Ballard displaced the progressivist optimism of the genetic engineers with a vision which reminds his readers that the first of their kind were the Nazi scientists of the concentration camps, carrying out ethnic purification with all the fervour of a fundamentalist ache to return to the original Adam. *The Drowned World* ended with its questing protagonist blind and heading for the new Eden, 'a second Adam searching for the forgotten paradises of the reborn sun'.

In *High-Rise* (1975), he dealt more directly with the devolutionary mutations induced by the modern high-tech habitat. It is probably no coincidence that its year of publication coincided not only with unprecedented levels of industrial unrest, but also with the erection of a number of complexes for living whose function was to cater to the material needs of inhabitants to such levels of repletion that, serene in the security of their concrete community, they could regard the outside world as so much redundant space. That year too witnessed talk of a new rising underclass, terrorist attacks, and growing racial tension. Like Lessing's *The Memoirs of a Survivor*, Ballard's novel was in part a response to the events of the time in its depiction of a technologically advanced world thrown back by a holocaust into primitive tribal mentalities and where existence is ultimately the withdrawal into the blank minimalism of the survivor. Lessing's novel, however, did offer an alternative symbolic world of Jungian archetype and a vision of salvation through psychic and spiritual transcendence. Not so Ballard's.

To its inhabitants, the fictional world of High-Rise had seemed for a time to be perfect: air-conditioning conduits, elevators, garbage disposal chutes, and electrical switching systems, we are told, 'provided a never-failing supply of care and attention that a century earlier would have required an army of tireless servants'. Despite this and because of it, however, the High-Rise world is one whose inhabitants are dying through their failure in mutational adaptation to their own self-created environment. The new involuntary Luddites are not displaced labourers but the recipients of automated care. Their environment has bred a new type 'who thrived like an advanced species of machine in the neutral atmosphere . . . thrived on the rapid turnover of acquaintances, the lack of involvement with others, and the total sufficiency of lives which, needing nothing, were never disappointed'. Technology has ushered in an era of absolute Smylesian self-reliance and, in an imaginary compression of evolutionary process, produced a new being, more machine than man, able to blend unobtrusively with the new environment. As always in nature, however, adaptive failures and genetic throwbacks muddy the clean arc of advancement and the environment created by *homo faber* becomes uninhabitable to *homo sapiens*. The psychological impulses of the old order erupt into a primitive tribal-style blood-letting. Barbaric furies are unleashed from the dark Darwinian swamp on which High-Rise is built: a centre-point whose foundations reach down into ancient pestilential spores.

5 NATION AND NEW IDENTITIES

> History may be servitude,
> History may be freedom. See, now they vanish,
> The faces and places, with the self which, as it could, loved
>   them,
> To become renewed, transfigured, in another pattern.
>
> (T. S. Eliot, 'Little Gidding')

Enoch Powell proclaimed in 1969 that 'the life of nations no less than that of men is lived largely in the imagination'.[1] Like the disease of the hypochondriac, it would seem that Britain too exists mainly in the mind. In fact, since the earliest development of the Western European nation states, vernacular literatures have been central in shaping, challenging, or reinforcing images of nation and national identities. 'Literature', even as the best that has been thought or said, has never been canonized on purely aesthetic grounds for, in practice, aesthetic values have always been bound up with moral, political, or religious considerations. During the period covered by this book, the concept of a unified nation underwent profound changes, and so too did that of its national literature. Britain is now poised on the brink of further change as it goes 'into Europe'. Malcolm Bradbury's *Dr Criminale* (1992), set in 1990, summed up the mood of transition at the close of the period:

Streetwise historians were announcing the End of History, journos like me were noting the Close of the Cold War, politicians everywhere were talking of the New World Order—especially those in the New World. Marxism and the command economy were plainly dying of terminal exhaustion. On the other hand liberal capitalism wasn't doing so well either . . . in Brussels Napoleonic dreamers were reinventing Europe, if they could just find out where its edges started and stopped. There was conflict in Yugoslavia, independence rioting in the Baltics, ethnic and tribal tension everywhere.

As consensual identification with nation was modified by a trend of cultural identification with localities—of region, ethnic groups, gender, race, class—the question of value in literature or indeed the very constitution of English literature became problematic. In the eighties growing numbers of minority groups in Britain began to demand the recognition of their own distinct voices as part of the national culture. The fragmentation of consensus opened up furious debates in the literary and academic world over the legitimation of aesthetic value and about the role and function of literature in the formation of national identity. Some prominent voices argued for a rehabilitation and renewed defence of the older consensus about the constitution of good literature, others proclaimed the end of a pernicious hegemony which had always functioned through the deliberate exclusion of significant cultural groups. For the former, the fragmentation of value reflected the narcissism of a society whose members could only recognize as good that which reflected their own interests: gender, class, race, or ethnicity. For the latter, however, the notion of objective and transcendent aesthetic value had simply been exposed as the cultural imperialist myth of the White male leisured and professional classes. Either way, literary value was pushed out of the consensual golden world envisaged by the postwar settlement and into the politically confrontational world of 1990.

Debates about the contentious grounds for identifying literature actually entered the popular press in the late eighties in response to government proposals for a new National Curriculum to be taught in all state schools in England and Wales. Simply in geographical terms, 'English literature' is difficult to identify. Not only is it now to be distinguished from 'literatures in English', but the United Kingdom itself is a complex historical composite of different nations and peoples. National identity has always been an arena of contested meaning. George Orwell, however, noted in 1940 that the economic and political domination of one nation, England, had produced an idea of Englishness which tended imperially to subjugate or subsume others, even though 'our islands' are called by six different names: 'England, Britain, Great Britain, the British Isles, the United Kingdom and, in very exalted moments, Albion'.[2] Fierce debates arose in the eighties about the constitution of English literature, however, because a mythic Englishness was challenged by a variety of economic, social, and political changes. From the mid-seventies there would be a polarization of politics and a fragmentation of cultural consensus which would finally bring apparently incommensurable value-systems into open conflict. Even the quiet groves of the English academy would resound with the new turbulent uprisings.

Whatever the reality of national identities in the present, however, the imaginary space of nation is often a sealed one where old images linger on, like Larkin's 'Show Saturday', something 'That breaks ancestrally each year into | Regenerate union . . .'. Their persistence was captured in comic vein in David Lodge's novel of transatlantic 'academentia' set in 1969, *Changing Places* (1975), when the ambitiously professionalized American Morris Zapp learns that his British counterpart has no doctoral qualification: 'They have a different system in England, Morris. The Ph.D isn't so important,' he is assured. Zapp responds, however, with bemused incredulity: 'You mean the jobs are hereditary?' However wide of the mark Zapp may seem (and some might say, not very), the point is less that his comment is grounded in an empirically observable distinction between the British class system in the seventies and its more meritocratic American equivalent, than that it implies a persevering feudal image of the British nation as bound anachronistically to a system of fixed aristocratic privilege. 'Nation' is never simply the now of political and geographical space, but always a concept with its own narrative history. England now and for ever may exist in imaginary space as a feudally hierarchized 'sceptred isle', a 'green and pleasant land', or 'teeming' earth of kings by divine right, even when the actual physical space is girdered by deindustrializing conurbations and the travestied nationalism of football hooliganism, or riven by the kinds of urban disorder and racial conflict which erupted in Brixton in 1981, and across the entire country by the middle of the decade.

Because 'nation' exists in imaginative space, however, the founding origins of its narratives of identity tend to be buried and, though constructed as pragmatic fictions, may come to take on the essential and unchanging aspect of myth. Poets have sometimes conceived of their task as to 'purify the dialect of the tribe', a preservation or recovery of a mythically pristine identity even though national cultures are always highly impure conglomerations. Edmund Spenser had complained in *The Shepheard's Calendar*: 'now they have made our English tongue a Gallimaufry or hodge podge of all other speeches'. One wonders what he would have made of the fugal variations on the native song of Larkin, Hughes, Hill, or of the assertion of regional- and class-consciousnesses in the song of Tony Harrison's 'V', the renascent Scottish or Welsh nationalism of Ian Crichton Smith or Dannie Abse, the Northern Irish 'guttural', as Heaney calls it, of the Ulster poets, and the Creole rhythms of Anglo-Caribbean poets such as Grace Nichols? Conscious of the need to preserve what Eliot had referred to as a regional 'diversity within unity' (of nation), Donald Davie wrote a cycle of poems on those Old High Tory bastions of Englishness, the Shires. In his Essex cycle, he wrote of 'Humiliation, corporate and private', of a contaminated English language which reflects 'the new adulterations' of a 'shrunken world'. He is conscious of the paradox involved in attempting to preserve the linguistic essence of a disappearing England in verse which: 'Fears the inauthentic | Which invades it on all sides | Mortally. The style may die of it, | Die of the fear of it, Confounding authenticity with essence' ('Epistle: To Enrique Caracciolo Trejo'). The heavily stressed 'Mortally' is a reminder to himself that language is a human system which must inevitably change, die, and newly evolve; that his fear of foreign contamination may in itself precipitate the linguistic body into a paralysis which hardens into the very rigor mortis he fears. Similarly, 'Confounding' actually confounds two meanings: the recognition that authenticity may be confused with essence, history abandoned to myth, but also that essence itself (as an apparently absolute but possibly provisional concept) may confound (defeat) authenticity as the acceptance that, in the words of Wallace Stevens, it must change. Davie knows his Englishness may be an unregenerate myth, but he prefers to be at the end of a dying tradition than to accept a demythologized and contaminated history.

Debates about the Englishness of English literature divided the critical institution throughout the eighties. Edward Said attacked the academy of 'English letters' for preserving outworn imperialist myths of nation. In one essay, the English department is viewed as a reliquary where monuments are 'canonised into rigid dynastic formation, serviced and reserviced monotonously by a shrinking guild of humble servants'.[3] Said's argument drew substantially on the work of the French historian Michel Foucault, which was concerned with the relations between knowledge and power and the construction of institutional spaces (like literature) which legitimate cultural and national myths. Foucault's own analyses focused on the 'other' excluded by such essentialist myths of identity and reintroduced Nietzsche's concept of the 'will to power' as the disguised impulse which lies behind the apparently objective images of cultural knowledge. In Foucault's eyes, power was omniscient but not omnipotent: the powerless could reverse the discourses of the colonizer in order to confirm identities of their own, but they could not simply escape from them. His ideas were widely disseminated and fed into the burgeoning literary debate about national identity. So, for example, in the 1988 anthology entitled *The New British Poetry*, one could view the voice of 'Black Britishness', heard throughout, as a Foucauldian 'reverse discourse'. In John Agard's 'Listen Mr Oxford Don', for example: 'I'm not a violent man Mr Oxford don I I only armed wit mih human breath I but human breath I is a dangerous weapon . . . I making de Queen's English accessory I to my offence.' Agard's alternation of Creole with 'Standard English' reminds the academic custodian that the legacy of the British Empire is a new hybrid, a second generation half-caste, 'a simple immigrant I from Clapham Common': his too is the voice of the national literature in the eighties.

This mixing and meshing of voices and discourses and contestation of values has sometimes been understood as the cultural identity of post-modernism. Other commentators in the eighties, such as Fredric Jameson, analysed the tendency rather more pessimistically as the inevitable condition of late capitalism where the depthless surfaces of consumer culture have invaded all physical and imaginary space, producing an art which mixes kitsch and nostalgia, plundering ethnic and historical forms, but under the pressure of a consumer hedonism unconcerned about historical connection or depth of meaning. Yet it became evident that the post-modern critique of essential and unified subjectivity, and its assertion of the self as an aesthetically shaped and ever-revisable script, could be valuable in loosening fixed notions of national identity for those seeking to reclaim their own lost histories or to shape new identities in the future. Post-modernism has been described as the 'romance of the marginal', and certainly in this decade, as never before in Britain, voices from the edge began to demand recognition by the centre and the right to author their own lives through a truly democratic extension of the political vocabulary of the liberal state.

Grace Nichols, who came to Britain from Guyana in 1977, was another writer concerned to reverse cultural stereotypes as a means of asserting her own voice. In *The Fat Black Woman's Poems* (1984), she brought a defamiliarizing eye to the customs and ceremonies of Englishness as they are set in the context of her memories of the islands of her childhood. What she is, however, transforms where she is, rather than the other way round. Her fat black woman goes shopping in London, stares at the freezing thin fashion mannequins in their power-dressed invincibility, reminisces about the 'soft and bright and billowing' clothes which are nowhere to be found, and cursing in Swahili–Yoruba, concludes that when it comes to fashion 'the choice is lean | Nothing much beyond size 14.' By remaining large and bright, however, she refuses to take up less space and can assert 'the power to be what I am, a woman, charting my own futures', laughing 'cause your head's too small | for your dreams', refusing the exhortations of politicians, and promising instead to put her 'X against a bowl of custard'.

David Dabydeen, however, in the *New British Poetry* (1988), cautioned that 'peasantry is in vogue'. The 'huddled together memories' hoarded against 'the opulence of our masters' in 'a winter of England's scorn' can all too easily feed liberal White culture's desire for a sentimentalized 'otherness' which keeps its own boundaries safe and clear, or one into which it can pour its own sense of marginalized disaffection. The ubiquitous concept of the 'other' which emerged in criticism at this time was a handy container in which could be poured any category which seemed to imply marginalization in relation to whatever was constructed as dominant. The position of the other might at times be occupied by members of ethnic minorities, women, 'transgressive' sexualities, passion, poetry, post-colonial writing, criminals, insanity, or even anyone over 60. What began as a concept with a respectable history in political and existential philosophy ended as an overworked catchphrase for any cause or position claimed to be radical.

Indeed, hasty conflation of unlike orders of being was a temptation to which progressive criticism often succumbed in the post-modern eighties. A common mistake in the decade of textuality was to regard the formal disruptions of contemporary avant-garde or fantastic writing as bearing ontologically the same subversive status as existentially disruptive political action in the world outside the text. It is difficult to assess the tendency. On the one hand, modes of the fantastic and the post-modern certainly offered new possibilities of self-expression for those increasing numbers of writers who experienced themselves outside traditional images of national identity. On the other hand, as the New Right seemed ever more invincible during the eighties, and socialism confused, in retreat, and unable to compete with the populism of the Thatcher regime, it does not seem to be entirely coincidental that the dissent of middle-class intellectuals should express itself through the language of abstruse theory or a literary preference for fantastic otherness or linguistic *jouissance*.

There was a dangerous tendency in the various critiques of reason, which circulated during the eighties, to regard alterity or otherness as a sublime space outside the law, offering redemption from the Enlightenment Fall into consciousness, and recoverable through madness, aesthetic experience, transgressive practices, or some version of the idea of returning to the body. It seems, however, that as the New Right strengthened its position in the eighties and as Mrs Thatcher was returned to power with each successive general election, so too the fantastic became more pervasive in literature, concepts of otherness in theory, and the linguistically constructivist in criticism. If physical space could not be transformed, the power of the imaginary or a new supra-rational sublime must be heightened and politicized. In this mode, post-modernism bears a striking resemblance to some forms of Romanticism.[4] But as transgression became vogueish, analogy was all too easily mistaken for causality. Poets were to be seen as the acknowledged legislators of the world and a post-Romantic revolutionary political significance claimed for a semi-mystical linguistic otherness locked into the Sybilline contours of the post-modern or post-colonial literary text. The metaphors of fluidity and the hybrid generic mixes which appeared in the post-modern and feminist writing of the eighties were sometimes seized on in late countercultural fashion as sublime expressions of new and undreamt-of possibilities of identity. The heady optimism of this literary multiculturalism challenged earlier myths of identity, but in its resolutely anti-materialist (and often anti-rationalist) mode, as we shall see shortly, often created more than a few of its own.

Some of these problems were evident in Salman Rushdie's post-modern and fantastic *Shame* (1984) (significantly written after the deportation of the Shah and the revival of the Islamic revolution with the return from exile of Ayatollah Khomeini in 1979). The novel covered the period from 1947 to the present and fantastically reconstructed a central episode in Pakistan's internal political history: a family quarrel between Iskander Harrapa (Bhutto) and the successor who executed him (Zia). After the fantastic exploration of the concept of splitting to examine the consequences of Indian Independence of 1947 in *Midnight's Children*, the focus of *Shame* was on the subsequent attempts at reintegration and restoration. The novel suggests that in the subsequent construction of Pakistan, the claim to absolute truth of Islamic revivalism functioned as the political weapon of a nationalist politics which simply reproduced the oppressions of the imperialist order from which it claimed to have liberated its peoples. Language, myth, and story are central in this:

So-called Islamic 'fundamentalism' does not spring, in Pakistan, from the people. It is imposed on them from above. Autocratic regimes find it useful to espouse the rhetoric of faith, because people respect that language, are reluctant to oppose it. This is how religions shore up dictators; by encircling them with words of power, words which the people are reluctant to see discredited, disenfranchised, mocked.

Rushdie's text is therefore post-modernistically fluid in the extreme. Recognizing the 'desire of every artist to impose his or her vision on the world', he is anxious to distance as far as possible the techniques of his own fiction from those of militarist nationalism or repressive theocracy.

Conscious of his own status as translated man, Rushdie uses the image of migrancy to bind political content and formal aesthetic. Other dissident voices march 'in from the periphery of the story', those of the women and of Indian legend, both suppressed under the new nationalist regime. The fixity of the *logos* as the foundation of the theocratic state is undermined through parody of the Koran. Fictional and historical characters are indiscriminately mixed, so too are levels of discourse. Metaphors are surrealistically literalized (imaginative space literally becomes the geographic space of nation). The conventions of Western psychoanalysis, popular horror fiction, and Indian cinema are conflated as Sufiya's *shaman* at her father's tyrannical and demagogic rule materializes in her body as somatic blushing and finally and violently as a fantastic demonic werewolfism. The temporal and spatial laws of realism are spectacularly ignored and the ontological coherence of the historical narrative self-consciously split apart. Vehicle and tenor of metaphor change place to illustrate Rushdie's belief that migrants experience a 'triple disruption' in recognizing not only that the real is fabulated but that it can be taken apart, unmade, and remade. However, despite the appeal of such imaginary fluidity and of the concept of migrancy as a way of representing personal identity, it seemed somewhat inadequate as a means of opposing violent and repressive nationalisms. Rushdie draws on the familiar Foucaultian idea of turning around a negative identity, that of marginality or migrancy, and conferring on it a positive agency. But the identity to be espoused is so fluid and shifting one cannot see at all how it could effectively oppose a triumphally repressive nationalism.

Fluidity may be a desirable alternative to fixity, but does not in itself entail a coherent politics, though it may stimulate new ways of thinking about identity and ethics. Novels like *Shame* present such issues through images, metaphors, and perspectivally shifting narratives of nation and identity, rather than politically correct or coherent theories and concepts. However, in the post-structuralist eighties any writer producing fluid and disruptive texts might be proclaimed politically progressive. This assumption bears instructive comparison with the debate about the relations between politics and literature in the early part of the period. A major problem for many of the political dramatists of the late sixties and early seventies, for example, was in justifying at all the presentation of any ambiguity or psychological complexity particularly to ideologically engaged critics who regarded this as an unnecessary distraction from the political message of the plays. Trevor Griffiths felt the need actually to warn those seeking in political theatre either political correctness or strict correspondence to theoretical models or revolutionary functionalism, that all drama must be 'analytical and descriptive . . . I'm not really interested in propaganda theatre. Though it has a function, I'm not really sure it has a function in the society *we* live in.'[5] Griffiths distanced himself here and elsewhere from a crude agitprop theatre, or the sort of shock tactics favoured at the time by Howard Barker, for example, for whom ambiguity and analysis were indeed the problem and not the cure. As a character in his play *The Hang of the Gaol* (1978) argued:

We are in England, and in England you may think a man a liar but you are better not to call him one. This is called maturity. The more mature you are, the less you use the word you want. The purpose of wrapping meanings up in cotton wool is to stop them hurting. This is a very sick and bandaged race.

Though sharing the aim of exploding the national character, postmodernists would embrace the very cure which Barker had diagnosed as the national disease.

Griffiths, however, was certainly not (then) a post-modernist, but one of a group of dramatists who showed that psychological complexity did not have to be sacrificed to political analysis, but was indeed essential to any understanding of the desire for or the resistance to social or political change. He wrote one of the most powerful plays of the seventies, which actually debated as its central concern, the efficacy of art in challenging stereotypes of nation and national identity. *Comedians* was produced in 1975 before the very last, painfully suspended, and rattling breaths of the old consensus. It dramatized the conflict between the reformist humanist thinking which had motivated the post-war welfare settlement and the new hatred arising from those whom it had inevitably excluded (and which would be expressed even more provocatively in the eighties in the television figure of Yosser Hughes in Alan Bleasdale's *Boys from the Blackstuff*). The inspiration for Griffiths's play was actually a television series called *The Comedians* which recycled stale racist and sexist stereotypes, but in a confrontational vocabulary which seemed to represent the efflorescence of what Griffiths took to be a new and frightening mood of political hate. The play was set in a night school for comedians, who were preparing for their first public début under the humane and pedagogic eye of Eddie Waters, a retired comedian himself whose message is that comedy must rise above prejudice, art is an aspect of ameliorative education, and that 'a joke that feeds on ignorance starves its audience'.

The members of his class, including a Jew and two Irishmen, explode their own cultural stereotyping through the complex emergent psychological subtext of the rehearsal, but revert to its crudest forms in the contest itself, once under the corrupting pressures of commercial competition and the audience expectation of the working-man's club. Liberal idealism is fine in the comradely atmosphere of the classroom, but ineffectual in the world of market capitalism. The highlight of the play is the club performance of Gethin Price, who has already 'refused his consent' with a vicious parody of Waters's optimistic ameliorism and who proceeds, during the contest, to shock with a brilliant but nihilistic mime acting out the real violences of two nations: a skinhead smashing the culture of the upper classes in an unmitigated expression of class hatred. To Waters's subsequently dismayed 'it was drowning in hate', Price replies that 'truth is a fist you hit with'. Waters attempts to justify a liberal reformist aesthetic in an account of his psychologically disturbing erotic responses on a visit to a concentration camp, but his expiatory narrative of complicity cannot entirely displace the force of Price's violent refusal of compromise. Price's honesty is a commitment to destructive exposure and his act is one which eschews any belief in the reparative or cathartic effects of dramatic art. The audience is left with alternative but equally pessimistic images: on the one hand an authentic but destructive aesthetic built on hate and on the other an art of consolation which is founded in deception. Griffiths's play is a sober counterweight to a naïvely optimistic revolutionary poetics which fails to analyse the psychological power of reactionary myths or the inevitable complicity of art in a market economy which produces deep and violent social division.

Post-Modernism and the Nation State

Tom Nairn in fact suggested two years later (1977), as we have seen, that national consensus had disintegrated to such an extent that the 'break-up of Britain' was imminent and with it the demise of Englishness as the valid description of a state of mind transcending regional, class, and subcultural difference. The development of Welsh and Scottish nationalism, the immigration into the United Kingdom since the fifties of the overseas people of its former dominions and the rise of new cultures around ethnic identities, the growing influence of American popular culture and Japanese technology, the Troubles in Northern Ireland, and the entry into the new European Community in 1975 are just some of the reasons why this might appear to be the case. Monetarist ideas were creeping into the Cabinet and the centre was failing to hold: Labour was splitting into a left wing increasingly active in local government and a right wing which would help to found the new Social Democratic Party in 1981. Margaret Thatcher had won the Conservative leadership in 1975 and set about using the IMF crisis to boost her campaign to move the party toward free-market economics. As the left moved toward demands for genuine democratic representation within a socialist economy and the right toward a declaration of war on corporatism, each registered a withdrawal from the post-war consensus and the beginning of a new era of polarized conviction politics and subcultural confrontation.

What did Englishness continue to mean in this context? George Orwell's essay 'England, Your England' had summed up the national character as an 'obstinate clinging to everything that is out of date and a nuisance . . . addiction to hobbies and spare-time occupations, the privateness of English life . . . the liberty to have a home of your own'. His nation of decent, home-loving and suburban amateurish dilettantes, however, was invoked in 1940 in the context of a threat of takeover by a technocratically harnessed and imperialistic national socialism. But, like all national identities, neither was his Englishness absolutely anchored to that earlier moment. English reserve was in any case a legacy of that national identity promoted by an imperial civil service, with its view of the foreigner as exotically other and in need of safe containment, a threat both outside but also potentially within the national psyche as a lurking evolutionary throwback. But it was a convenient myth to rehabilitate for the eighties, and the very perpetrators of the change from a national ethos of amateurism and public-spiritedness to one of hard-nosed professionalized acquisitiveness were the same rhetoricians who most often invoked both the pre-1939 myth of privacy and the post-1939 sense of national decency. Thatcher's economic privatization was very different from Orwell's 'private life' and it might seem that the former's acquisitive entrepreneurialism should logically entail the eradication of his romantic 'Englishness'. But the shift of emphasis from economic libertarianism to Victorian values required a reincarnation of the ideology of the private life, of the Englishman's home as the moral centre to be protected by the new authoritarian populism. Presented in the eighties in a crusading spirit, the shift also involved the investiture of Thatcher as second Britannia, reclothed in Churchill's ceremonial military garb of the forties and in his image as wartime leader and saviour of the values of the nation.

Official policies on the arts at that time would also reflect the desire to resuscitate the image of 'Great' Britain, though one honed into the lean and streamlined efficiency of the monetarist economy. The Arts Council published its report in 1985 under the title of 'A Great British Success Story'. Literature was reviewed as integral to an 'arts industry' existing to provide employment, leisure, and distraction, or to persuade tourists of the greatness of the 'British Heritage'. The document closed with explicit recommendations to potential buyers that 'our product offers excellent value'. The unspoken message, of course, was that the Arts Council itself had lost the relative autonomy of its pre-Thatcher years and become yet another managerial arm of the state. Commercial populism had converted the Victoria and Albert Museum into the sensationalist Saatchi and Saatchi 'ace caff with quite a nice museum attached' in another attempt to market the nation through its arts. In fact, such crude revitalization of Victorian values did little to obscure the reality of industrial unrest, of fragmenting subcultures and economic division which surfaced savagely in the middle of the eighties. These were the images of nation preferred by those writers who seriously addressed its ailing condition.

Unlike some other nations and empires in the eighties, however, Britain did not suddenly or cataclysmically break up. Even before the Thatcherite shift from welfare corporatism to free-market monetarism, underlying economic and social trends were producing tendencies toward cultural fragmentation that would simply surface more dramatically from 1975 to 1990. Throughout the entire period 1960–90 industry was shifting from Fordist mass production to forms of consumer-oriented flexible specialization using new technologies and a freer floating workforce. As manufacturing production declined (Britain became a net importer of manufactured goods during the period), service industries expanded, so that some economists viewed Britain in the eighties as a post-industrial nation whose basic commodity was the fluid and endlessly interpretable one of knowledge. In all senses the economy seemed to be more complex and less stable. Dickensian anatomies of the ills of the industrial age along the lines of *Hard Times* would give way to the satire of the 'futures' trading of a 'sign economy' in Malcolm Bradbury's *Rates of Exchange* (1983). Mrs Gaskell's *North and South*, as we saw earlier, would be recalled but intertextually displaced in David Lodge's examination of the collisions of mutually uncomprehending industrial and post-industrial cultures and economies in *Nice Work* (1988).

It was not simply the British economy which was changing. Though Britain remained a class-ridden society, the composition and lifestyles of its classes were changing rapidly, the middle classes becoming considerably more heterogeneous in educational background, and the working class more fluid, as increased numbers in secure employment were encouraged to become homeowners whilst others joined the ranks of an unemployed underclass. Gender remained an important social issue. In the eighties there would be a backlash against the feminist gains of the seventies and an attempt to strengthen the functionalist picture of the nuclear family headed by the breadwinning male and serviced by the unpaid housewife and mother.

The reality, however, was that even if women still did most of the domestic work, fewer and fewer families conformed to this image and more women than ever had entered the workforce. Indeed, all markers of national and social identity were involved in change. A new internationalization of culture provided a countercurrent to the Thatcherite attempt to rearm the nation state. Global money markets, multinational corporations (twenty of the top thirty companies in the eighties), the continuing world spread of American popular culture, and the growing involvement in Europe weakened the grip of the state. Even recessions, since the sixties, were inevitably worldwide. Throughout the economic and cultural spheres, the relevance of autarky seemed to be diminishing. There was a revival also of environmental politics in both radical ecologist and more reformist modes, and this too entered popular consciousness as another stimulus to global awareness. State socialism seemed to have collapsed throughout Europe by the early nineties.

Added to this was what economists have seen as the space–time compression effect of technologized late capitalism (instant world media coverage, satellite links, telecommunications and electronic information circuits, world marketing).[6] Such globalizations produced disorientation, however, and again this fed into the desire for recovery or construction of local or regional identities, ethnic revivalisms, minority politics, and single-issue pressure groups: all means of asserting identity through difference and outside nineteenth-century conceptualizations of the nation state. The American social theorist Daniel Bell proclaimed that the nation state was indeed in crisis, 'too small for the big problems of life, and too big for the small problems of life'.[7] Global dislocation entered the post-modern and post-colonial literary work of the decade, while the search for local community was expressed in the burgeoning minority group and regional writing of the period. Whereas disaffected writers in the sixties tended to explore the possibility of recovering an essential and authentic self through revelation or by throwing off layers of inauthentic social control (the repression model), those of the later seventies and eighties tended to renounce this archaeological model and to accept that significance must be made and shaped rather than simply discovered (the productive or aesthetic model).

Poetry of the 'Inner Émigré'

Throughout the period Northern Ireland came increasingly into prominence as one of the manifestly dark and troubled areas of British identity. In 1976 the leading Ulster poet Seamus Heaney resigned his post at Queen's University, Belfast, to take up residence in the Republic, declaring in *North* (1975), 'I am neither internee nor informer | An inner émigré . . .'. Efforts made to build a new peace movement in Northern Ireland were largely overwhelmed. There was escalating tension generated by renewed IRA activity and tougher reprisals by the security forces now bolstered increasingly by the largely Protestant Royal Ulster Constabulary and Ulster Defence Regiment. The British armed presence was growing and Britain faced continuous difficulties with the International Court of Human Rights over its policy of internment without trial. In Scotland and Wales, Devolution Bills had been proceeding through parliament and became laws in 1978, though both were finally defeated and the dismantling of the Union agreement with Scotland of 1707 did not take place. It was evident, however, that many of the 'Celtic Fringe' were not happy with fringe status. Elsewhere, too, the United Kingdom was looking increasingly less united. If the nation had never actually spoken with one voice, by the end of the seventies it was to become impossible even to retain the pretence of choral harmony.

Seamus Heaney was to become the figurehead of what came to be known as the Ulster Renaissance, reminding English audiences too, of their own condition of inner *émigré*: their dispossession of the imperialistic myth of an imaginary glorious and unified national identity. Indeed, in 1976 he delivered a lecture in California entitled 'Englands of the Mind' which examined the state of mainstream English poetry (Hughes, Larkin, and Hill) and pronounced it to be suffering from an introspective obssession with the recovery of a lost 'native identity'. The image used in the lecture, of poets who can only look in and not up to England, diagnosed a sort of literary curvature of the spine induced by deepening recognition of loss of imperial power, failure of economic nerve, and the diminishing role of Britain in world and European affairs. Hughes, Larkin, and Hill become emblematic, all three hoarders and shorers of what they take to be the real England . . . possessed of that defensive love of their territory which was once shared only by those poets whom we might call colonial . . . Their very terrain is becoming consciously precious . . . a confirmation of an identity which is threatened.[8]

It seemed that even the self-appointed native poets now suffered from a beleaguered sense of being internal *émigrés*, self-consciously aware of inhabiting an Englishness which is increasingly more a marginal enclave of the past than a reality in the foreground of the present.

Heaney himself writes as an Irishman with an awesome sense of inherited responsibility to 'forge the uncreated conscience of the race', a quotation from Joyce with which he ended his 1974 Royal Society of Literature lecture entitled 'Feeling into Words'. Words are indeed central to his treatment of the theme of conscience: the 1974 poem 'A New Song' had declared 'our river tongues must rise' and flood 'with vowelling embrace, | Demesnes staked out in consonants'. But words are a threshold for Heaney, doors into the dark which open both ways. In 'The Other Side' (a poem about the simultaneous nearness and distance of two Catholic and Protestant neighbours in Ulster), the poet is always in a between world of violence and belonging, politics and art, fit and misfit. Even in the earliest poem 'Digging', his vocation dispossesses the poet of that land heaved and nicked by his labouring father, but it offers different means by which to reveal the 'living roots', or at least those which awaken menacingly, consolingly, in his head: 'Between my finger and my thumb | The squat pen rests; snug as a gun.' The poet's words are hinges, like Eliot's 'individual talent', between unconscious feeling and conscious tribal affiliation, physical sound and metaphysical concept, involuntary memory and intended technical effect. Words are seen as excavated from the pre-linguistic reservoir which is both the source of poetic craft and of cultural identity. Words become things in themselves, each with its own shape and feel, each a discrete entity, like a rock existing for itself; but also like a rock, each word takes its place in a landscape upon which human meanings have already been inscribed and mythic shapes long-since hewn. Moreover, from the earliest image of his own ambivalent digging with 'the squat pen' in a 'big coarse-grained navvy of a poem',

Heaney has conceived of himself as an excavator, but one who Neoplatonically discovers the shape of Ireland as a 'dark embryo' moulded out of a feminized earth of peat and bog, rather than honed from a classically masculinized marble.

For Heaney's between world is a no man's land, a feminine body to be taken, as he answers its 'mating call of sound' which 'rises to pleasure me'. In turn, he may be taken in himself, ingested like the sacrificial victim, as the Earth goddess 'tightened her torc on him I And opened her fen'. Heaney has said of Ireland that 'what we have is the tail-end of a struggle in a province between territorial piety and imperial power' (1974). Sexualized feminine and masculine emblems of colonized and colonizer carry the two poles of struggle in the poetry. Heaney himself hovers between, creating his own mythic power from the exploration of their shifting tensional oppositions. For women readers, however, the grafting of his myth of colonized Ireland onto traditional associations of the female body is somewhat problematic. Of course, as a Catholic Ulster poet, there are attractions for Heaney in identification with the feminine, and he is only one of many 'ex-centric' male writers of the period who have looked to femininity as a space in which to articulate their own sense of difference. Sometimes and paradoxically the female body is a vehicle for male guilt: 'Punishment' uses its pornographic images of the executed adulteress dug out of the bog to indict all men, Heaney included, for the imperialism of their patriarchal cruelty and dominance. The poem explicitly makes a connection between Irish Catholic women tarred and feathered for fraternizing with the enemy male and those bog women long ago sacrificed to tribal custom. But the emotional emphasis of the poem shifts to the self-punishment of the male himself: his sense, on the one hand, of guilt in relation to the tribe for his rational disengagement from the patriarchal scapegoating of the feminine, but, on the other hand, the liberal guilt of being voyeuristically and sexually caught up at all with such atavistic tribalism.

Heaney's voice is caught between complicated feminine and masculine identifications. Complicated, of course, because even the desired identification with the woman is suspect, an urge to see in the violated and mysterious other of the female body from the bog an image of his own condition of inner *émigré*. In fact, Heaney first started to use the image of the female body as his poetry took a more explicitly political turn after 1969, and as his search for identity took on a nationalistic and mythic aspect. But the casting of the feminine as metaphor for the colonized and the victim presents some difficulties. It was in 'Bogland' (1969) that he first discovered the feminized image of bog which would afterwards convey his feeling for words as 'bearers of history and mystery', for poetry as personal excavation and cultural reclamation from the unformed and unconscious, and for Ireland as a sacramental body of earth. The primordial and pre-linguistic 'unfenced country', 'melting and opening underfoot', part of the bog whose 'wet centre is bottomless', is also the imagistic starting-point for Heaney's own mythic construction of national identity. So founded, of course, his relation to his own male body (identified with the colonizer) must be ever insecure. The uncertainty appears in 'Funeral Rites' as the awkward and self-conscious 'shouldering' of the coffins 'of dead relations' or in 'The Tollund Man' as an identification with the 'bridegroom to the goddess': the decapitated Celtic 'peat-brown head' buried in Jutland to propitiate a maternal deity all too like Kathleen Ni Hoolihan, that feminine icon of mythic Irishness.

For all that Heaney avoids self-conscious formulation of his theme, his later poetry, fed by the feminist and post-colonial intellectual culture of the eighties, tended to move away from the earlier gendered mythic identifications. The poem 'Sheelagh na Gig' in *Station Island* (1984) is his swansong to the cult of Celtic feminine mystery, for here, no longer a 'bog queen', she has 'grown-up, grown ordinary'. Heaney's dilemma is one faced by all writers in his situation: how far to call up for nationalistic identification Yeats's bardic Ireland 'terrible and gay', but also potentially atavistic and reactionary? Alternatively, how far rationally to deconstruct those mythic sources which might, after all, turn out not only to be the lifeblood of a national culture, but, for a poet who feels that the community to which he belongs is 'Catholic and nationalist', also the very 'melt of the real thing' which is his own heart ('Hailstones', 1987). How to negotiate the contemporary *purgatorio*, between the exhortations of his predecessors—to 'Remember everything and keep your head', or to 'let go, let fly, forget', or, above all to write out of 'feeling, and I in particular, love' ('Station Island')?[9]

Political Theatre in the Seventies

The problem facing poets such as Heaney, Derek Mahon, and Paul Muldoon, writing with a pressure on them to forge a nationalistic renaissance, was that benign myths of the past may make for dangerous myths of the future. Each deals with the difficulty by creating borderlands where boundaries shift and may be redefined. Dramatists in the seventies took up similar themes, but capitalized on the capacity of theatre to expose the gap between words and actions and lay bare pernicious and nostalgic myths of national and imperial identity. The most immediate myth to be dissected and abandoned was the countercultural belief in the establishment of the new Jerusalem through a divestment of the shackles of false consciousness and a Rousseauistic rediscovery of spirit and nature. Howard Brenton waved an emphatic goodbye to its ethos in declaring that 'the truth is that there is only one society—that you can't escape the world you live in. Reality is remorseless. No one can leave.'[10] However, in 1967 the New Left Mayday Manifesto of Stuart Hall, Edward Thompson, and Raymond Williams had also declared a similar disaffection with the parliamentary road to socialism, arguing that every facet of British life was tainted with the sense of political failure masquerading as victory. Writers such as David Edgar, David Hare, Howard Brenton, Howard Barker, and Trevor Griffiths were to carve their drama out of this mood of disaffection with, and sense of the exhaustion of, conventional and alternative British politics. Unlike the preceding 'angry' dramatists, however, their theatre would be more specifically focused on an attempt to offer trenchant analysis of the stagnation and inequalities of Great Britain through an anatomy of its recent social and political history.

Before the rise of political theatre in the seventies, John Osborne had in fact continued through the sixties to express his anger at a declining and politically moribund nation, but it had never been grounded in a socialist critique of the Establishment. Jimmy Porter's railings against Alison's Tory background were always more of a rhetorically polished cry of Romantic self-expression against the repressive and stagnant tolerance of corporate mediocrity. His most Brechtian play was *Luther* (1961), but even here the figure of the great sixteenth-century individualist dissident who dared to stand out against Rome is approached, not so much in political and historical terms, as in those borrowed from that most individualistic of discourses, post-Freudian ego-psychology. Indeed, Osborne's Luther is a dramatization of Erik Erikson's study of a neurotically driven individual who attempts to resolve, on the stage of history, oedipal conflicts persisting into adulthood as cloacal obsession and psychosomatic ailment. Despite the use of Brechtian alienation effects, it is to psychoanalysis rather than Marxism that Osborne turns in order to raise the action to epic proportion. Religious fanaticism is presented as a futile attempt to escape, by sublimation, the bodies of the mother and the father. Luther, however, is presented as tragically heroic in his hubris, a lone male egotistical sublime struggling with internal demons as with the forces of social conformism ranged oppressively against him. He is a celebration of a heroic if beleaguered individualism in what his creator sees as an age of mediocre corporatism:

Unless I am shown by the testimony of the Scriptures—for I don't believe in Popes or councils—unless I am refuted by Scripture and my conscience is captured by God's own word, I cannot and will not recant, since to act against one's conscience is neither safe nor honest. Here I stand; God help me; I can do no more.

'More', as romantic individual conscience, was not enough, however, for the dramatists of the next generation. But then neither was the classic Marxist analysis of history as a teleological narrative propelled by economic class conflict. The French situationists were one supplementary intellectual influence, their critique described by David Edgar as 'less about the organisation of the working class at the point of production and much more about the disruption of bourgeois ideology at the point of consumption'. This differential analysis surfaced in the distinction made by Sandy Craig, one of the founders of the agitprop theatre company 7 : 84, between political drama which seeks reform of the liberal middle classes and political theatre which expresses the voice of the working class as the real progressive force in society. Though Brenton would talk of the theatre as a 'dirty place . . . there to bait our obsessions, ideas and public figures', he was, in fact, one of the first of his political generation to move out of fringe and on to the mainstream stage.[11] By 1974 he was talking confidently of the failures of fringe as an effective political weapon: 'A socialist government has to run the country, before a socialist theatre can dominate the theatre.'[12] In fact, the emphasis on 'bourgeois consumption' and, in particular, the issue of personal moral responsibility as the focus of political drama became more and more appealing to each of the prominent political dramatists of the seventies.

In 1978, the year which brought to an end the decade of political theatre, David Hare argued that its strength as a force for social change lay not so much in a facility for peddling 'gimcrack mottoes of the left' to the converted, but in the ability to expose the gulf between words and actions where moral analysis might be inserted. The dramatist can 'put people's sufferings in historical context', by focusing on those aspects of culture which are hidden or covered over by social myths.[13] Hare described here the *raison d'être* of his own highly articulate, scenically perspectival dramatizations of recent British history, and also, if implicitly, revealed his distaste for the psychologically starved cartoon creations of the agitprop movement which had taken to the streets in 1968. His concern to situate subjective suffering in the context of political analysis produced, in *Plenty* (1978), perhaps the most powerful dramatic representation in the seventies of the roots of national despair and personal anomie. Although most of his plays were set in enclosed environments (the university, a girls' school, a country house, the commuter belt of Guildford in Surrey), geographical place became a microcosmic location within which to explore the imaginary space of national identity.

In 'A Lecture' in *Licking Hitler*, Hare described himself as someone who writes 'tribal pieces, trying to show how people behaved on this island, off this continental shelf, in this century. How this Empire vanished, how these ideals changed.'[14] As in Shaw's *Heartbreak House* or Ibsen's *Ghosts*, the sets of Hare's plays provided visual symbols which conveyed with theatrical vitality the moral dilemmas of living in a corrupt and degenerate society. The exclusive girls' school in *Slag*, for example, is an entirely self-enclosed middle-class educational establishment where self-regarding obsessional narcissisms can be dressed up as progressive ideology or social concern. In fact, beyond the endless talk and self-congratulatory private discourse, and as in the Chekhovian drawing-room, nothing happens and no one changes. In the commercial middle-class world of *Knuckle* (1974), Curly, the Micky Spillane-type operator, deals in guns as an oedipal gesture designed to point to the immoral commercial weaponry of his father's business empire. Patrick, his father, meanwhile fashions an invincibly persuasive public persona out of the civilized nuance of the various Henry James novels he reads for cultural improvement and as an upmarket alternative to Dale Carnegie. Curly sees that, whenever a 'tiny little weed called morality' appears, the debonair Patrick is actually 'waiting with a cement grinder and a shovel to concrete it over', but he also comes to accept that his literal-minded youthful revolt is no match for his father's literary-sophisticated immorality. Indeed, he declares that morality 'cannot help us now', and sells out after all.

Hare's play *Plenty* (1978) most successfully dramatized the pain of living in a society whose ideals have become tainted and where existential purpose is provided only by fragmenting myths. The play presents a succession of scenes which trace key moments in British history from the Second World War to the immediate pre-Wilson era of 1962. Dramatic tension is beautifully maintained because the disrupted temporal ordering of historic moments virtually plots the psychological confusion and conflict of its central character Susan, whose moral relation to the events presented is left as an open-ended but compelling dilemma. The play is framed by scenes in France where Susan had felt absolutely existentially alive in her role as resistance fighter during the Second World War. She had believed utterly in the struggle for a new vision of society: the sun-drenched fields of plentiful wheat in rural France would continue in imaginative space as an icon of the harvest of freedom for which the war had been fought. This scene of bounty is immediately contrasted, in the temporal flow of the play, however, with a stripped room and locked packing-cases and the supine body of her naked husband as she prepares to leave him in 1962.

Images of plenty and famine are juxtaposed throughout in a narrative of events which draws public and private history together as Susan, married to a British diplomat after the war, comes to recognize that its morally justifiable deceptions have continued as the state-ordained 'glittering lies' and corruptions which are the real foundation of the post-war nation. The high point of the play is the diplomatic dinner on the eve of the Suez débâcle where Susan begins mentally to fall apart as she is literally confronted with the grotesque consumption of material plenty in the context of abject moral famine. But Susan herself is ambiguously presented, for her own moral void can only be fed by the utopian plenty of the past, and, in her nostalgia and yearning for the lost wartime enhanced and dramatic sense of being alive, she destroys not only herself but the lives of all around her. As in most of Hare's plays, the one honest character who sees the corruption can find only a destructive means of escape from it. As with that of the addictive rock singer Maggie of *Teeth N' Smiles*, however, Susan's honesty cannot be pure. Its infra-red exposure of moral corruption is flashed up in the frame of her own self-deceptive nostalgia. Because we must therefore judge her on actions which often appear hysterical, it is difficult to decide whether they are the gestures of a manipulative and narcissistic exhibitionist or those of an honest but uncompromising moral conscience. Her husband Brock, unable to carry the burden of her provocation any longer, delivers the speech on which our judgement hangs: 'Your life is selfish, self-interested gain . . . You claim to be protecting some personal ideal, always at a cost of almost infinite pain to everyone around you.' Yet he speaks to her as a father to an adolescent daughter. For Brock, if morality is not possible, manners will do. Hypocrisy preserves decency which is 'adult behaviour': but Susan prefers eternal adolescence. By remaining caught in 1945, she refuses to grow up. But in doing so she flaunts and therefore exposes the very roots of that nostalgia which has provided the foundational security of post-war British national identity. Because she is a woman, she cannot rail like Jimmy Porter, but as a hysteric she acts out in florid physical embodiment the hidden sicknesses of an entire society. The final flashback to France in 1945 is doubly ironic, as she announces those words whose prophecy the play has shown to be entirely misplaced: 'We have grown up. We will improve our world . . . There will be days and days like this.'

Like Hare, David Edgar also moved away from agitprop directness, 'thinking the politics you could get across were very crude', and toward a more morally nuanced political drama which might reveal how 'the world about us was getting more complicated'.[15] The play which earned him well-deserved mainstream acceptance was *Destiny* (1976), which covered roughly the same period of national history as *Plenty*, sharing too its epic model of theatre. Snapshots of significant moments in history are connected through an underlying psychologically subjective as well as politically objective documentary narrative logic. Edgar's focus, however, is specifically on the politics of race, and it provided the first serious and significant literary attempt to understand the fear, aggression, and nostalgia which had led to the formation of the National Front in 1967. Disturbingly too, a prominent member of the Establishment, Enoch Powell, had made a series of racially inflammatory speeches culminating in April 1968 in Birmingham, where he recalled, in a classically disguised but violent analogy, the ancient Roman Sibyl who had seen the prospect of the River Tiber 'foaming with much blood'. Moreover, Immigration and Race Relations Acts designed to defuse the subsequent tensions actually exacerbated racial conflict. In 1968 immigration was limited to those with patrial ties with existing British residents, and a discriminatory quota system was introduced with the result that families were split up and subjected to further suffering and conflict.

In Edgar's play *Destiny*, the phrase 'rivers of blood' was repeated as a leitmotif to convey the rootedness of racist violence in the insecurities bred by territorial nationalism. A measure of sympathy is accorded each of the characters, for the play reveals how the nationalism which arises in the context of the desire for belonging, security, and nurture can suddenly convert to a violent racism when these are threatened, as they would be, in the post-imperial phase of British history from 1947 onward. The Nation Forward Party of *Destiny* is an unstable conglomerate of fearful and disaffected right and left, working and middle classes, who temporarily suspend earlier ideological commitments, united in a negative desire to scapegoat the 'outsider' as the cause of their loss of esteem and security. At its Stratford-upon-Avon début and in the 1977 Aldwych production, the shoddiness and muddleheadedness of their conspiratorial affiliation were physically realized in the ramshackle set and the fudged attempts by various speakers to unite 'national' with 'socialist'. It was also made evident in the dramatic plot which finally reveals the extreme right-wing Major Rolfe to be a member of an entrepreneurial commercial syndicate which has deprived his former Sergeant Turner, erstwhile adjutant and new Nation Forward comrade, of his livelihood as a small-time antique dealer peddling icons of nostalgia from a small shop. Even Rolfe, however, stagestruck by a lingering vision of imperial heroics and mourning the execution of his son by the IRA, is also allowed some sympathy: we see the complex emotional hinterland hidden behind the monologic bigotry. There are no stage villains, and, to underline the need for understanding rather than caricature, Edgar gave the last words of the play to Adolf Hitler (whose birthday anniversary actually coincided with Powell's historical speech), at Nuremburg, 3 September 1933: 'Only one thing could have stopped our movement: if our adversaries had understood its principle, and had smashed, with the utmost brutality, the nucleus of our new movement.' To understand is not to forgive in this instance but not to understand is to be unable to mount effective political opposition.

Edgar's later play *Maydays* (1983, The Barbican) coincided with the attempt to revive imperial fantasies after the Argentinian invasion and occupation of the British colony, the Falkland Islands, in March 1982. The Prime Minister sent in a task force of 10,000 with the support of most of the British population, secured a highly questionable victory with the sinking of the enemy cruiser *General Belgrano* (which appeared to be leaving the exclusion zone at the time of attack), and by June had recovered Port Stanley, the Falkland capital. The British tabloid press, particularly the *Sun*, reached new heights of vulgar jingoism and, as Mrs Thatcher was transformed into the new Boadicea, so opinion polls pointed toward a Tory upsurge. Although the war was soon forgotten, it had revived nationalistic fervour and ensured that Thatcherism was here to stay. The title of Edgar's play now seems ironic in the extreme when viewed in its historical context: 'mayday' is the international distress call and the day of left-wing political celebration. Within the Labour Party, there seemed little to celebrate: the split between centre and left had widened; Callaghan had resigned in 1980; and Michael Foot, voice of the old left, had inherited a dispirited and ideologically riven party. Eric Hobsbawm had delivered an influential lecture entitled 'The Forward March of the Left Halted?', in which he argued that the old industrial working-class culture was disappearing and that if Labour was not to become a relic it must realign itself with progressive groups such as the environmental and peace movements, and revise its socialism for what came to be known as 'New Times'. Indeed the 1983 Labour manifesto uneasily cobbled together a commitment to the representation of the concerns of Greens, feminists, and gay rights groups, while trying to preserve older elements of statism and corporate planning despite their lack of popular appeal and the evident loss of union power and solidarity. With Labour in disarray and the Conservative Party riding high, the Tories gained a huge majority of 142 seats in the 1983 election. Mayday sounded more the note of distress than celebration.

Like *Destiny*, Edgar's later play again caught the mood of the time and drew on history to examine the political foundations of a contemporary crisis. Like Hobsbawm's lecture, the play examined the thesis that the left was moribund with old ideas, tied to a nineteenth-century model of industrial production which could no longer account for the late capitalist shift 'from the factory to the supermarket' and the possibility that 'the working class is owned by what it buys'. Self-consciously written at the moment of the resurgence of the economic libertarian right, its epic sweep suggested the need to return to an examination of the basic tenets of socialism and of personal moral responsibility. The post-war failures of socialism are understood in the context of a consumer society where the tension between the conformity required by collective politics and the individual desire for liberty which pulls against it is felt acutely by all who regard themselves as socialists of one kind or another. The panorama of international history is focused through its varying impact on the lives of a trio of characters who, for different reasons, defect from an organized left which is seen to draw its revolutionary impetus from the spontaneous and righteous energy of the people, but then to contain and cramp it by a deforming and devitalizing correctness: 'there is always . . . a fundamental contradiction between the urge to make men equal and the need to keep them free'.

This terrain had been dramatically covered by a number of plays in the seventies, most notable of them Trevor Griffiths's *The Party* (1974), but none had attempted the epic scale of *Maydays* which flashed through each of the public landmarks of post-war history from May Day 1945 to Greenham Common in the present. Griffiths's play was concentrated more narrowly on the aftermath of 1968, exploring the discussions at a party of left-wing intellectuals as scenes from the student uprisings of 1968 are flashed onto the wall of the fashionably located house in south-west London. Griffiths's play contrasted the inertia of the talk with images of the violence of the student action, a juxtaposition designed to affirm that both are founded on a hypocritical avoidance of acknowledgement of their own class complicity in the creation of a culture of the dispossessed: Chekhovian abysses open up as each of the characters builds a rhetorical bridge over the gap between professed principles and actual practices. Again, like Edgar's, the play allows sympathy but also apportions blame.

Each of these plays was sensitive to changes occurring in the nation of Great Britain which required new political thinking. They registered the break-up of political consensus but showed the right to be more effective in securing electoral support, capitalizing on the profound psychological fears and insecurities thrown up by the loss of unified national identity. Right and left are seen to be guilty of peddling nostalgia, but the former is seen to harness it as an extremely effective political weapon to cloak a radical shift of ethos and direction which would surface most emphatically in the full bloom of the enterprise eighties. Imagery of disease or corruption recurred in each play as emblematic of the condition of post-war Britain, and most emphatically in Howard Brenton's earlier *The Churchill Play* of 1974, produced at a crisis moment in political history: in the wake of the miner's strike, with a state of near chaos existing in Northern Ireland and escalating crime rates feeding a new mood of confrontation which was to signal the imminent collapse of consensus. Set in a political concentration camp in a futuristic 1984, the play opened dramatically with Sir Winston Churchill fantastically rising from his coffin as he lies in state in Westminster Palace Hall in 1965. The audience, however, was immediately plunged into a theatrical *mise-en-abyme* as the real was revealed to be a play rehearsal for a performance before a visiting parliamentary committee. Echoing *Hamlet* in its structure and disease imagery, and *Marat/Sade* in its theatrical anatomy of political violence, it also called up Ibsen's *Ghosts* in the revelation of Churchill–Britain's syphilitic inheritance, an 'infected marsh' which continues to rot at the foundations of its institutions of power and is revealed as the dark side of that supposed legacy of freedom which its wartime leader had bequeathed to the nation.

If *The Churchill Play* had been designed to shock, this was even more the case with Brenton's *The Romans in Britain* (1980), which became the subject of a court action over its representation of attempted homosexual rape (one of the few attempts to impose theatre censorship since the abolition of the Lord Chamberlain's veto in 1968). The depicted rape was itself a crude and in any case highly problematic metaphor for imperial violation. The play was not in the least concerned with sexual relationships but with political power and the history of nation which it represented as a series of brutal colonial occupations beginning in 54 BC on the brink of the Roman invasion of England, proceeding through the Saxon invasion of AD 515, and arriving through this oblique route in Northern Ireland in the present day. Little distinction was made between the various occupations, each shown to involve an assumption of superiority on the part of the colonizer which is actually betrayed as more barbaric than the culture of the colonized. As each conqueror is seen to rewrite history as self-flattering legend, the play posed the question, articulated explicitly in the words of the scornful Irishwoman who surveys Major Chichester's attempt to deny his imperial heritage: 'what nation ever learned from the sufferings it inflicted on others?' The stories constituting the national myths which are the comfort and security of one group obscure, by the writing out of history, the misery of those whom they dispossess. Each of the male political dramatists of the seventies arrived at this insight. It would be the turn of women dramatists in the eighties to take the analysis further, and to begin to construct a more optimistic map of possible national and super-national identities.

6 POST-CONSENSUS FICTIONS

> No fullness, no void.
>
> (Maurice Blanchot, *The Writing of the Disaster*)

During the mid- to late seventies critical battles raged about the future of the novel. Academics argued about whether formally innovative novels were morally thin, their dazzling manners set against dwindling matter; liberal critics saw the self-reflexive disembeddedness and multiple perspectivism of modern life as inimical to the continuation of consensual panoramic fictions which had an intellectual grip on the entire social world; a new invasion of self-reflexivity in the shape of the autonomous linguistic structures posited by structuralist and post-structuralist theory seemed to threaten the referential and thus moral dimension of fictional prose. Microcosms were fashionable, attested to by the increasing popularity of, for example, the campus novel, that genre arising out of the new student generation of the sixties, or what became known (somewhat derogatorily) as the 'Hampstead' novel with its anatomy of the relationship in the context of changing liberal bourgeois mores. In a fragmenting society, it seemed impossible to construct typical or representative characters, so that some feared the demise of realism altogether. Both realism and the novel, of course, are still with us, and the apocalypticism of the critics was, perhaps, in part the projection of an ending which might confer retrospective significance upon their own contingent confusions in a commercially driven culture more interested in sales potential than aesthetic worth.

In the eighties, however, the novel took a distinctly fantastic turn, as we have seen in *Shame*, often combining a magic realist use of spatial and temporal dislocation with essayistic narratorial intrusion and with Chinese-box effects such as characters in fictions reading fictions about their own lives or of allegorical representations metamorphosing into primary levels of reality. Julian Barnes's novel *Flaubert's Parrot* (1984), for example, comically pursued metaphysical and psychological questions of personal identity in an obsessive quest for the truth about the life of Gustave Flaubert. The delayed fictional punchline is the revelation by Braithwaite (the country doctor-questing narrator) of the paranoid identification of his own relationship with his adulterous wife with that of Emma Bovary and her fictional husband. The quest for the real Flaubert is a journey of attempted self-discovery and clarification of the reasons for his own wife's sexual betrayal. He pursues the quest with the fury of a jealous lover. The narrative spins with manic propulsion through a catalogue of Flaubert memorabilia, bestiaries, philosophic *aperçus*, disquisitions on critics, even on parrots (the inspiration and subject for Flaubert's *Un cœur simple*) as diverse, obsessive, and baffling as the treatment of whales in *Moby Dick*. Like Melville's novel, too, it arrives at the conclusion that the more you find, the less you know. Lives cannot be rationally dissected and contained: complicated fictional transferences always occur between subjects and objects of biography as between friends and acquaintances in everyday life. Language is always more an instrument of invention than discovery, and even then usually more a pragmatic than a poetic one. It is 'a cracked kettle on which we beat out tunes for bears to dance to, while all the time we long to move the stars to pity'.

The late Romantic Braithwaite discovers, however, that there seems to be no categorically imperative and universal truth existing in the spheres of ethics, cognition, or art. Prejudice, irrational belief, and contingent desire propel human behaviour. Truth has ever been the invention of a self which is never free from servitude to irrational forces within and social and institutional pressure from without. American writers such as Thomas Pynchon had been obsessed with the theme for some time. *The Crying of Lot 49*, for example, was influential, with its obsessive quest and hesitation between interpretations, its hovering on the borders of the paranoiac and the sacred. The Dickensian imagination of Peter Ackroyd caught this interest in anti-detective detection in *Hawksmoor* (1985), in a Gothic detective fiction which placed an Inspector Bucket-type rationalism (that of Nicholas Hawksmoor) at the centre of a (Borgesian) labyrinthine plot which hesitates, like Pynchon's story, between supernatural (onto-logical) and sociopsychological (epistemological) explanation. Ackroyd plays on the analogous possibilities of architecture (struc-tures in physical space), fiction (verbal structures which occupy real and imaginary space), and the supernatural, as intimations of differ-ent and autonomous orders of being.

The eighteenth-century murders committed in the discharge of his Faustian pact by Wren's assistant architect Nicholas Dyer are cir-cumstantially doubled in the twentieth century even in details such as the names of the victim and the pattern of the crimes. Hawksmoor, however, is tormented by traces and clues which still lead nowhere and eventually, like Pynchon's Oedipa, begins to lose his highly valued but inadequate powers of reason, brought to the edge of a madness induced by the Burkean intuition of a sublime 'pattern so large that it remained inexplicable'. Ackroyd's literary joke is, of course, hardly new. Jorge Luis Borges's story 'Death and the Com-pass' (1964) involved a ratiocinative detective whose semiotic in-toxication led him on the trail of a serial murder plot which finally required his own death to complete its artistically perfect order. The idea of being written into a story and subsequently dispensed with on completion of the plot had also appeared in Muriel Sparks's *The Comforters* in 1961. In each case an analogy is drawn between the sublime other-worldliness of fiction and that of the supernatural with the novelist existing as divine architect in a world of text. Hawksmoor's investigations also lead to his death because, like Dyer, he has fulfilled the function assigned to him in this particular plot. Ackroyd spells out the analogy from the start. Dyer himself begins his seventeenth-century narrative with instructions to his architec-tural draughtsman to 'keep the structure intirely in Mind as you inscribe it . . . I have imparted to you the Principles of Terrour and Magnificence.' 'Terrour and Magnificence' are also the central char-acteristics of the sublime, and Dyer's edifices, dedicated to Satan, will be replicated in that verbally wrought house fit only for unfree characters which is Ackroyd's own post-modern 'architexture'.

Along with the Borgesian fantastic, the magic realism of writers such as Gabriel García Márquez began to influence the British novel in the eighties. Fantastic worlds sprang up all around. David Lodge parodically revitalized the medieval romance quest in *Small World* (1984). Antonia Byatt prefaced her novel *Possession: A Romance* (1990) with a quotation from Nathaniel Hawthorne's *The House of the Seven Gables*: 'when a writer calls his work a Romance, it need hardly be observed that he wishes to claim a certain latitude, both as to its fashion and material, which he would not have felt himself entitled to assume, had he professed to be writing a Novel', and which continues by justifying the practice as a means to 'connect a bygone time with the very present that is flitting away from us'. Byatt, like Ackroyd, and like John Fowles earlier, creates a doubling of worlds, self-consciously textual in their pastiche formulation, and connected (again) by a literary anti-detective detective plot (invaded by motifs from the genre of romance) which exposes the literariness of history in its protagonist's quest for a buried history of literature.

The idea of recovering buried histories was the theme too of Graham Swift's *Waterland* (1983), another meditation on the disconnection of versions of the past, of the psychological compulsions rationalized into official narratives, and of the lives and experiences thereby written out. The waterland of the fens is also an image of the fragility of our conscious construction of who and where we are, a crazy paving of reclaimed earth whose borders are ever shifting, ever succumbing to the fluid tides of past denial which erode and sometimes flood this floating world. Crick, the history teacher, whose own personal past has returned to overwhelm the dry land of his pedagogic Whig progressivism, recognizes that history, 'if it is to keep on constructing its road into the future, must do so on solid ground': the rationalistic grounds, however, which have led throughout modernity from revolution to terror. Furthermore, even without this catalogue of horror, he knows with Freud, that earlier avatar of the ambiguities of modernity, that 'the more you try to dissect events, the more you lose hold of what you took for granted in the first place'. To excavate for bedrock with the tools of reason is only to dicover endless layers of sediment; to look for a linear causal sequence of events, a determining motor-force or grand narrative of history, is like drawing provisional channels along a strand and then waiting for the return of the tide. The solid land of empirical fact or rational enquiry, like the fen country, threatens ever and thanetically to return to the magically onomatopoeic 'silt': 'a slow, sly, insinu-ating agency . . . which shapes and undermines continents'. Swift's philosophical rejection of positivistic history and rationalistic theory is imaged in the poetic resonance of his central symbol. Its narrative realization, however, is effected through his own powers as histor-ical storyteller to create a family saga of place, a tale of region rather than nation, peopled, rather like Flannery O'Connor's tales of Southern grotesques, by compellingly credible though utterly eccen-tric characters irreducible to psychoanalytic or sociological cliché. Here was yet another fictional assault on the legacy of Enlightenment, of faith in the rationality of the self and the inevitability of historical progress. And just as the fens defy the human imposition of bound-ary, so too, throughout the eighties ecologists and environmentalists would continue to question the instrumental assumptions of modern science that our relation to nature must be as a controlling and consuming subject confronting an inert and available object.

Like these writers, post-modern thinkers such as Foucault, and communitarian moral philosophers such as Alisdair MacIntyre, were influential in their challenge to reflectionist theories of truth, or what Richard Rorty has referred to as the notion of mind as a 'Glassy Essence'. Instead, language is viewed as a constructive tool through which the powerful impose on the world as truth their own versions of history. Both Foucault and MacIntyre withdrew from Enlighten-ment assumptions and turned to pre-modern philosophy for alternat-ive models of the good life. While Foucault recommended a return to the pre-modern Greek concept of *technē*, or self-conscious artistic making as a model for authentic living, MacIntyre advised the re-habilitation of an Aristotelian and Augustinian sense of virtue: both Foucault and MacIntyre emphasized the provisionality or humanly fabricated quality of truth. Similarly, that other child of the Enlight-enment, the novel (grounded in assumptions of the primacy of empirical sense-experience, the achievement through rational analy-sis of self-knowledge, and the existence of a moral and epistemo-logical correspondence between contingent surface and universal order) seemed also to be reeling in a post-Enlightenment world where such certainties were breaking down. In politics, liberal consensus and the concept of democratic representation, inherited from the great *philosophes* of the eighteenth century, were under stress; in philosophy, deconstructionists were showing how rhetoric subverts rather than supports logic, how all meanings undo themselves, and how there can be no non-complicit transcendent position outside language from which to proclaim universal truths; in science, the stable and ultimately mathematically fathomable universe was claimed to be simply one of many possible worlds whose nature was not amenable to formulation in the terms of Newtonian materialist physics.

Indeed, it is not surprising that the novel too seemed to be breaking up. On the one hand were those writers attempting to extend Enlightenment vocabularies by taking over traditional forms but speaking from displaced perspectives of race, class, gender, or ethnicity; and on the other were writers more interested in exploring, either apocalyptically or with greater optimism, the representational consequences of what seemed a disintegrating eighteenth- and nineteenth-century inheritance or the beginning of a new political, philosophical, or scientific paradigm. As assumptions underlying the consensual orders of realist aesthetics were challenged but future alternatives seemed difficult to imagine, a number of creative writers, as well as philosophers, returned to pre-Enlightenment forms: for example, playing on the dialogic potential of the novel by fragmenting it into unresolved contestatory discourses, or presenting multiple levels of worlds within worlds as Edmund Spenser had done in *The Faerie Queene*, or generating the effect of nested worlds through extended similes and metaphors as Milton in *Paradise Lost*, or kaleidoscopically staging confrontations of levels of artifice as in the courtly masque or Restoration comedy or the play-within-a-play of *Hamlet*. Such tendencies had been evident since the early seventies, but writers in the eighties were more inclined to see as a virtue what had previously been cause for apocalyptic gloom: the end of what Lukacs had seen as the representative typicality of the novel, the rise of the grotesque and eccentric, the break-up of universal representativeness into culturally differentiated styles and voices; the construction of cosmologies which defy known laws of space and time; the carnivalesque which disturbs ontological and elemental categorization.

Nationhood continued to be a dominant concern, though the nation and its history were more likely to be presented through the perspectives or voices of dislocated observers or displaced narrators (in Amis, Ishiguro, Ballard, Trevor, Kelman, Gray, Mo) or located in a physical space outside the British Isles (Boyd, Naipaul, Farrell, Rushdie, Jhabvala, Chatwin, Roberts, Golding) or in the temporal no man's land of historical pastiche (Fowles, Ackroyd, Unsworth, Golding, Winterson), or the self-reflexively intertextual world of literariness itself (Lodge, Rhys, Brookner, Byatt). Microcosms were increasingly giving way to macrocosms, to intergalactic empires existing in cosmic space or anti-patriarchal imaginary kingdoms (Carter, Winterson, Lessing, Weldon). As we shall see, the fantastic burgeoned as the macrostructural equivalent of metaphor: a means of talking about what has not yet been named by expressing it through analogies which, temporary and specious as they might be, were still capable of defamiliarizing and challenging normative assumptions about the constitution of the real. Was the turn to fantasy simply more evidence of the effects of a consumer culture built on the continuous stimulation of desire, where communal goals and traditional moralities are sacrificed for the narcissistic pleasures of the private imagination and the projection of psychic interiority? Or did it represent a continuing Romantic celebration of the imagination as a space outside commercial culture where new worlds could be envisaged and new voices heard? In fact, cosmological fantasy was most in evidence in novels written by writers concerned less with realistic or nostalgic analysis of the break-up of consensus than with those anxious to forge or explore new possibilities of subjective identity. It is always easier, of course, to talk about new identities than to live them, and post-modernist theorists such as Lyotard had warned of the potentially Fascistic consequences of attempts to graft the sublime onto the real. Even so, the capacity of the fantastic and grotesque to disturb the familiar and to leave unresolved the implications of that disturbance is undeniable. Both remain important means of unsettling stereotypes of identity and gesturing toward new possibilities of imaginary and historical existence.

New Cosmologies: Feminism and the Fantastic

The last national conference of Women's Liberation was held in Birmingham in 1978. The movement itself had failed, legislatively at least, to realize the political aims of the early seventies, and by the eighties internal eruptions of cultural difference and the rise of a more fragmented identity politics emphasizing differences between women such as class, race, sexual orientation, and ethnicity would lead to the coining of the expression 'post-feminism'. The term, however, seemed singularly inappropriate when applied to the world of literary publishing, for the eighties saw a feminist or at least 'woman-centred' publishing boom on an unprecedented scale. Virago had been founded in 1973 to be followed by a stream of other women's presses such as Pandora, Everywoman's Press, Sheba. By the eighties, however, the independent woman had become a buoyant consumer market and, after a series of take-overs, feminist publishing went mainstream. Literature would continue to be an important means of sustaining consciousness-raising, even if opposition looked, at times, more like big business and although many of the fictions published might appear to be old-fashioned and unexciting personal confessions of what it was to be a woman.

One of the distinctive features of the women's movement since the early seventies, however, had been a close and self-reflexive relation between theory and practice. Women's writing (even if avowedly non-feminist) in the seventies had tended to focus on themes of motherhood, the contradictions of women's roles, and an often confessional search for 'authentic' experience which reflected the politics of the women's movement and the theorizations of academic feminists. Romance continued to be popular even as it was (partially) dissected, as in the novels of Anita Brookner, a surprising Booker Prize winner with *Hotel du Lac* (1984), who strongly repudiated all attempts to see her work as feminist and declared that the novel was 'a love story pure and simple: love triumphed over temptation'.[1] Edith Hope, writer of traditional romance and the novel's romantic heroine, believes women read her fiction because it gives them a sense of power and importance otherwise absent from their lives. Her analysis is actually congruent with a number of feminist dissections of romance published in the eighties, but, unlike theirs, it asserts a belief in the essential stasis of this condition of eternal femininity. Like all Brookner's heroines, before and after, Edith looks to heterosexual romance and the discovery of the ideal (fatherly) man who will heal the childhood wounds of negligent parents and allow her to grow up and become an autonomous adult. The novel abounds with negative images of voracious and theatricalized femininity from which Edith flees into writing and into the disastrously idealized arms of the sadistic and misogynistic Mr Neville. Romance is portrayed as the infantilized projection of women who have never been allowed to grow up: Brookner, however, perversely denied that any feminist conclusion might be drawn from this.

Brookner's fiction is elegantly crafted and intelligent, though hardly innovative. There was, however, an eager market for traditional writing of this kind, feminist or otherwise, and romance continued to flourish. Changes were under way, however. In the eighties academic feminism had taken a post-modern turn, beginning with the development of a self-conscious awareness of the contradiction at the heart of its attempt to define a new epistemology: that women were on the one hand seeking equality for and recognition of their existing gendered identities while at the same time arguing that this femininity had been socially constructed and must be dismantled along with the patriarchal institutions shaping it. At this theoretically sophisticated level, there seemed no longer any point in trying to liberate an essential or authentic female self gagged and bound by the thought-policemen of social control: confessional authentic experience came under the chopping block of deconstructionist philosophic logic. However, the problem which then appeared (as Virginia Woolf had recognized during the first wave of feminism) was: once you've killed the 'Angel in the House', what do you put in her place? Woolf herself conjured up the fantastic Orlando, a transsexual body unashamedly crossing boundaries of space and time and guiltlessly transgressing those of custom and social convention. S/he would be reincarnated, though now in the garb of magic realism, the carnivalesque, and the new science, and in the wake of the gender theories of Julia Kristeva, Jacques Lacan, Michel Foucault, and Mikhail Bakhtin, in the most innovative feminist fiction of the eighties. Indeed, it is arguable that fictional writing by women has done as much to disseminate awareness of feminist theory as the more obviously analytic commentary of academic critics.

Transgression is a concept attached to guilt cultures, because it implies the existence of cultural boundaries which become even more clearly demarcated once transgressed. The world of the eighties, however, was much closer to what sociologists would see as a 'shame' culture. Here, social control is effected through the need for self-esteem and the fear of being revealed to be inadequate when measured against cultural norms. It plays on the need for public approval, existence in the gaze of others, rather than the confrontation with the self-punishing private conscience or the hidden confessor, which is the essence of the guilt culture's conformity to fixed moral or religious precepts. The feminist novel of the early seventies rejected the naïvely ungendered liberationism of the sixties by tackling themes such as motherhood, rape, or 'growing up a girl' in order to help free women, as traditional bearers of the domestic and emotional, from their inheritance of moral guilt about the transgression of 'normal' boundaries of femininity. As women increasingly entered the public world, feminist writing in the eighties seemed to have as its political aim the liberation of women from shame, focusing less on the confessional consciousness-raising which removes private guilt through collective sharing than on the attempt to reconstruct the female body as a physical space which could resist the projection onto it of public images of desirable and acceptable femininity. In 'Professions for Women', Woolf recognized that she had 'pressed up against' something, the female body, which she found impossible to express. Historians have since shown how the emancipations of modernity actually brought the female body under greater social control as the Welfare State intruded into what had formerly been regarded as the sphere of the private. Women were made to feel ashamed of bodies which were not safely contained within the functional but decently disguised parameters of reproduction or of decorously attractive femininity. Consumer capitalism has reinforced this 'hysterization'. As French feminists such as Hélène Cixous thus called for a new writing and assertion of the female body, many British women in the seventies and eighties began to think about their own relation to the body. Feminists such as Simone de Beauvoir in *The Second Sex* (1949) had described the construction of the female body as always immanent, a place of mystery and objectification held in the transcendent subjective gaze of male knowledge, constituted as 'other' than and therefore threatening to it, requiring ever-vigilant containment.

The increased focus on hysterical illnesses such as anorexia nervosa and the obsession with reducing and slimming were a testimony to anxieties about gender identity which were focused on the female body. Slimming obsessions reflected a desire to keep the female body small, childlike, and non-threatening: equally a commodity in the private sphere as in the public. Brigid Brophy wrote a novel about the complex gender investments in cultural formulations of the ideal body, the title *Flesh* stamped across its decoratively Rubenesque cover. Margaret Drabble's early novels explored femininity by focusing on the physical and psychological effects of motherhood. Her first heroine in *A Summer Birdcage* (1963) had complained that 'you can't be a sexy don', whereas the academic Rosamund of *The Millstone* (1965), regarding pregnancy as a punishment and delighted that her body mechanically snaps back into place after birth, even refuses (in what is psychoanalytically termed 'the flight from womanhood') to acknowledge that the birth of her baby is a physical process. To be in an unavoidably female (parturitional) body is to be 'trapped in a human limit', for the maternal body is a reminder of the mortality and dissolution of the flesh and a memory of the frightening mergence of earliest nonidentity. Thus Rosamund writes her scholarly and scientific doctoral thesis on (platonic) love poetry and strenuously avoids the messy intimacy and threatening physicality of sex itself. A later Drabble narrator, Jane Grey (dethroned majesty) of *The Waterfall* (1969), utterly transgresses cultural taboos and actually begins an affair in her post-parturitional bed, seeking to transform her male lover into the mother she feels was never her own. Both are almost destroyed by her passionate belief in the possibility of romantic dissolution. It is finally brought under control only through the ironic and distancing effect of narration itself: not for Drabble the *jouissance* of immolatory *écriture feminine*. Images of water, fluidity, merging, recur throughout, tying the ideology of romance as a pathology to the female body, but suggesting that its cure may come through the disruptive effects of linguistic form: irony, parody, shifts of narrative voice. Barely post-modern, the novel does, however, suggest the need for women to 'rewrite' their own bodies: this would become almost a catchphrase (and the title of a novel by Jeanette Winterson) of feminist theory and fiction in the eighties and nineties.

Writers in the eighties such as Fay Weldon, Angela Carter, and

Jeanette Winterson would caricature the psychoanalytic assumptions underpinning the social welfare control of the female body, and subvert images of acceptable femininity by building their fictions around grotesque giantesses, indeterminate hybrids, bodies which laid bare the hidden relations between the physical and the imaginary by defying the laws of time and space: bodies monstrous and sublime. Fay Weldon's *Life and Loves of a She-Devil* (1983) was televised and became one of the best-known of such Gothic fantasies. Its heroine Ruth has 'tucks taken in her legs' and total body surgery to transform her monstrous bulk into a shape resembling that of her husband's lover, petite romantic novelist Mary Fisher. But all of this is in order that she may avenge his marital betrayal and achieve, not love, but 'power over the hearts and pockets of men'. Because Ruth's ungainly body has refused decently feminine physical containment, her person has been shamed by a reflexive refusal of social acceptance. So, if society deems her monstrously outside its bounds, she is able to use that psychological monstrosity in turn to punish society: but only, however, once her body conforms to norms of femininity. In a parody of the Frankenstein myth, she re-creates herself with the aid of medical technology as a conventionally desirable and physically petite female form. Thus armed, she steps into the power side of that sado-masochistic equation which is her marriage, and, recalling that 'hell hath no fury like a woman scorned', proceeds to wreak revenge on husband Bobbo by inflicting on him the masochistic, tortured, and unrequited desire which had been her own lot in life. She proposes to do for women what Jesus did for men: 'He offered the stony path to heaven: I offer the motorway to hell. I bring suffering and self-knowledge'. Each of Weldon's novels, in fact, revisits similar terrain. In *Puffball* (1980), for example, the pregnant Liffey recognizes her victimization through the body as she watches with horror the cold steel of her husband's knife slice into the swollen globes of puffball mushrooms. Weldon's somewhat slapstick Gothic fictions suggest that the limits of her characters' desires are the limits of their worlds. The underlying structure of this desire changes very little, always will to power, will to romance, will to consume. There seems little hope of change, though occasionally, and if women refuse complicity in their own victimization, the gendered poles of master and slave may, at least fantastically, be shifted or reversed.

Weldon writes post-modern Gothic but it is finally harnessed to the exposure of power relations in the world of the domestic. Michele Roberts, Jeanette Winterson, and Angela Carter pushed the limits of the fantastic much further, collapsing distinctions between worlds, gender boundaries, or even a stable concept of transgression. Each attempted to imagine the no place which Michel Foucault, in the preface to *The Order of Things* (1970) called the 'heterotopia'. There he argued that utopias are consolatory and unfold in stable space whereas heterotopias are disturbing and 'destroy syntax in advance, and not only the syntax with which we construct sentences but also that less apparent syntax which causes words and things . . . to hold together'.[2] The concept recurred in a variety of literary contexts in the post-consensual eighties. It was echoed in Rushdie's notion of the 'migrant' and in Bruce Chatwin's philosophic-travel-fiction 'nomad' as the description of a universally and damagingly contained and curtailed human impulse in *The Songlines* (1987).

Perhaps nowhere was it so emphatically articulated, however, as in Jeanette Winterson's *Sexing the Cherry* (1989). What was most distinctive about Winterson's text, perhaps, was her introduction into the feminist grotesque of cosmological ideas from the new physics. Ian McEwan had engaged some of the new ideas about time in earlier, avowedly feminist-friendly, psychological horror stories such as 'Solid Geometry' and more extensively, though wedded more to a Bergsonian sense of subjective temporal relativity, in his novel *The Child in Time* (1987). In each of his fictions, in fact, he reveals how the child in each of us is abducted by an instrumentally rationalist state whose premises are derived from the mathematics of Newton and the logic of Descartes. Explored in his fiction as an alternative, is the potential of ideas from the new physics to generate a concept of spacetime where 'nothing was nothing's own' (*The Child in Time*) and where 'relationality' becomes a moral and political as well as ontological condition. In a later novel, *The Black Dogs* (1992), patriarchal rationalism is indicted as the philosophical underpinning of those modern forms of social engineering which have bequeathed to us the 'black dogs': Winston Churchill's name for his periods of acute depression, expanded here as a metaphor for the dark legacy of the Holocaust and the horror at the heart of Western civilization. Like Winterson's, each of these novels directly addressed the power dimensions of gender relations, but McEwan's commitment to a psychologically realist exploration of power relations was rather closer to Weldon's domestic grotesque than to the cosmologically heterotopic and ludic fantasy of Winterson.

Sexing the Cherry gives an opening indication of its intellectual concerns in two prefatory statements, the first a version of the Sapir–Whorf hypothesis that time is an effect of language, and the second a reference to the insights of the new science that matter is mostly 'empty space and points of light'. The question is posed: what do these insights suggest about time and about the reality of our world? Winterson returns to the image at the end of the novel, describing the firmament above us, but whose light may be the trace of stars which travel so fast that they are millions of years extinct by the time we see them. Here is a 'new Heaven, new earth', where the 'most real, the best-loved and the well-known are only hand-shadows on the wall'. The novel engages intertextually throughout with a number of earlier literary cosmogonies such as Milton's epic poem *Paradise Lost*, whose shadowy presence is evident on a number of levels— each of which posits new physical and spiritual worlds and invokes the sublime as the only mode in which they might be imagined. Winterson's imaginary universe, however, rejects both the physics, faith, and gender assumptions of Milton's. In her fiction, historical events are divided between the period of the seventeenth-century Interregnum from the Puritan seizure of power through the beheading of the King to the empty spaces and light of the Plague and the Great Fire, and a present-day narrative in which (as in *Hawksmoor*) doubles of the historical characters find their contemporary experiences uncannily looping back in time.

The events of the novel effectively cover the beginning and what may turn out to be the beginning of the end of Enlightened modernity: the Newtonian physical universe; Cartesian dualistic metaphysics; and a political, philosophical, and religious regime which privileges mind over body, man over woman, and separates matter absolutely from spirit. The novel begins in a period poised between old and new worlds: a medieval religious universe and a modern scientific one. With the rise of the new science in the seventeenth century, a feminized nature, superstitiously feared as the Devil's habitat and periodically contained through the burning of witches, was transformed into a mechanical universe requiring dissection, demystification, and naming of parts. Indeed, the burning of witches ceased abruptly at the end of the seventeenth century as the Newtonian and Cartesian world-views took over and nature, and woman, came to be those inert objects (body, material, emotion) set against the active rational subjectivity of the male. Virginia Woolf had written in *Three Guineas* in 1938 that 'Science, it would seem, is not sexless'. Indeed, for Woolf, Newtonian science, separating body and mind, man and woman, reason and emotion, spirit and matter, is decidedly male. But Winterson is writing in the midst of both a second wave of feminism whose energy has been in the service of a deconstruction of gender polarities and a second scientific revolution which has blurred such fixed dualities as matter and mind and there-fore resonates with the potential for dissolving others, including those of gender.

The seventeenth-century events of the novel are narrated within a post-Einsteinian relativistic universe (and self-conscious fabulation) of new science which entails that event and narration, model and reality, theory and matter are indistinguishable. The world of matter is no longer an inert stasis whose patterns can be repeated in the mind, but an everchanging network of possible universes which can only, sublimely and imaginatively, be glimpsed in their non-mathematical otherness. Division and its overcoming is the theme of the novel. The severing of the King's head from his body is one of many images of a burgeoning world of modernity caught up in deformative dualisms, even as it is still bound to the lost plenitude of the past and longs for a sublime condition of wholeness in the future. The healing of the split is the quest of the Dog Woman's foundling son, resonantly named Jordan, who is implicated in a romantic search for the twelfth princess Fortunata. The name calls to mind the Roman Fortuna, whom Machiavelli had seen as the cruel goddess of an unpredictable nature whose power must be trapped by men for their own cultural ends. But it is used also in the novel as an image of romantic yearning for discovery of and completion by the other which will return us to a primordial and pristine self undivided by gender: 'if the other life, the secret life, could be found and brought home, then a person might live in peace and have no need for God.'

Jordan's mother, meanwhile, is a grotesque reincarnation of Defoe's Moll Flanders, dishing out 'advice to the ladies', surrounded like Milton's female Sin with her brood of hungry dogs, a giantess whose grotesque body and Rabelaisian spirit flamboyantly transgress the Puritan denial of flesh (another splitting), the Cartesian repudiation of the body, and the Newtonian mechanization of nature. Witch-like, timeless, and indomitable, she turns back as weapon on a patriarchal world its cultural stereotypes of woman as Imago: unleashed physicality which can devour and destroy the male sex. Indeed, the novel resounds with Freudian jokes as Dog Woman asserts her freakish autonomy, horticulturally castrating one suitor in a pruning operation to encourage a healthier sapling growth in the place of his ugly and unruly branch. Her pre-modern body, however, also exists within a post-modern and post-Newtonian fictional universe where Borgesian paradoxes are realized, temporal causality breaks down, and appparent chaos breaks up into proliferating little narratives of order. In this new universe of the imagination, all is possible, time is no longer an order of the clock (Newtonian image *par excellence*), and magic realist universes of language occupy physical space on earth. Indeed, whole kingdoms are wiped out by love and, *pace* Swift, why then should sunlight not be extracted from cucumbers?

Winterson's novel inverts Burke's image of the implicitly masculine sublime by embodying it in the grotesque female form of the Dog Woman. How can Dog Woman, however, stand for a glimpse of that possibility of magnificent otherness which is in nature and ourselves, unencompassable by visual imagination or conceptual understanding? For this is indeed what the aestheticians of the eighteenth century understood by the idea of the sublime (and indeed, the sublime was always implicitly gendered masculine just as the beautiful in its inherently submissive and conformist mode was inevitably gendered feminine). Dog Woman, in fact, is not an isolated example of such reversal in recent fiction. Equally grotesque and beyond the bounds of possibility (and established conventions of gender and aesthetics) was Angela Carter's bird-woman Fevvers in *Nights at The Circus* (1984), another giantess who romps through history defying space and time, unavoidably a body, her yawn 'opening up a crimson maw the size of that of a basking shark', forever staring at reflections in mirrors or reflecting back the gaze of others in the bottomless abyss of eyes which open up universes, 'sets of Chinese boxes, as if each one opened into a world into a world into a world, an infinite plurality of worlds'. Carter's fiction, here and in other texts such as *The Passion of New Eve* (1977), is more self-consciously grounded than Winterson's in a knowing play with ideas of the Freudian revisionist Jacques Lacan, for whom self is always an endless pursuit of reflections in the eyes of others, love a desire for the desire of the other, gender an unstable category bounded by struggles for power where what is within can never entirely free itself from dependency for definition on what is without. Women are dependent on men for identification as bodies, and although they may wield those bodies as weapons, like men, too, they can never step out of image and into real. Nature has never existed and nurture is all. Bodies always come complete with meanings and there can be no pristine pre-linguistic wholeness to recover. Whereas Winterson's novel invents a sublime world where women can achieve some autonomy through imaginative comic reversal, Carter's is an ever-picaresque place of disguise, dodge, and complicity with no escape: a circus.

Both, however, construct plots (and grotesque bodies) which are reflexive of an endlessly transforming, deviating, non-causal, relative universe. Whereas Carter's fictions seem to call for the sort of interpretative and epistemological framework offered by psychoanalysis, however, Winterson's try to graft feminist possibility onto the sublime cosmology of the anti-materialist new physics of the eighties. It is likely, as more popular extrapolations and translations of the new science render it at least crudely available to the layperson, that there will be much more of this sort of fictional fantastic in the nineties. James Joyce recognized that relativity theory had overturned causality and changed the novel, just as Dickens, in *Bleak House* and other fictions, built his endlessly proliferating but often finally entropic plots from Darwinian notions of chance, mutation, and endless transformation. Since then, science has been drawn to an obsession with origins that are even more primal, and, though the theories of Big Bang are written in a language of theorems remote from Darwin's colourful and imaginatively metaphoric prose, their implications are beginning to resonate in the late twentieth century with something of the mythic force that evolutionary theory carried for the Victorians.

Scientists have always worked with metaphors available in the culture to attempt to communicate their discoveries. As with other areas of knowledge, in science, too, from 1960 to 1990 aesthetic metaphors were prominent. The relativity theories proposed at the beginning of the century produced a Kuhnian paradigm shift in scientists' perceptions of the physical universe. The mutually excluding properties of quantum physics proposed a reality which is entirely remote from common sense, and in which nature becomes the flickering pictures of our relation to what cannot be seen or even imagined. In the nineteen-nineties the immutable order of Newtonian physics, preserved even against the challenge of Darwinism, is finally giving way to the unpredictable and random world of quantum theory, superstrings, catastrophe, and chaos. The metaphor from aesthetics most often used to describe this new cosmos is that of the sublime. At the centre of the new physics is the conviction that there is a radical discontinuity between what can be visualized and what is theoretically possible: imaginative hypothesis and material reality are no longer opposed poles and, by extension, neither are body and mind.

Though this new universe is radically uncertain, it does offer release from the fixity of the inert physicality of the Newtonian world as from the entropic predictions of the second law of thermodynamics. Its randomness, as the chaos theorists have suggested, is one which promises new possibilities of order; unpredictable and ever open, these possibilities constitute post-modern little narratives which break up and disrupt the deterministic wheel of those grand narratives of scientific modernity. Reinstated is the centrality of imagination, creativity, and the possibility of a transformed human agency. As two well-known British mathematical physicists have announced: 'Materialism is dead.'[3] One can see the attraction here for writers interested in the projection of different orders of being; of translated, nomadic, exiled, protean, 'chutnified', transgressive, miscegenated identities; of post-colonial transitional states; or the imaginary third sex beyond gender.

Accordingly, cosmic versions of the fantastic have been prominent also in fictions by male writers, though more often expressive, particularly in the earlier half of the period, of an apocalyptic sense of ending, of disintegration, rather than sublime possibility or comic vision. Ballard's and Burgess's fictions of a purgatorial or devolutionary universe have already been mentioned. Angus Wilson's novels of the sixties and seventies always combined an element of bellicose fantasy with his professedly liberal though often defensively hierarchical social vision. *The Old Men at the Zoo* (1961), published in the first year that Britain applied for Common Market membership, might have been a prophetic denunciation of Maastricht. It combined a nostalgic Little England fear of the foreign with a vision of nuclear Armageddon as a bureaucratically muddled Britain succumbs to the military might of an armed Europe. Fantasy recurred as psychic threat also in his ambitious *No Laughing Matter* (1967), which interwove pastiche of modernist fiction, European drama, and the family sagas of Galsworthy in order to present sixty years of conflictual and declining British history. The wider analysis, however, is filtered through a satire of those manners which disguise the true violences of English middle-class family life, as husband and wife Mr and Mrs Matthews prey on each other and, savagely but nonchalantly, inflict untold psychic damage upon their offspring. Ostensibly presenting a grotesque version of Freud's tragic liberal vision of the world, the novel falls prey itself, however, to a fantastic teratogenesis of the mother who is presented at once as an over- rather than unsexed Lady Macbeth and a predatory Eagle with snapping beak who terrorizes her children.

In the eighties, however, male writers too, and not only Salman Rushdie, perceived the advantages of the fantastic for presenting dislocated worlds or politically motivated dissections of the nation. Two prominent Scottish voices, Alisdair Gray and James Kelman, drew on fantastic strategies to construct a defamiliarized vision of their native Glasgow, motivated, as the title of one of their novels suggested, by *A Disaffection* (1989). Of the two, Kelman's is closer to confessional realism, though the absence of the use of identifying quotation marks or spatial indentation weaves dramatic dialogue and the Glaswegian inner stream of consciousness of its declassed teacher-narrator into a surreal flow inextricably blurring the boundaries between inner and outer worlds. Nothing can take discrete form because anomie is the essence of all, indigenous art cannot impose meaningful identity ('these pipes have got fuck all to do with Scotland'), love fails, drink provides only temporary escape, and the readily available hooliganism which is the only politics of the young is too active and therefore too positive a statement of the nihilism summed up in the last words of the book, 'Ah fuck off, fuck off'.

Gray's *Lanark* (1981) presents a similar vision of the impoverished inertia of city life, processed through the obsessive and somatically displaced psychic life of artist *manqué* Duncan Thaw. Here though, the city is set against an even more fantastic projection of urban space which is the realm of Unthank, a purgatorial extension of Thaw's city in which the psychic afflictions of modern life take on even more bizarre physical manifestations. *Lanark* is a systematized narrative extension of the locally literalized metaphors which have become a hallmark of magic realism. Thaw's real schizoid retreat from feeling in a world which presents too much horror and squalor is somatically discharged in the virulent atopic eczema which erupts over his body and in the symbolically significant breathing disease of asthma with which he is also afflicted. Both illnesses are medically authenticated responses to the pollutions, mental and physical, of the modern world, but in Unthank dualism collapses entirely and florid corporeal change is not simply a sign of psychological distress, but a materialized sickness of the soul. Duncan's *alter ego* Lanark succumbs to the deadly condition of 'Dragon-skin' in a metamorphosis which places his monstrous being utterly beyond the reach of technologized medical science. Only sunlight could cure him, but there is no sun in the darkness visible of this modern hell.

Winterson's fantastic is far removed from these. Dog Woman too is remarkably hideous, but, partaking of the sublime, she both requires submission to and inspires awe at human potential rather than despair at its actual condition of squalor. In a world caught between the collapsing plots of religion on the one hand and materialist science on the other, pure tragic determinism or pure comic optimism tend to be fantastically suspended and the formal and ethical vacuum filled by the grotesque. It is our late modern version of the sublime, expressing that which cannot be named and which continues to confront us with the limits to our linguistic constructivism. Although this mood has flourished within the novel, it has appeared also in some of the drama of the eighties. The world which can be named and that which is beyond naming were incisively and comically brought together as Acts 1 and 2 of *Cloud Nine* (1979), Caryl Churchill's comparison of the sexual politics of the Victorian values of family life in a British colony in nineteenth-century Africa with those of the liberated sex-role play of bourgeois libertarian present-day Britain. The gay movement had gathered force in Britain in the seventies, inspired by the 1969 Stonewall rebellion in New York with its rejection of tolerance and its militant demand for equality. Churchill's play brought the new sexual politics into the theatre by setting them against a more traditional socialist feminist analysis of patriarchy, and concluding somewhat ambivalently that 'Everything is upside down when you reach cloud nine': the politics of the sublime might produce more than one variety of derangement. In her play, cross-gender and cross-race casting in the production combined with temporal dislocations in the plot, doubling of actors, and pastiche of Victorian song, in order to forestall easy stereotyping. Indeed, as Churchill has said in interview, her exploration of the new politics of sexual ambiguity prompted accusations that her work was too philosophical and aesthetic and not sufficiently political.

The play in fact set an analysis of what she calls the 'softcops' shaping imperial patriarchal identity (the 'ideological state apparatuses' of religion, family, education) in Act 1, with the confusing post-modern politics of desire in Act 2. In Act 1, a classically Freudian model of sexuality as repression is the perfect model for understanding a world where the fear of women and their identification with the Dark Continent to be kept under control is linked to a homosocial bonding which inevitably covers a homophobic fear of sexual contamination by the feminine which includes the less-than-manly man. The most enlightened character can only manage to see his homosexuality as the burden of 'a man born crippled', the disease of the invert rather than the sin of the devil. In Act 2, fantasy becomes overt, indicated through temporal dislocation as the play leaps forward one hundred years while the characters only age by twenty-five. All seems changed utterly in this brave new world: sex is a fine art endlessly and openly discussed in a realm of polymorphous sexual identities, of parodic roles to be tried on and taken off, and because there is no 'right way to do things you have to invent one'. Yet, underneath the fluidity of desire, the bending of gender, and the progressive reconstructions of identities freed from anatomical sex, women still do most of the domestic work, children still struggle with parents who cannot accept their behaviour, and orgasms continue to be faked to bolster machismo: the most fluid forms of relationality are still caught up in violent struggles for power and recognition.

Caryl Churchill's work throughout the eighties continued to be suspicious of 'cloud nine' political thinking. *Top Girls* (1983), for example, continued the sexual politics debate by showing, through the rise of the Thatcherite new woman Marlene, the ease with which the politics of equality can lead simply to imitation of the oppressor rather than the dismantlement of his values. Churchill's committed suspicions were embodied in the most innovative and vigorous drama of a decade which, however, saw the decline not only of political theatre but of new plays generally. From 1970 to 1985 new writing formed 12 per cent of all plays performed on the mainstage of London and regional repertory theatres: between 1985 and 1990 this fell to 7 per cent. Because of severe cuts in funding, many touring companies disappeared. Indeed, the only increase in theatre seemed to be in the numbers of women dramatists and with Churchill, writers such as Pam Gems, Nell Dunn, Sarah Daniels, and Timberlake Wertenbaker revitalized theatre as a medium for ideas (in an age of the musical spectacular). Their investigation of the gender indifference of the prominent socialist dramatist generation of the seventies addressed important absences in that earlier critique, just as the seventies' writers had in turn taken up and exposed the political blindnesses of the disaffected liberals and Angry Young Men of the late fifties and early sixties.

Beyond the Imperial Fiction

By the late eighties literary theorists began to turn their attention away from an obsession with trying to define the post-modern to a concern, particularly after the publication of Edward Said's book *Orientalism* (1978), with definitions of the post-colonial. Like most 'post'-conditions, this one too partly derived its identity from what preceded it: the colonial condition and the colonial novel of the sixties and seventies, the years when the British Empire was finally dismantled. The rise and fall of British imperialism in India had appeared as the focus in the seventies of a number of novels concerned with the construction of history and national identity. Paul Scott's *The Raj Quartet* repeated the Forsterian sexual image of rape at the centre of a fiction which explored imperialism as the 'unsexing of a nation' in the words of the rape victim, Daphne Manners. Lust as sex without love is approached, with seduction through deception, as forms of violation which also stand as images of colonial dominance and imperial power. The title of the book is taken from a painting which depicts an Indian prince offering a jewel to Queen Victoria against a backdrop of the map of India unfurled by Disraeli. Racial, sexual, and class prejudice conspire, as in Forster's *A Passage To India*, against the recovery of any final truth about the circumstances of the rape, and at the centre of the quartet is the insight of Emerson that 'man is explicable by nothing less than all his history'. Man, like history, is therefore finally not explicable at all.

J. G. Farrell's *The Siege of Krishnapur* (1973) also drew innovatively on established ingredients of the genre, deploying a Forsterian narrative detachment and a symbolically resonant talent for the description of place, but combining them with a self-conscious subversion of the stereotypical features of popular imperial fiction to give an account of the effects of the Indian Mutiny of 1857 on the lives of a group of British characters and particularly the Collector of Krishnapur. The Collector has recently returned in adulatory spirit from the Great Exhibition, but his Victorian optimism about scientific progress and the spread of civilization collapses after the siege, so that its rational foundations seem naïve and inadequate and its culture an ornamentation of the rich to disguise their real inner ugliness. His Eurocentric perspective has been challenged in its confrontation with the dead of Krishnapur, and it becomes overwhelmingly apparent that a civilization which had regarded everything which came before as 'a mere preparation for us' must now acknowledge that it may simply be an 'afterglow of them'. The Collector's former Arnoldian liberalism is shattered as he comes to recognize that 'a people, a nation, does not create itself according to its own best ideas, but is shaped by other forces of which it has little knowledge'. Self-conscious voyeurism on the part of the novelist suggests both a complicity with the arch-detachment of the British, but also a recognition that empires, like novels, are finally built out of what is shut out of and suppressed within the consciousness of those who build them.

In a collection of essays written in 1987, Hayden White wrote that

it is only from our knowledge of the subsequent history of Western Europe that we can presume to rank events in terms of their world-historical signifi-cance, and even that significance is less world-historical than simply West-ern European, representing a tendency of modern historians to rank events in the record hierarchically from within a perspective that is culture-specific, not universal at all.[4]

The novels of Scott and Farrell, though innovatory, remained broadly within the Eurocentric paradigm, challenging but remaining situated within the consciousness of the British characters. This tendency of earlier fictions of empire was questioned in the 1980s by the literary attention given to the problems and existence of post-colonial peoples whose histories had been subsumed by and identities forcibly generated in relation to former colonial powers. The winding-up of the British Empire accelerated after Suez in 1956 and continued steadily through the Macmillan period and into the sixties. By 1990, however, roughly two-thirds of the world was in a condition of post-coloniality, and a number of important writers from the former col-onies were born or were resident in Britain during the period 1960–90.

The title of Gray's otherworld, Unthank, sums up the condition of the post-colonial person: the need to refuse to thank the colonizer, to repudiate nation or independence as a gift bestowed by a benign sovereignty. For writers such as V. S. Naipaul or Salman Rushdie, however, that English liberal culture which is inauthentic is also the intellectual environment which had framed their sense of existential and creative identity. For writers like them, voice became a problem to be pursued through dislocated and often highly self-conscious narratives. An interesting work which looked forward to later post-colonial themes of displacement and the problem of authenticity was Jean Rhys's *Wide Sargasso Sea* (1966). The novel was originally entitled 'The Revenant' and Rhys seemed something of a revenant herself, disappearing in 1939 to return in the sixties from the 'far-off edge' to publish after years of silence a novel imbued at every level with the sense of displacement and of belonging to no world. Yet prophetically and proleptically she caught what would come to be the dominant literary concerns of the next twenty-five years: the feminist theme of the suppressed 'madwoman in the attic'; the structuralist rediscovery of 'intertextuality'; the post-modern critique of commerce, rationalism, and linearity; and the post-colonial concern with boundaries, language, translation. A White West Indian who had returned to England in 1927, she found in the repressed Victorian English spaces of *Jane Eyre* a powerful metaphor for her own sense of being an inner *émigré*. Bertha is less fleshed out than vocalized in as Antoinette, now given the necessary attributes of self-identity: her own haunting and lyrical narrative voice, a specific history (post-slave Dominica of the 1830s), and a sense of agency (the fire at Thornfield a planned act of cultural arson, a consumption by the vivid, sunlit flame-colours of the West Indies of a grey, class-ridden, and patriarchal England where it had always 'rained that day').

Antoinette, conscious from the first that 'there is always the other side', describes her garden on the island, 'the tree of life grew there', but her paradise is already lost, eaten by the genetic worm of madness and the double dispossession of being outcast from the commercially driven logic of White colonial culture but unacceptable as a Creole to the magical native one with which she feels affinity. Rochester speaks in a narrative voice whose strangulated rationality disguises his colonizer's fear of succumbing to a necromancy perceived as essentially feminine: sexual, exotic, irrational, too much heat, light, colour. Through it he controls the conflict of being torn between a fascination with uncovering and possessing what it hides in order to fill his own lack, and the fear of losing an over-defended masculine autonomy to be overwhelmed by and incorporated into what might be too dark altogether. Rhys offers another image of the rationalized male gaze confronting the threatening mystery of the female body (woman, insane, colonized). She draws intertextually on the fire and light imagery of *Jane Eyre* but extends its opposition of dutiful and altruistic rationalized Christian humanism versus passionate self-fulfilment into the post-colonial spaces of masculine–reason–commerce–colonizer opposed to feminine–emotion–slave–colonized. This interconnecting network of oppositions draws out the ambiguity of the relations of each to the other, the fears, projections, and anxieties which lock men and women as colonizer and colonized into tortured co-dependency.

If Rushdie is a writer who has explored the positive potential as well as the anxiety of being a translated man, a migrant, a master, and victim, V. S. Naipaul has been more concerned with the metaphysical legacy of colonialism as the yoking of heterogeneous cultures by violence together. For him, the post-colonial writer carries the uneasy and comically indissoluble burden of the complicitous secret sharer. If Rhys is a revenant, however, Naipaul is more of a remnant, writing out of the guilt of a first generation of West Indian writers fast being superseded by the more confident assertions of a later, second generation whose perspective arose out of the independence of the 1960s. Naipaul has been criticized by post-colonial theorists for his alignment with English liberal culture, for his assertion, for example, that everything he had ever done in relation to the Caribbean, Conrad had done first in his treatment of Africa. Even the title of his autobiographical fiction *The Enigma of Arrival* (1987) is reminiscent of the theme of Conrad's *Heart of Darkness*. In another essay, he describes his relation to writing in terms which again, and as a variety of 'talking cure', echo Marlow's justification for his narrative to the seafaring audience in the gloom upon the Thames: 'to become a writer, that noble thing, I had thought it necessary to leave. Actually to write, it was necessary to go back. It was the beginning of self-knowledge.'[5]

Naipaul was born in Trinidad to East Indian parents and began to explore the cultural splitting and longing for home which afflicts the eponymous hero of his third novel *A House For Mr Biswas* (1961) who, literally born the wrong way round, cannot therefore inherit his parents' Hindu culture but feels equally excluded from that of the Caribbean. The potential for violence as well as for myth-making in this situation was given fiercest expression in *Guerrillas* (1975), which intertextually invoked another Brontë novel, *Wuthering Heights* (the name which Jimmy Ahmed gives to his commune), in a fictionalized exploration of the activities of the Trinidadian Black Power leader Michael X, who was executed in the year of its publication. Although neither he nor Trinidad is actually named in the novel, many reviewers treated it as a documentary account, and Naipaul actually wrote an essay on the killings in Trinidad for the *Sunday Times* (1980). He saw the undirected anger of its peoples in the sixties as the perfect ingredient from which the volatile Michael X (Jimmy Ahmed in the novel) could narcissistically concoct his myth of dispossessed tribal hero and charismatic political leader. Indeed, Naipaul's novel is another text which displaces its author's own self-conscious anxiety about fictional exploitation into a self-reflexive concern with the relations between history, fiction, and myth, and their connection with power and sexuality.

In the struggle for power, myths are lethal weapons. Jimmy Ahmed, fashioning himself in the terms of an outcast Heathcliff, tries to turn history into a romantic autobiography which, like that of Emily Brontë's character, involves the violation of a White middle-class Englishwoman (sexually and then homicidally) who is herself in the grip of a decadent sexual fantasy about the mysterious otherness of the native male body. Historical action throughout is premissed on narcissistic fantasy: there are no real guerrillas as such except as a metaphor for the psychological state which possesses every character in the novel. The murder of Jane occurs when she is exchanged as a gift to propitiate the fury of the slum-boy Bryant with whom Jimmy has a homosexual relationship. Indeed, the revolutionary commitment to economic redistribution which is signified by the existence of the commune breaks down repeatedly into the corrupt circulation of sexual favours. As in most forms of sexual abuse, each of the abused becomes in turn the abuser of another. Ironically, it is Bryant, the stunted psychopathic slave at the bottom of the pile who causes the death of Jane, the insouciant and affluent Englishwoman behind whom 'lay the certainties, of class and money'. Such certainties produce a brutal and egotistic blindness to the impotent desperation around her. Thus blind, however, she is also vulnerable, and her decadent fantasies of sexual kicks are subsumed by the more terminal fantasies in the rage of the impotent which she has failed even to notice. The metaphor of rape so often used to convey the act of colonial possession becomes a controlling symbol for the pervasive psychological corruption induced in all colonial societies: in colonizer, colonized, and in the writer who is caught between them.

Each of the three principal characters is caught in a narcissistic psychological fantasy of identity which dangerously mythicizes history. Even the liberal, Roche, is confronted in the radio interview with his corruption of politics into an 'art for art's sake' pursuit of random and indiscriminately chosen radical and political causes simply because they are radical and a convenient hook therefore on which to hang the frustrated and narcissistic idealisms of his own ineffectual life. Although post-colonial in its focus, the underlying themes of *Guerrillas* are those which we have seen in so many of the liberal novels of the seventies: the dangerous implications of grafting fictions onto history; the buried psychosexual motivations for political action and, in particular, terrorism (as in Lessing's *The Good Terrorist* and Muriel Spark's *The Only Problem*); the proliferation of violence; and the entropic state of liberal culture. By the eighties, as revealed in the work of Salman Rushdie, such self-conscious anxieties in turn become the focus of self-conscious parody: self-exile must itself be exiled in order to pave the way for a new, fluid world, as the boundaries of the present dissolve into the spaces of many possible fictional futures. Ironically, of course, one of these would be a violent containment of Rushdie himself by what would appear, from a liberal perspective, to be forces of reaction and retrogression. The event lent a sobering historical gloss to the exuberance of his post-modern aesthetic sublime, and suggests one reason, at least, for the need to situate English literature in its 'Backgrounds':

Outsider! Trespasser! You have no right to this subject! . . . I know: nobody ever arrested me. Nor are they ever likely to. *Poacher! Pirate! We reject your authority. We know you, with your foreign language wrapped around you like a flag: speaking about us in your forked tongue, what can you tell but lies?* I reply with more questions: is history to be considered the property of the participants solely? In what courts are such claims staked, what boundary commissions map out the territories? (*Shame*)

No doubt after 1990, and as Europe breaks into new disruption and reformulation, the claims, boundaries, and territories of the map of both literature and its backgrounds will change once again.

CONCLUSION
CULTURAL DEMOCRACY OR THE
DEMOCRATIZATION OF CULTURE

> Only when difference has its home, when the need for belong-
> ing in all its murderous intensity has been assuaged, can our
> common identity begin to find its voice.
>
> (Michael Ignatieff, *The Needs of Strangers*)

The cultural ideal of welfare capitalism until 1976 was broadly one
of cultural democracy: the maintenance of a common culture through
education, good literature, and state subsidies for the Arts. Throughout the eighties, however, there was a steady shift of emphasis toward the rather differently inflected concept of a democratization
of culture: the emergence of a plurality of voices, the embrace or
acceptance of irreconcilable difference, the acknowledgement of a
multiplicity of cultures or subcultures each with its own orders of
value and social and aesthetic norms. Throughout the sixties, on
both the right and the left, there was still a strong commitment to the
goal of a common culture and the assumption that literature was a
'common pursuit' (the phrase taken by F. R. Leavis from T. S.
Eliot's earlier essay 'The Function of Criticism'). In 1958, in an
essay entitled 'Culture is Ordinary', Raymond Williams had criticized
the selectivity of the cultural tradition espoused by Eliot and Leavis
and dismissed out of hand Clive Bell's notion of civilization, referring
to it as 'this extraordinary fussiness, this extraordinary decision to
call certain things culture and then separate them, as with a park
wall, from ordinary people and ordinary work'. Williams repeatedly
asserted that culture is ordinary, that 'the making of a society is the
finding of common meanings and directions, and its growth is an
active debate and amendment under the pressures of experience,
contact, and discovery, writing themselves into the land'. Culture is

shared but subjectively experienced and 'remade in every individual mind'. Three years later, in *The Long Revolution* (1961), he argued that literature, like all art, is a 'very powerful means of sharing', for 'through the art the society expresses its sense of being a society . . . even in our own complex society, certain artists seem near the centre of the common experience'.[1]

From the late sixties, however, we have seen how the forces of culture tended to become centrifugal rather than centripetal. Proliferation of cultures rather than homogeneity of culture was to be the condition of the future. The last two chapters have indicated the gradual emergence of a range of new literary voices highly self-conscious of their dislocated or oblique relation to the previous cultural consensus. Even in the early sixties, however, it was clear that the old consensus was coming under strain for a variety of reasons: the rise of popular music subcultures with varying ethnic roots including folk and a continuing diverse jazz culture; the flowering of 'pop poetry', such as the Mersey Sound and the Children of Albion, with links to the counterculture; the expansion of higher education and growing student demands for relevance in literary criticism coinciding with a decline of gentlemanly belletrism and the rise of criticism as a newly professionalized university discipline; the appropriation of consumer images in pop art; developments in television and popular satire. These are just a few of the artistic and intellectual developments of the decade which contributed their challenge to earlier conceptualizations of a common culture. By the seventies it was evident too that economic divisions were not the only barriers to a common culture and that other distinctions of race, gender, ethnicity, age, and region would be articulated forcibly in the eighties, bringing with them the recognition that identity is not determined through labour alone.

Such recognitions produced something of a crisis in the teaching and study of literature, for, in the new world of multicultural difference, to insist on the superiority of one variety of culture was to invite accusations of élitism, ethnocentricity, sexism, racism, or class authoritarianism. Hence the 'explosion' of English, as its study was no longer pursued within a frame of cultural democracy grounded in the consensual acceptance of shared aesthetic value, but was caught up in the kaleidoscopic frames of intersecting networks of cultural as well as social change: technological changes giving rise to new media art forms, political changes stimulating new national and post-colonial literatures, and economic shifts which reflected the decline of Britain as an imperial and even world-industrial power and the rising influence of a new global Americanized media culture. Though committed to a common culture, the post-war consensus had actually facilitated the emergence of a diasporic plurality of subcultures which would fragment from within its fragile compromises. Increasingly after the mid-seventies, the concept of representative democracy was to come under strain as more and more social groups claimed the right to speak for themselves, within their own terms and with their own distinctive voices. The idea that 'great literature' is great because it speaks for all would be attacked from a variety of new positions. As the enterprise culture of the eighties further encouraged an ethos of individualism, so traditional collective cultures of dissent associated with both the middle and the working classes would find their boundaries challenged and their rhetoric requiring renewal.

By the nineties it seemed to a number of observers that Britain was entering an unprecedented crisis in the legitimation of traditional cultural values and of its constitutional liberal democracy. The 'post'-mood deepened, for if the sixties saw the end of empire and the seventies that of the post-war welfare consensus, the nineteen-eighties seemed to bring to a close a range of theoretical models and institutions which had formed the backbone of an earlier modernity: Fordism, industrialism, Marxism, Keynesianism, state communism. Belatedness stalked through the times, and in much imaginative writing futuristic or fantastic impulses were set against an equally powerful nostalgia or anxiety of influence, often held in tension by a tone of ironic or parodistic self-consciousness. We have seen that some writers espoused a gradualist vision which saw the last thirty years bringing to fruition trends apparent throughout the twentieth century (the late modernists), while other more apocalyptic thinkers saw the period arriving at the edge of a radically new age (the post-modernists).

It is difficult to evaluate the claims of each side except perhaps to say that the desire for holistic judgement belongs with the tradition of the former, and the assertion of its impossibility or undesirability with the latter. Throughout this book I have tried to maintain a (healthy?) rational scepticism and a rather more post-modern perspectivism: I would suggest it might be wise simply to view the period, culturally at least, as caught somewhere between these two poles. In literature, the apocalypticism of the radical-break view of contemporaneity was evident as early as 1962 in the preface to Alvarez's *The New Poetry*. Almost immediately, however, it was repudiated as arrogant sensationalism in Robert Conquest's temperate preface to his second *New Lines* anthology of 1963. Conquest's preference was for the (Yvor Winters's style) commitment to literature as a rational judgement of broadly universal experience. Indeed, Conquest was not the only writer to express the view that

it seems both egotistical and insensitive to proclaim that the circumstances of modern life are so different from any thing that has gone before that they open up hitherto unsuspected psychological depths to be exploited, or expose entirely new methods and attitudes, beyond such variation and novelty as have come in generation and generation in the past.

Equally pervasive, however, was the mood expressed by Doris Lessing's Anna in *The Golden Notebook* of 1962: 'I don't want to be told when I wake up, terrified by a dream of total annihilation, because of the H-bomb exploding, that people felt that way about the cross-bow. It isn't true. There is something new in the world.'

Writers continued to argue both sides of the case throughout the period and, as with everything else, rhetorical self-consciousness became part of the equation. Was there something new or was the real change actually in the rhetorical and generic conventions themselves, so that the discourses of apocalypse seemed more seductive than those of rational progress? Just as cosmologists preferred to talk about the intelligible as opposed to the real universe, literary theorists such as Roland Barthes began to talk about history in the same terms. History as much as culture was opened to negotiation: viewed as a network of stories through which experience is formulated and understood. The history teacher of Graham Swift's novel *Waterland* (1983) explained to a sceptical student,

All right, so it's all a struggle to preserve an artifice. It's all a struggle to make things not seem meaningless. It's all a fight against fear. . . . I don't care what you call it—explaining, evading the facts, making up meanings, taking a larger view, putting things into perspective, dodging the here and now, education, history, fairy-tales—it helps to eliminate fear.

Fear is eliminated through the reclamation of experience: what is it to write if not to reclaim history? C. S. Lewis once said that 'literature heals the wound, without undermining the privilege, of individuality'. Perhaps more than anything else, the literature of our time serves to remind us of the nature and fact of such privilege.

Throughout 1960–90 different groups and individuals seized on the metaphor of reclamation to describe their own cultural and social struggles. The ensuing fragmentation of culture may be viewed as a positive extension of the vocabularies of liberal democracy: as the release of opportunities for the negotiation of new identity scripts and the construction of new selves in a more genuinely democratic, if more separatist, culture. But less optimistic interpretations are also available. If the underlying economic divisions and organization of political power are regarded as unchanged, then it may seem appropriate to hold a rather more sceptical attitude toward the capacity of aesthetic or post-modern language games to undo authoritarian state politics or gross economic inequalities. Salman Rushdie's *Shame* (1984), though post-modern in form, had painted such a pessimistic, Nietzschean reading of Darwin in its portrayal of the relations between knowledge and power in the construction of the narratives of history:

History is natural selection. Mutant versions of the past struggle for dominance; new species of fact arise, and old, saurian truths go to the wall, blindfolded and smoking last cigarettes. Only the mutations of the strong survive. The weak, the anonymous, the defeated leave few marks . . . history loves only those who dominate her; it is a relationship of mutual enslavement.

Whether or not Rushdie is right, it is evident in retrospect that the most distinctive feature of the period 1960–90 was an intensification of cultural pluralization even as politics itself seemed to become more monologically authoritarian. In 1971, in an essay which engaged with the dilemmas of the 'novelist at the crossroads' and well before the era of multiculturalism, David Lodge noted that 'we seem, indeed, to be living through a period of unprecedented cultural pluralism which allows, in all the arts, an astonishing variety of styles to flourish simultaneously'.[2] By 1990 writers were often less sanguine about this state of affairs, convinced either that such pluralization was only apparent, operating within the framework of a silently repressive state authority, or that it was real but had thus fragmented effective and concerted opposition to the authoritarian state, or (and most pessimistic of all) that it was simply another facet of that stimulation of incessant desire for the new integral to consumer capitalism.

Literature has continued, however, to be defended as a vital ingredient in a democratic culture, requiring a readerly relation of imaginative identification with otherness which is the basis of human sympathy and responsible citizenship. Within this perspective, to recognize that the foundations of liberal democracy have been radically challenged and are in the process of being energetically extended does not entail that the edifice built upon them must one day inevitably collapse. Literature is seen to be part of the process of challenge and extension, for it can supply an important corrective to the increasing tendency of Western liberal cultures to be blind to the necessity for establishing an ethical foundation for politics which defines needs and conceives of equality in more than purely material terms. Perhaps this is the most valuable lesson to be learnt from studying English Literature, with its backgrounds, at this particular historical moment.

NOTES

Chapter 1

1. W. H. Auden, in *Encounter*, 12 (Apr. 1959), 139.
2. Arnold Wesker, quoted in Charles Marowitz and Simon Trussler (eds.), *Theatre at Work* (London, 1967), 88.
3. Anthony Sampson, *The Essential Anatomy of Britain: Democracy in Crisis* (London, 1992), 11.
4. Tom Nairn, *The Break-Up of Britain* (London, 1977).
5. Sam Beer, *Britain against Itself: The Political Contradictions of Collectivism* (London, 1982), 139.
6. Margaret Thatcher, quoted in *The Times*, 19 Jan. 1985.
7. Margaret Thatcher, quoted in the *Guardian*, 28 Mar. 1982.

Chapter 2

1. Lionel Trilling, 'On the Teaching of Modern Literature', in *Beyond Culture* (Harmondsworth, 1967), 19.
2. Marshall Berman, 'Sympathy for the Devil: Faust, the '60s, and the Tragedy of Development', in *American Review*, 19 (1974).
3. D. H. Lawrence, 'Morality and the Novel', *Calendar of Modern Letters* (Dec. 1925).
4. Betty Friedan, *The Feminine Mystique* (New York, 1962).
5. Robert Hewison, *Too Much: Art and Society in the Sixties 1960–1975* (London, 1988), 26.
6. Anthony Sampson, *Essential Anatomy of Britain*, 16, 154.
7. Robert Conquest, *New Lines* (London, 1956), 215.
8. Andy Warhol, in *Encounter*, 12 (Apr. 1959), 52.
9. P. L. Berger and T. Luckmann, *The Social Construction of Reality* (Harmondsworth, 1971); Hayden White, *Metahistory* (Baltimore, 1973); Erving Goffman, *The Presentation of Self in Everyday Life* (Harmondsworth, 1969).
10. Quoted in Alan Sinfield, *Literature, Politics and Culture in Post-War Britain* (Oxford, 1989), 269.
11. John Berger, *Ways of Seeing* (Harmondsworth, 1972), 146.
12. F. R. Leavis, *Nor Shall My Sword* (London, 1972).

13. Fred Inglis, *Radical Earnestness: English Social Theory 1880–1980* (Oxford, 1982), 21.
14. Richard Hoggart, quoted in C. H. Rolph (ed.), *The Trial of Lady Chatterley* (Harmondsworth, 1990), 100.
15. Martin Kettle, in the *Guardian*, 3 (Apr. 1993), 25.
16. Tzvetan Todorov, *The Fantastic: A Structural Approach to a Literary Genre*, trans. Richard Howard (Cleveland, 1973), 168.
17. Salman Rushdie, *Imaginary Homelands* (London, 1991), 394.
18. C. S. Lewis, *An Experiment in Criticism* (London, 1961), 85.
19. John Osborne, in *The Times*, 14 Oct. 1967.
20. E. P. Thompson, *Writing by Candlelight* (London, 1980), 248.

Chapter 3

1. Christopher Booker, *The Neophiliacs* (London, 1969), 304.
2. W. H. Auden, *The Dyer's Hand* (London, 1963), 85.
3. Ted Hughes, interviewed in *London Magazine* (Jan. 1971).
4. John Crowe Ransome, 'Criticism Inc.', in *The World's Body* (New York, 1938).
5. Peter Fuller, in Boris Ford (ed.), *The Cambridge Cultural History: Modern Britain* (Cambridge, 1988), 141.
6. John Robinson, *Honest to God* (London, 1963), 52.
7. D. Riesman, *The Lonely Crowd* (New Haven, Conn., 1961).
8. Iris Murdoch, *Metaphysics as a Guide to Morals* (London, 1992), 21.
9. Harold Pinter, in *Paris Review Interviews* (Harmondsworth, 1972), 312–13.
10. Walter Benjamin, *Reflections* (New York, 1986), 209–10.
11. Iris Murdoch, 'The Sublime and the Beautiful Revisited', *Yale Review*, 49 (1959), 271.
12. Ead., *Metaphysics as a Guide to Morals*, 506.
13. Ead., interviewed in Heide Zeigler and Christopher Bigsby (eds.), *The Radical Imagination and the Liberal Tradition* (London, 1982), 229.
14. Ead., *Metaphysics as a Guide to Morals*, 97.
15. Harold Pinter, in *Sunday Times*, 3 Mar. 1962.
16. Edward Bond, quoted in Simon Trussler (ed.), *New Theatre Voices of the Seventies* (London, 1981), 31.
17. Id., *A Companion to the Plays of Edward Bond* (London, 1978), 22.
18. Ted Hughes, in Keith Sagar (ed.), *The Achievement of Ted Hughes* (Athens, Ga., 1983), 36.
19. Octavio Paz, *The Other Voice: Poetry and the Fin-De-Siecle* (Manchester, 1992), 151.

20. Anthony Burgess, interviewed in Rosemary Harthill (ed.), *Writers Revealed* (London, 1989), 17.
21. Geoffrey Hill, in John Haffenden (ed.), *Viewpoints* (London, 1981), 89.

Chapter 4

1. Mercia Eliade, *The Myth of the Eternal Return*, trans. Willard R. Trask (New York, 1965).
2. The Tynan–Ionesco debate is discussed in Martin Esslin's *The Theatre of the Absurd* (London, 1962).
3. George Steiner, *Language and Silence* (Harmondsworth, 1967), 15.
4. Antonin Artaud, *The Theatre and its Double*, trans. Victor Corti (London, 1970), 7.
5. Muriel Spark, 'My Conversion', *Twentieth Century*, 170 (autumn 1961), 63.
6. E. P. Thompson, *The Poverty of Theory* (London, 1978), 47.
7. Quoted in Michael Schmidt and Grevel Lindop, *British Poetry since 1960: A Survey* (Oxford, 1972), p. ix.
8. Theodor Roszak, *The Making of a Counter Culture* (London, 1970), 77–8.
9. Jan Kott, *Shakespeare our Contemporary* (New York, 1965).
10. Tony Harrison, interview with John Haffenden, in *Bloodaxe Critical Anthologies*, 1. *Tony Harrison*, (Newcastle, 1991), 232.
11. Ibid. 231.
12. Karl Popper, *The Logic of Scientific Discovery* (London, 1968), 111.
13. B. S. Johnson, *Aren't You Rather Young to be Writing your Memoirs?* (London, 1973).
14. Paul Feyerabend, *Against Method* (London, 1975), 27, 307.
15. Doris Lessing, *New Statesman*, 1 Dec. 1961, pp. 822–4.
16. Ead., 'The Small Personal Voice', in Tom Maschler (ed.), *Declaration* (London, 1957), 24.
17. A. Alvarez, *The New Poetry* (Harmondsworth, 1962), 26.
18. Jonathan Raban, *Soft City* (London, 1974), 10.
19. Sigmund Freud, 'Hysterical Phantasies and their Relation to Bisexuality', *Standard Edition*, ix. (London, 1957), 146.

Chapter 5

1. Enoch Powell, *Freedom and Reality* (London, 1969), 245.
2. George Orwell, 'England Your England', repr. in Frank Kermode *et al.* (eds.), *The Oxford Anthology of English Literature*, ii. (Oxford, 1973).

3. Edward Said, 'Opponents, Audiences, Constituencies and Community', in Hal Foster (ed.), *Postmodern Culture* (London, 1985), 135–59.

4. See my *Practising Postmodernism/Reading Modernism* (London, 1992) for a full discussion of post-modernism, including its relations to Romanticism.

5. Trevor Griffiths, in *Plays and Players*, 19/7 (Apr. 1972).

6. See E. Soja, *Postmodern Geographies: The Reassertion of Space in Critical Social Theory* (London, 1988); David Harvey, *Consciousness and the Urban Experience* (Oxford, 1985) and *The Condition of Postmodernity* (London, 1989).

7. Daniel Bell, 'The World and the United States in 2013', *Daedalus*, 116/3 (1987), 14.

8. Seamus Heaney, 'Englands of the Mind' (1976 lecture), in *Preoccupations* (London, 1984), 150–1.

9. See id. 'Feeling into Words' (1974 lecture), in *Preoccupations*, 41–60.

10. Howard Brenton, *Theatre Quarterly*, 5/17 (1975), 10.

11. Id., in *Plays and Players*, 19/5 (Feb. 1972).

12. Id., quoted in Catherine Itzin, *Stages in the Revolution* (London, 1980), 198.

13. David Hare, 'On Political Theatre', repr. in introd. to *The Early Plays* (London, 1992), 5.

14. Id., 'A Lecture given at King's College, Cambridge' (1978), in *Licking Hitler* (London, 1978).

15. David Edgar, in *Theatre Quarterly*, 9/33 (1979).

Chapter 6

1. Quoted in John Haffenden, *Novelists in Interview* (London, 1985), 73.

2. Michel Foucault, *The Order of Things* (London, 1970), p. xviii.

3. Paul Davies and John Gibbon, *The Matter Myth* (London, 1991), 7.

4. Hayden White, *The Content of the Form: Narrative Discourse and Historical Representation* (Baltimore, 1987), 9–10.

5. V. S. Naipaul, *Finding the Centre* (Harmondsworth, 1985), 40.

Conclusion

1. Raymond Williams, 'Culture is Ordinary', repr. in *Resources of Hope* (London, 1989); id., *The Long Revolution* (Harmondsworth, 1961), 40, 47.

2. David Lodge, 'The Novelist at the Crossroads', in Malcolm Bradbury (ed.), *The Novel Today: Contemporary Writers on Modern Fiction* (London, 1977), 100.

APPENDIX

The list below suggests some of the reasons why 1976 may be regarded as a watershed in the period 1960–90. It was the point at which a number of shifts occurred across a range of political, cultural, social, and intellectual movements and formations, so that the broad culture of consensus increasingly begins to give way to one of dissensus.

Consensus: 1960–1976

Official Political Culture
   welfare capitalism and Keynesian corporate planning
   political consensus
   Fordist industrial production economy
   Arnoldian cultural ideals
   growing influence of American political and mass media culture

Alternative Cultures
   New Left
   counterculture, hippies, and anti-psychiatry
   Rastafarianism and popular music subcultures
   emphasis on essentialist liberation, art, spirit
   critique of rationalization and scientific method
   belief in spaces outside commercial and consumer capital which promise
      unity and integration through aesthetic experience

Literary Cultures
   commitment to the ideal of a 'common culture'
   fears of the exhaustion of liberalism in debates on the novel
   location of value in the sphere of personal relations
   New Criticism stimulates renewed interest in modernism
   idealism tempered by self-conscious irony
   critique of rationalism
   interest in violence and Apocalypse
   emergence of voices of difference: class, gender, race
   Lady Chatterley trial confirms literary consensus

Dissensus: 1976–1990

Official Political Culture

end of consensus and rise of acquisitive individualism

enterprise culture and monetarist economics

authoritarian populism

post-Fordism and shift toward service economy

publicity and increased power of the commercial press

strong influence of America on popular culture

'heritage' culture

new European orientation in international politics.

Alternative Cultures

abandonment of countercultural idealism

theorizations of cultural complicity and post-modernism

nihilistic subcultures such as punk

parody and pastiche

'new times' socialism modifies labour–capital economism

environmentalism continues but appropriated by the right

emergence of 'identity politics'

Literary Cultures

loss of faith in untainted space for art or belief

art unavoidably complicit with official cultures

anti-foundationalism and post-modernism

anti-essentialism and social constructivism

increasingly commercially driven literary culture

rift between academic criticism and the literary marketplace English explodes

controversy over the constitution of the National Curriculum

crisis of value and consensual aesthetics

powerful new 'voices' of gender and post-colonialism

growth of cultural studies

challenge to distinctions between 'mass' and 'high' culture

fantasy, parody, self-consciousness, and the grotesque

Arts Council rhetoric of 'good culture' tempered by arguments for 'leisure funding'

deregulation of the media

publishing takeovers and disappearance of small presses

'theory' revolution in the academy

Salman Rushdie affair suggests end of literary consensus

CHRONOLOGY

1960   John F. Kennedy elected US president. *Lady Chatterley* trial. Daniel Bell introduces the term 'post-industrialization' to describe the economic trends of the West, *New Left Review* launched. Peter Hall becomes director of the Shakespeare Festival Theatre; R. D. Laing publishes *The Divided Self*.

       Pinter's *The Caretaker* performed; Ted Hughes, *Lupercal*; David Storey, *This Sporting Life*; Stan Barstow, *A Kind of Loving*; Kingsley Amis, *Take A Girl Like You*; Sylvia Plath's first volume of poetry *Colossus* published; Charles Tomlinson, *Seeing is Believing*.

1961   Government announces bid to join Common Market. Russia launches first man into space. Bertrand Russell's Committee of 100 begins demonstrations against nuclear weapons. First exhibition of pop art at the 'Young Contemporaries' exhibition. Spate of 'What's Wrong With Britain' publications. The new political satire launched with the revue 'Beyond the Fringe'; RSC is founded under Peter Hall's direction. Raymond Williams publishes *The Long Revolution*; C. S. Lewis, *An Experiment in Criticism*; George Steiner, *The Death of Tragedy*; Simone de Beauvoir's *The Second Sex* published in Britain.

       Evelyn Waugh, *Unconditional Surrender*; Shelagh Delaney's *A Taste of Honey* performed; Richard Hughes, *The Fox in the Attic*; Angus Wilson, *The Old Men at the Zoo*; V. S. Naipaul, *A House For Mr Biswas*; Beckett's *Happy Days* performed at the Royal Court; Muriel Spark, *The Comforters*; John Osborne, *Luther*; Thom Gunn *My Sad Captains*; Iris Murdoch, *A Severed Head*.

1962   Cuban Missile crisis, Commonwealth Immigration Bill, Pilkington Committee on the future of television. First James Bond cinematic extravaganza *Dr No* and surge of interest in spy thrillers related to the Cold War; New Wave cinema shown in Britain: Resnais, Truffaut, Antonioni; Thomas Kuhn, *The Structure of Scientific Revolutions,*

       Burgess, *A Clockwork Orange*; Edward Upward, *In the Thirties*; Alvarez, *The New Poetry*; J. G. Ballard, *The Drowned World*; Doris Lessing, *The Golden Notebook*.

1963   Kennedy assassinated, crisis in Vietnam erupts, Profumo scandal, Philby identified as the 'third man' in the Burgess and Maclean affair of 1951, Robbins report on the expansion of higher education, the Beatles first hugely successful year and pop takes off, *Encounter* issue *Suicide of a Nation?* (ed. Arthur Koestler), Mary Whitehouse begins her 'Clean up Television' campaign, GB refused entry into the Common Market. John Robinson's controversial *Honest to God*; National Theatre opens at the Old Vic; 'Dark cinema': Orson Welles, *The Trial*; Pinter-scripted *The Servant*; E. P. Thompson, *The Making of the English Working Class*; Michael Horovitz, *Declaration*; W. H. Auden, *The Dyer's Hand*.

   Robert Conquest, *New Lines 2*; Spark, *The Girls of Slender Means*; Fowles, *The Collector*; B. S. Johnson, *Travelling People*; Philip Hobsbawm and Edward Lucie-Smith, *A Group Anthology*; Nell Dunn, *Up the Junction*; David Storey, *Radcliffe*; Margaret Drabble, *A Summer Birdcage*.

1964   Harold Wilson takes office as PM, President Johnson sworn in, death of Winston Churchill, Libraries and Museums Act, Centre for Cultural Studies opens at Birmingham University. Swinging London emerges; huge success of David Hockney in New York exhibition; Margot Fonteyn takes 89 curtain calls; the Beatles are the first pop group to play at the Carnegie Hall and the *New Statesman* leads with 'The Menace of Beatlism'; Denys Thompson, *Discrimination and Popular Culture*; Theatre of Cruelty season at the RSC.

   Larkin, *The Whitsun Weddings*; B. S. Johnson, *Albert Angelo*; Golding, *The Spire*; Peter Brook directs Weiss's *Marat/Sade* play; Peter Schaffer, *The Royal Hunt of the Sun*; John Osborne's *Inadmissable Evidence* at the Royal Court; Orton, *Entertaining Mr Sloane*.

1965   USA bombs Vietnam and the war escalates, the Rhodesian crisis and UDI declared; India and Pakistan at war, the 'Cultural Revolution' begins in China. Capital punishment abolished in Britain, Jennie Lee appointed as the first Minister for the Arts and the Government publishes 'A Policy for the Arts'. CAST formed: first agitprop theatre group, the People Show and others follow; Albert Hall poetry reading: The Children of Albion; Jan Kott's *Shakespeare our Contemporary* influences theatrical approaches to Shakespeare.

   Sylvia Plath, *Ariel* and *Collected Poems* published posthumously; Bradbury, *Stepping Westward*; Pinter, *The Homecoming*; Bond, *Saved*; Basil Bunting, *Briggflatts*; Fowles, *The Aristos*; Lodge, *The British Museum is Falling Down*; Drabble, *The Millstone*.

1966   Financial crisis; *Cathy Come Home* televised by the BBC; Juliet
Mitchell's 'Women: the Longest Revolution' appears in *New Left
Review* and suggests first glimmerings of the second wave of the
Women's Movement. Susan Sontag, *Against Interpretation*.

Orton, *Loot*; Fowles, *The Magus*; Seamus Heaney, *Death of a
Naturalist*; B. S. Johnson, *Trawl*; Graham Greene, *The Comedians*;
Paul Scott, *The Jewel in the Crown*.

1967   Legalization of abortion and homosexuality, Enoch Powell's 'Rivers
of Blood' speech, reconstruction of the Arts Council as a politically
independent body, failure of attempt of industrial-relation reform
proposals 'In Place of Strife'. Underground magazine *Oz* launched;
'The Dialectics of Liberation' conference in the Round House; New
Left Mayday Manifesto; George Steiner, *Language and Silence*.

Stoppard, *Rosencrantz and Guildenstern are Dead*; Hughes,
Wodwo; Gunn, *Touch*; Angus Wilson, *No Laughing Matter*; Jean
Rhys, *Wide Sargasso Sea*; Andrew Sinclair, *Gog*; Orton, *The Ruffian
on the Stair* and *The Erpingham Camp* at The Royal Court.

1968   Robert Kennedy and Martin Luther King assassinated; Soviet invasion of Czechoslovakia; student demonstrations across Western
Europe; the Six Day War in Israel; beginning of Vietnam peace
talks; papal encyclical letter on birth control *Humanae Vitae*. Theatre
censorship abolished and emergence of many new fringe groups;
collapse of Ronan Point and planning crisis; Peter Brook, *The Empty
Space*; Lindsay Anderson's film *If*.

A. S. Byatt, *The Game*; Kingsley Amis, *I Want it Now*; Spark, *The
Driver's Seat*; Osborne, *Time Present* and *Hotel in Amsterdam*;
Geoffrey Hill, *King Log*.

1969   British troops sent into Northern Ireland; Stonewall rebellion for gay
rights in New York; Open University conceived; Divorce Reform
Act linked to Matrimonial Property Act. Edward Bond season at the
Royal Court.

Fowles, *The French Lieutenant's Woman*; Orton, *What the Butler
Saw*; Lessing, *The Four-Gated City*; Heaney, *Door into the Dark*;
Drabble, *The Waterfall*; B. S. Johnson, *The Unfortunates*; Horovitz
(ed.), *Children of Albion: Poets of the Underground in Britain*; Peter
Nicholls, *The National Health*; Bond, *Narrow Road to the Deep
North* opens; Douglas Dunn, *Terry Street*; Tomlinson, *The Way of a
World*.

1970   Conservatives returned under Heath in General Election; Radio Three constituted; plans finalized for Milton Keynes, the last of the new towns; Equal Pay and Sexual Discrimination papers leading to 1975 Acts are published. Roszak's *The Making of a Counter Culture* published in Britain; Jeff Nutall, *Bomb Culture*; Germaine Greer, *The Female Eunuch*; Foucault, *The Order of Things* translated; Brook, *A Midsummer Night's Dream* opens at Stratford; *Oh! Calcutta!* devised by Kenneth Tynan.

   Hughes, *Crow*; Murdoch, *A Fairly Honourable Defeat*; David Mercer, *After Haggerty*; Howard Brenton, *Cheek* and *Fruit* performed; David Hare, *Slag*; David Storey, *Home* and *The Contractor* at the Royal Court; David Lodge, *Out of the Shelter*.

1971   Internment without trial in Northern Ireland; Industrial Relations Bill to curb unofficial strikes; Open University goes into operation; Britain withdraws east of Suez; curbs on immigration begin. Alvarez, *The Savage God*.

   Spark, *Not to Disturb*; Gunn, *Moly*; B. S. Johnson, *House Mother Normal*; Osborne, *West of Suez*; Burgess, *MF*; Lessing, *Briefing for a Descent into Hell*; Simon Grey, *Butley*; *Lay-By* by Hare *et al.* performed; David Caute, *The Occupation*; Piers Paul Read, *The Professor's Daughter*; Pinter, *Old Times*.

1972   Heath announces direct rule in Northern Ireland and abolishes Stormont; school-leaving age raised to 16; miners win victory in strike. Hull Truck and 7 : 84 theatre groups form; John Berger responds to Kenneth Clark's conservative *Civilisation* with his Marxist *Ways of Seeing*; F. R. Leavis's embattled *Nor Shall My Sword*.

   Stoppard, *Jumpers*; John Berger, *G*; Heaney, *Wintering Out*; Elizabeth Jennings, *Relationships*; Angela Carter, *The Infernal Desire Machines of Doctor Hoffmann*; Storey, *Passmore*; Bond, *Lear*; Charles Wood, *Veterans*; Charles Tomlinson, *Written on Water*.

1973   Watergate erupted in USA, Franco resigned, oil crisis, world recession; inflation at 23 per cent, the three-day week, GB joins EEC.

   Murdoch, *The Black Prince*; B. S. Johnson, *Christy Malry's Own Double-Entry*; Martin Amis, *The Rachael Papers*; Greene, *The Honorary Consul*; Lessing, *The Summer Before the Dark*; Spark, *The Hothouse By the East River*; J. G. Farrell, *The Siege of Krishnapur*; Ballard, *Crash*; Schaffer's *Equus* at the National Theatre; Trevor Griffiths, *The Party*; Pinter, *Landscape and Silence*; Bond, *The Sea* at the Royal Court; Christopher Hampton, *Savages*; Brenton, *Magnificence*; Bennett, *Habeas Corpus*; Hare, *Brassneck*.

1974   IMF crisis continues, President Nixon resigns, Greek junta resign, Labour victory in election and Wilson returns as PM after Heath calls state of emergency, record trade deficit and inflation, Welsh and Scottish devolution enters the political agenda.

Larkin, *High Windows*; Stoppard, *Travesties*; Bond, *Bingo*; Lessing, *Memoirs of a Survivor*; Hare, *Knuckle*; Brenton, *The Churchill Play*; Ballard, *Concrete Island*; Burgess, *The Napoleon Symphony*; David Rudkin, *Ashes*; Douglas Dunn, *Love or Nothing*; Tomlinson, *The Way In*.

1975   North Sea oil starts to flow, Margaret Thatcher elected leader of the Conservative Party, unemployment passes 2 million, Equal Pay and Sex Discrimination Acts, tax-free child benefit introduced, radical Toryism (monetarism) surfacing. Monstrous Regiment (feminist theatre group) formed; Paul Feyerabend, *Against Method*.

Malcolm Bradbury, *The History Man*; Ballard, *High Rise*; Lodge, *Changing Places*; Heaney, *North*; Naipaul, *Guerrillas*; Christine Brooke-Rose, *Thru*; Ian McEwan, *First Love, Last Rites*; Pinter, *No Man's Land*; Martin Amis, *Dead Babies*; Murdoch, *A Word Child*; Hare, *Teeth N' Smiles* (performed); Hare, *Fanshen*; Bond, *The Fool*; Barker, *Stripwell*.

1976   Callaghan becomes PM after Wilson's resignation, Carter elected president of USA, public expenditure cuts, attempts to begin peace movement in Northern Ireland fail, punk hits the headlines. National Theatre opens with a new building on the South Bank of the Thames.

David Edgar, *Destiny*; Gunn, *Jack Straw's Castle*; Hughes, *Season Songs*; Spark, *The Takeover*; Pam Gems, *Dusa, Fish, Stas and Vi*; Heaney's lecture 'Englands of the Mind' delivered in California; Caryl Churchill, *Light Shining in Buckinghamshire*.

1977   Silver Jubilee of Queen Elizabeth; Lib–Lab pact. Poetry Society's first national competition.

Hughes, *Gaudete*; Carter, *The Passion of New Eve*; Pam Gems, *Queen Christina*; Bond, *The Bundle*; Mary O'Malley, *Once a Catholic*; Bennett, *The Old Country*; Drabble, *The Ice Age*.

1978   Devolution Bills for Scotland and Wales defeated; 'winter of discontent': strikes and shutdowns; ban on sport and contact with South Africa; last national conference of Women's Liberation in Birmingham. Riverside theatre opens in Hammersmith; E. P. Thompson, *The Poverty of Theory*; Edward Said, *Orientalism*.

Stoppard, *Professional Foul*; Murdoch, *The Sea, The Sea*; Greene, *The Human Factor*; Barker, *The Hang of the Gaol*; Hare, *Plenty*; Hughes, *Cave Birds*; Charles Tomlinson, *The Shaft*; Amis, *Success*; Burgess, *1985*; McEwan, *The Cement Garden*; Hare, *Licking Hitler*; Pinter, *Betrayal*; Tony Harrison, *From the School of Eloquence*; Hill, *Tenebrae*; Byatt, *The Virgin in the Garden*; Gems, *Piaf*.

1979   Ayatollah Khomeini returns from exile to lead Islamic Revolution after the deportation of the Shah, transport workers strike and gain pay awards, wave of 'Decline of Britain' publications, Government defeated and Margaret Thatcher becomes PM, Arts Council grant cut by 1 million by incoming government, Thatcher takes belligerent line on GB's financial contribution to the EEC at the Dublin summit. Lyotard's *The Postmodern Condition* published in France.

Golding, *Darkness Visible*; Hughes, *Moortown*; Dunn, *Barbarians*; Churchill, *Cloud Nine*; Heaney, *Fieldwork*; W. S. Graham, *Collected Poems*; Michael Longley, *The Echo Gate*; Naipaul, *A Bend in the River*; Spark, *Territorial Rights*; Fay Weldon, *Praxis*; Craig Raine, *A Martian Sends a Postcard Home*; Lessing, *Shikasta*.

1980   Prior's Trade Union Act to prevent secondary picketing and discourage closed shops, Housing Act to promote sales of council houses, large rises in public-sector pay after Clegg enquiry, trade figures show that more workers are employed in service than manufacturing industries; first legally elected Zimbabwean state.

Golding, *Rites of Passage*; Burgess, *Earthly Powers*; Lodge, *How Far Can You Go?*; Brenton, *The Romans in Britian*; Drabble, *The Middle Ground*; Murdoch, *Nuns and Soldiers*; Weldon, *Puffball*; Julian Barnes, *Metroland*; Tony Harrison's *The Oresteia* performed in the ancient Greek theatre of Epidaurus.

1981   SDP formed, Reagan elected president of USA; Iran hostages released, race riots in Brixton and elsewhere, IRA hunger strike and the death of Bobby Sands, British Nationality Bill, *The History Man* televised, 'special relationship' between Reagan and Thatcher and agreement to allow US Cruise missiles into Britain, severe cuts in university funding brings the era of Robbins to an end.

Rushdie, *Midnight's Children*; D. M. Thomas, *The White Hotel*; Alisdair Gray, *Lanark*; Danny Abse, *Way Out in the Centre*; Harrison, *Continuous: 50 Sonnets from the School of Eloquence*; Brookner, *A Start in Life*; McEwan, *The Comfort of Strangers*; Spark, *Loitering With Intent*; Charles Tomlinson, *The Flood*; Burgess, *Earthly Powers*; Dunn, *St Kilda's Parliament*.

1982   Trade Union Act bans unlawful strikes, Falkland War and Foreign Secretary Carrington resigns, highest unemployment ever (over 3 million and 13.4 per cent of the population), Public Lending Right authorized. RSC opens at the Barbican.

Morrison and Motion, *The Penguin Guide to Contemporary British Poetry*; Gunn, *The Passages of Joy*; Elizabeth Jennings, *Celebrations and Elegies*; William Boyd, *An Ice-Cream War*; Brookner, *Providence*.

1983   Thatcher returned in General Election, Kinnock elected Labour leader, Greenham Common women's peace camp resists attempts to disband it, Tory privatization policy begins to be put into practice, oil prices cut by OPEC for the first time.

Rushdie, *Shame*; Graham Swift, *Waterland*; Edgar, *Maydays*; Bradbury, *Rates of Exchange*; Paul Muldoon, *Quoof*; Brookner, *Look at Me*; Churchill, *Top Girls*.

1984   Miner's strike; Thatcher remains hostile to a European Monetary System at the Fontainebleau summit; IRA bombing of the Grand Hotel in Brighton.

Amis, *Money*; Heaney, *Station Island*; Barnes, *Flaubert's Parrot*; Brookner, *Hotel du Lac*; Carter, *Nights at the Circus*; Tomlinson, *Notes from New York*; Boyd, *Stars and Bars*; Gray, *1982* and *Janine*, Lessing, *The Diaries of Jane Somers*; Lodge, *Small World*; Spark, *The Only Problem*; Ballard, *Empire of the Sun*; Churchill, *Softcops*; Nell Dunn, *Steaming*; Craig Raine, *Rich*.

1985   Miner's strike defeated after one year, Arts Council document 'A Great British Success Story', Church of England report 'Faith in the Cities', *The War Game* shown on television after twenty-year ban, records show widening gap between rich and poor since 1979, unemployment peaks.

Harrison, 'V'; Peter Reading, *Ukelele Music*; Grace Nichols, *The Fat Black Woman's Poems*; Peter Ackroyd, *Hawksmoor*; Byatt, *Still Life*; Lessing, *The Good Terrorist*; Barry Unsworth, *Stone Virgin*; Jeannette Winterson, *Oranges are Not the Only Fruit*; Rose Tremain, *The Swimming Pool Season*; Hare and Brenton, *Pravda*; Dunn, *Elegies*.

1986   Stockmarket Big Bang, race riots, Local Government Act curbs power of local councils, agreement to build channel tunnel, Chernobyl disaster increases anxieties about nuclear energy, BBC and government in conflict over reporting of IRA and broadcast criticism of government policy, *Spycatcher* incident, UGC cuts to universities and UFC set up, polytechnics move out of local government control.

Kingsley Amis, *The Old Devils*; Ishiguro, *An Artist of the Floating World*; Brookner, *A Misalliance*; Weldon, *The Shrapnel Academy*.

1987   Thatcher wins third election; collapse of SDP; stockmarket crash wipes 24 per cent off stock prices; Cleveland case raises questions about the extent of child abuse. Gilbert and George exhibition at the Hayward: images of contemporary (enterprise) Britain.

Churchill, *Serious Money*; Drabble, *The Radiant Way*; Chatwin, *The Songlines*; McEwan, *The Child in Time*; Naipaul, *The Enigma of Arrival*; Winterson, *The Passion*; Penelope Lively, *Moontiger*; Tony Harrison's 'V' televised and created national debate concerning morality, obscenity, and poetry.

1988   The poll-tax proposed by Nicholas Ridley, Education Act recommends national core curriculum, Thatcher's speech in Bruges attacks idea of the 'united nations of Europe', national deficit largest ever at 20 billion, The journal *Samizdat* formed by writers and intellectuals as a voice of liberal protest.

Lodge, *Nice Work*; Rushdie, *The Satanic Verses*; Lessing, *The Fifth Child*; Swift, *Out of this World*; *Small World* televised.

1989   Reagan retires and Bush elected president of USA; collapse of communism in East Europe gathers momentum; government criticized over NHS restructuring, over the King's Cross tube disaster, and the Community Tax; fatwa against Rushdie; Labour renounces unilateralism over nuclear arms; ecology issues foregrounded in the European elections and new concern with quality of life and the environment.

Amis, *London Fields*; David Caute, *Veronica or the Two Nations*; Ishiguro, *The Remains of the Day*; Winterson, *Sexing the Cherry*; James Kelman, *A Disaffection*; Barnes, *History of the World in 10$\frac{1}{2}$ Chapters*; Drabble, *A Natural Curiosity*; Tremain, *Restoration*; Weldon, *The Cloning of Joanna May*; *Nice Work* televised.

FURTHER READING

The place of publication is London unless otherwise specified. Because of the range and large numbers of writers discussed in the course of this study, there is no reference here to critical writing on specific authors. Listed below are sources which provide a useful general introduction to the period. Sources for backgrounds are organized under chapter headings, specialized studies of the literature of the period under the headings of Fiction, Drama and Theatre, and Poetry.

Chapter 1

Many of the books here provide background material relevant to issues pursued throughout the book but are included in this first section as useful introductory accounts of the period.

For cultural, political, and economic surveys of the period 1960–90, see: Brian Appleyard, *The Pleasures of Peace: Art and Imagination in Post-War Britain* (1989); Michael Ball *et al.*, *The Transformation of Britain: Contemporary Social and Economic Change* (1989); H. Bennington, *Change in British Politics* (1984); Christopher Booker, *The Seventies: Portrait of a Decade* (1980); Patrick Dunleavy *et al.*, *Developments in British Politics*, iii (1990) concentrates mainly on the decade of the nineties; Boris Ford, *The Cambridge Cultural History: Modern Britain* (1992), covers the arts generally from 1945; W. H. Greenleaf, *The British Political Tradition*: i. *The Rise of Collectivism* (1983), ii. *The Ideological Heritage* (1983), iii. *A Much Governed Nation* (1987) are invaluable and detailed accounts of the construction and history of post-war politics; Stuart Hall, *Policing the Crisis*; Stuart Hall and Martin Jacques, *New Times: The Changing Face of Politics in the 1990s* (1989) is a late Marxist account of Thatcherism and the crisis of the left; David Held, *Political Theory Today* (1991); David Marquand, *The Unprincipled Society* (1988); Arthur Marwick, *British Society since 1945* (2nd edn., Harmondsworth, 1990) and *Culture in Britain Since 1945* (Oxford 1991), both useful overviews by a social historian; W. N. Medlicott, *Contemporary England* (1976); Kenneth O. Morgan, *The People's Peace: British History 1945–1989* (1990) is an invaluable and detailed account of domestic political history; Anthony Sampson, *Anatomy of Britain* (1962) and *The Essential Anatomy of Britain: Democracy in Crisis* (1992); Alan Sinfield (ed.), *Society and Literature 1945–1970* (1983) and *Literature, Politics and Culture in Post-War Britain* (Oxford, 1989); Alan Sked and Chris Cook, *Post-War Britain: A Political History* (Harmondsworth, 1984).

Studies of the sixties, including discussions of the myths of the decade and cultural histories: Christopher Booker, *The Neophiliacs* (1969) is still fascinating as a chronicle of the Faustianism of the sixties written from within the decade; Christie Davies, *Permissive Britain* (1975); Robert Hewison, *Too Much: Art and Society in the Sixties 1960–1975* (1986) is one of the best guides to the era; Gerald Howard, *The Sixties* (New York, 1991); Bernard Levin, *The Pendulum Years: Britain and the Sixties* (1970); Sara Maitland, *Very Heaven: Looking Back on the Sixties* (1987) is a feminist, largely anecdotal account of the decade; Bart Moore-Gilbert and John Seed, *Cultural Revolution? The Challenge of the Arts in the Sixties* (1992), a collection of essays covering popular as well as high culture; C. P. Snow, *The Two Cultures and the Scientific Revolution* (1959); D. Widgery, *The Left in Britain 1956–1968* (1976). Political studies of the decade and 'condition-of-England' statements: Richard Crosman, *Labour and the Affluent Society* (1960); Arthur Koestler (ed.), *Suicide of a Nation?*, special issue of *Encounter* (July 1963). On the Profumo affair: Anthony Hartley, *A State of England* (1963); Brian Inglis, *Private Conscience—Public Morality* (1964); Clive Irving *et al., Scandal* (1963). Contributions to and accounts of the counterculture: Robert Bryan *et al., Laing and Anti-Psychiatry* (Harmondsworth, 1972); David Caute, *Sixty-Eight: The Year of the Barricades* (1988); David Cooper (ed.), *The Dialectics of Liberation* (1968); Colin Crouch, *The Student's Revolt* (1970); Paul Goodman, *The Empire City* (New York, 1964); R. D. Laing, *The Divided Self* (1960) and *The Politics of Experience and the Bird of Paradise* (1967); Timothy Leary *The Politics of Ecstacy* (1968); Herbert Marcuse, *Eros and Civilisation* (New York, 1962) and *One-Dimensional Man* (New York, 1964); Norman O'Brown, *Love's Body* (New York, 1966).

On Thatcherism and the New Right, see: N. P. Barry, *The New Right* (1987); B. Campbell, *Iron Ladies* (1987); S. E. Finer, *Thatcherism: Personality and Politics* (1980); D. Green, *The New Right* (Brighton, 1987); K. Hoover and R. Plant, *Conservative Capitalism* (1988); D. Smith, *The Rise and Fall of Monetarism* (Harmondsworth, 1987); Hugo Young, *One of Us* (1989).

On the women's movement, see: M. Barrett, *Women's Oppression Today* (1980); D. Boucher, *The Feminist Challenge: The Movement for Women's*

Liberation in Britain and the USA (1983); Jane Lewis, *Women in Britain Since the War* (1992); M. Wandor, *The Body Politic: Women's Liberation in Britain* (1972); Elizabeth Wilson, *Only Halfway to Paradise: Women in Post-War Britain 1945–1968* (1980).

On financing the arts, see: Brian Appleyard, *The Culture Club: Crisis in the Arts* (1984); Harold Baldry, *The Case for the Arts* (1981); R. Hutchinson, *The Politics of the Arts Council* (1982); Janet Minitan, *The Nationalisation of Culture: The Development of State Subsidies to the Arts in Great Britain* (1977); Roy Shaw, *The Arts and the People* (1987); John Sutherland, *Fiction and the Fiction Industry* (1987).

Chapter 2

See Anthony Giddens, *Modernity and Self-Identity: Self and Society in the Late Modern Age* on institutional self-reflexivity. On the disaffections of the age see Daniel Bell, *The Cultural Contradictions of Capitalism* (1976); Irving Howe, *The Decline of the New* (1971); Michael Ignatieff, *The Needs of Strangers* (1984); Bernice Martin, *A Sociology of Contemporary Cultural Change* (1981). On television and the mass media, see G. Goldie, *Facing the Nation: Television and Politics 1936–1976* (1977); Marshall McLuhan, *Understanding Media* (1964); P. Marnham, *The Private Eye Story* (1982); the *Pilkington Report of the Committee on Broadcasting* (HMSO, 1962); J. Treneman and D. McQuail, *Television and the Political Image* (1961); John Whales, *The Politics of the Media* (1980). On pop art, see: M. Crompton, *Pop Art* (1970), Dick Hebdige, 'In Poor Taste: Notes on Pop', *Block*, 8 (1983); Lucy Lippard, *Pop Art* (1970). On subcultures and cultural fragmentation, see S. Hall and T. Jefferson, *Resistance through Rituals* (1970); Dick Hebdige, *Subculture: The Meaning of Style* (1979); George Melly, *Revolt into Style* (1970); J. Savage, *England's Dreaming: Sex Pistols and Punk Rock* (1991); Alan Sinfield, *Literature, Politics and Culture in Post-War Britain* (1989); D. Strinati and S. Wagg (eds.), *Come on Down? Popular Media Culture in Post-War Britain* (1992). On Larkin: *Selected Letters 1940–1985*, ed. Anthony Thwaite (1992); Blake Morrison, *The Movement: English Poetry of the Fifties*. Useful historical accounts of the Rushdie Affair are S. Maitland and L. Apignanesi, *The Rushdie File* (1989); Daniel Pipes, *The Rushdie Affair* (New York, 1990). On censorship see Arts Council Report, *The Obscenity Laws* (1969); John Sutherland, *Offensive Literature: Decensorship in Britain 1950–1982*.

Chapter 3

Martin Buber, *Hasidism* (1948); Roger Caillois, *Man and the Sacred* (1959); Henry Clark, *The Church under Thatcher* (1993); D. L. Edwards, *The Honest to God Debate* (1963); Julian Huxley, *Religion without Revelation* (1959); Daniel Jenkins, *The British: Their Identity and their Religion* (1975); Iris Murdoch, *Metaphysics as a Guide to Morals* (1992); Jonathan Raban, *God, Man and Mrs Thatcher* (1989). On self and modernity, D. Frisby, *Fragments of Modernity* (1985); *Identity: The Real Me* (ICA, document 6); J. Rutherford (ed.), *Identity* (1990); Stephen Spender, *The Struggle of The Modern* (1973); Charles Taylor, *Sources of the Self* (1989); Alan Young, *Dada and After: Extremist Modernism and English Literature* (Manchester, 1981). Critiques of psychoanalysis: Ernest Gellner, *The Psychoanalytic Movement* (1985); Christopher Lasch, *The Culture of Narcissism* (1979) and *The Minimal Self* (1984); Alisdair MacIntyre, *After Virtue* (1984); Philip Rieff, *The Triumph of the Therapeutic* (1966).

Chapter 4

On the aesthetics of silence, see: Peter Brook, *The Empty Space* (1968); Martin Esslin, *The Theatre of the Absurd* (1962); Susan Sontag, *Against Interpretation* (New York, 1966); George Steiner, *On Difficulty and Other Essays* (1978). On New Left and new subjectivities: Eric Hobsbawm, *The Forward March of Labour Halted?* (1981) and *Politics for a Rational Society* (1989); E. P. Thompson, *Warwick University Ltd.: Industry, Management and the Universities* (Harmondsworth, 1971); M. Wiener, *English Culture and the Decline of the Industrial Spirit* (Cambridge, 1981); Nigel Young, *An Infantile Disorder? The Crisis and Decline of the New Left* (1977). On critiques of method, see: R. Bernstein, *Beyond Objectivism and Relativism* (Oxford, 1984); Paul Feyerabend, *Against Method* (1975); Arthur Koestler, *The Ghost in the Machine* (1967); M. Polyani, *Personal Knowledge* (Chicago, 1959); Alfred North Whitehead, *Science and the Modern World* (1925).

Chapter 5

On the nation and theories of nationalism: B. Anderson, *Imagined Communities* (1983); H. Bhaba (ed.), *Narrating the Nation* (1990); Andrew Gamble, *Britain in Decline* (1990); M. Hastings and S. Jenkins, *The Battle for the Falklands* (1983); Robert Hewison, *The Heritage Industry* (1987); D. Massey, 'A Global Sense of Place', *Marxism Today* (1991); K. Robins, 'Traditions and Translations: National Culture in its Global context', in

John Corner and Sylvia Harvey (eds.), *Enterprise and Heritage* (1991); Edward Said, 'Narrative and Geography', *New Left Review*, 180 (Mar. 1990). On post-industrialization and new times: Andrew Gamble, *Britain in Decline* (1990); S. Hall, *The Hard Road to Renewal* (1988); S. Hall and M. Jacques, *New Times* (1989); A. Touraine, *The Post-Industrial Society* (New York, 1971). On issues of race and identity: M. Anvar, *Race and Politics: Ethnic Minorities and the British Political System* (1986). On Britain and Northern Ireland: M. MacDonald, *Children of Wrath: Political Violence in Northern Ireland* (Cambridge, 1986). On Britain and Europe: R. Dahrendorf *et al.* (eds.), *Whose Europe?* (1989); S. A. George, *An Awkward Partner: Britain in the European Community* (1990).

Chapter 6

On the post-modern debate, culture, theory, criticism: Ian Adam and Helen Tiffin, *Past the Post: Theorising Post-Colonialism and Postmodernism* (1990); Alex Callinicos, *Against Postmodernism: A Marxist Critique* (1989); Jim Collins, *Uncommon Cultures: Popular Culture and Postmodernism* (1989); Mike Featherstone, *Consumer Culture and Postmodernism* (1991); Michel Foucault, *The Archaeology of Knowledge*, trans. A. M. Sheridan Smith (1978); see also *The Foucault Reader*, ed. Paul Rabinowitz (Harmondsworth, 1986); David Harvey, *The Condition of Postmodernity* (Oxford, 1989); J-F. Lyotard, *The Postmodern Condition: A Report on Knowledge*, trans. Geoffrey Bennington and Brian Massumi (Manchester, 1986); Christopher Norris, *What's Wrong With Postmodernism?*(1990); Richard Rorty, *Philosophy and the Mirror of Nature* (Oxford, 1980). On post-modernism and literature, see: Jonathan Arac, *Critical Genealogies: Historical Situations for Postmodern Literary Studies* (New York, 1987); Bernard Bergonzi, *Exploding English: Criticism, Theory, Culture* (Oxford, 1990); Malcolm Bradbury and Judy Cooke (eds.), *New Writing* (1992); Christine Brooke-Rose, *A Rhetoric of the Unreal: Studies in Narrative and Structure especially of the Fantastic* (1981); Victor Burgin, *The End of Art Theory: Criticism and Postmodernity* (1986); Christopher Butler, *After the Wake* (Oxford, 1980); Linda Hutcheon, *A Poetics of Postmodernism* (1989); Frank Kermode, *History and Value* (1984); Brian McHale, *Postmodernist Fiction* (1987); Patrick Parrinder, *The Failure of Theory: Essays on Criticism and Contemporary Fiction* (1987); Edward Said, *The World, the Text and the Critic* (Cambridge, Mass., 1983); George Steiner, *On Difficulty and Other Essays* (1978); Patricia Waugh, *Practising Postmodernism/Reading Modernism* (1992). On post-colonialism: Gayatri Spivak, *In Other Worlds* (1990) and *The Post-Colonial Critic* (1990).

General Writing on Fiction

Useful journals: *Granta, London Magazine, London Review of Books, Stand, Literary Review*.

Bernard Bergonzi, *The Situation of the Novel* (Harmondsworth, 1970); M. Bradbury and D. Palmer (eds.), *The Contemporary English Novel* (1979); Anthony Burgess, *Urgent Copy* (1968); *Granta, iii. The End of the English Novel* (1980); N. Gerrard, *Into the Mainstream* (1989); John Haffenden, *Novelists in Interview* (1985); Alan Kennedy, *The Protean Self: Dramatic Action in Contemporary Fiction* (1974); Frank Kermode, *Continuities* (1968); David Lodge, *Language of Fiction: Essays in Criticism and Verbal Analysis of the English Novel* (1966); id., *The Novelist at the Crossroads* (1971); id., *The Modes of Modern Writing* (1977); Alan Massie, *The Novel Today: A Critical Guide to the British Novel 1970–1989* (1990); J. A. Sutherland, *Fiction and the Fiction Industry* (1978); D. J. Taylor, *After the War: The Novel and England Since 1945* (1993); Patricia Waugh, *Metafiction* (1984) and *Feminine Fictions* (1989); Heide Ziegler and Christopher Bigsby, *The Radical Imagination and the Liberal Tradition* (1982).

General Writing on Drama and Theatre

Useful journals: *Gambit: International Theatre Review, Plays and Players, Theatre Research, Theatre Quarterly*.

P. Ansonge, *Disrupting the Spectacle: Five Years of Experimental and Fringe Theatre in Britain* (1975); John Arden, *To Present the Pretence: Essays in Theatre and its Public* (1977); C. W. E. Bigsby (ed.), *Contemporary English Drama* (1981); Peter Brook, *The Empty Space* (1968); J. Bull, *New British Political Dramatists* (1984); Richard Allen Cave, *New British Drama on the London Stage 1970–1985* (1987); Colin Chambers and Mike Prior, *Playwright's Progress: Patterns of Postwar British Drama* (Oxford, 1987); Judith Cook, *The National Theatre* (1976); Sandy Craig, *Dreams and Deconstructions: Alternative Theatre in Britain* (1980); David Edgar, *The Second Time as Farce: Reflections on the Drama of Mean Times* (1988); John Elsom, *Postwar British Theatre* (1979); Trevor Griffiths and Margaret Lewellyn-Jones, *British and Irish Women Dramatists Since 1958* (Milton Keynes, 1993); Ronald Hayman, *The Set-Up: An Anatomy of English Theatre Today* (1973); Helene Kayssar, *Feminist Theatre* (1984); Susan Rusinko, *British Drama from 1950 to the Present* (Boston, 1989); Michelene Wandor, *Look Back in Gender: Sexuality and the Family in Post-War Drama* (London, 1987).

General Writing On Poetry

Useful journals and poetry magazines: *Poetry Review, PN Review, Agenda, Review, Stand, New Review.*

C. Bedient, *Eight Contemporary Poets* (1974); Donald Davie, *Thomas Hardy and British Poetry* (1973); S. Deane, *Celtic Revivals: Essays in Modern Irish Literature 1880–1980* (1985); John Haffenden, *Viewpoints: Poets in Conversation* (1981); Ian Hamilton, *The Modern Poet: Essays from 'The Review'* (1968); Edward Larissey, *Reading Twentieth Century Poetry: The Language of Gender and Objects* (Oxford, 1990); Peter Jones and Michael Schmidt (eds.), *British Poetry since 1970: A Critical Survey* (1980); Edna Longley, *Poetry in the Wars* (Newcastle, 1986); John Lucas, *Modern Poetry from Hardy to Hughes* (1986); John Mole, *Passing Judgement: Poetry in the Eighties; Essays from Encounter* (Bristol, 1989); J. Raban, *The Society of the Poem* (1976); Michael Schmidt and Grevel Lindop, *British Poetry since 1960: A Survey* (Oxford, 1972); Anthony Thwaite, *Poetry Today: 1960–1984* (1984); G. Thurley, *The Ironic Harvest* (1974); A. K. Whitehead, *The British Dissonance* (1983) (on alternatives to modernism in British poetry).

INDEX

abolition of theatre censorship 118, 177
Abortion Act 118
Abse, Danny 152
absurdism 111–12
Ackroyd, Peter, *Hawksmoor* 180–1, 192
Adorno, Theodor 60
Agard, John 153
agitprop theatre 158, 169–70, 173
Alvarez, A. 26, 60, 63, 137, 143, 211
Amis, Kingsley 122, 128
Amis, Martin 46, 48, 63, 185
   London Fields 33
   Money 24, 30–3
Anderson, Perry 4, 49
Apocalypticism 98, 101, 102, 104, 106,
   129–30, 138–9, 147, 179, 184, 197,
   210, 211
Arden, John 8, 10
Arendt, Hannah 114
Aristotle 183
Arnold, Matthew 11, 36, 47, 202
Artaud, Antonin 80, 111, 112–13
Arts Council, the 4, 161–2
Auden, W. H. 8, 68, 70
   The Dyer's Hand 60–1
Augustine, St 1, 2, 42, 95, 145, 183
Ayer, A. J., *Language, Truth and Logic*
   128–9

Bacon, Francis 113
Bakhtin, M. 187
Ballard J. G. 48, 185, 197
   The Drowned World 147
   High Rise 147–8
Barker, Howard 158
Barnes, Julian, *Flaubert's Parrot* 71, 180
Barth, John 70
Barthes, Roland 38, 211
Bartlett, Elizabeth 87
Beauvoir, Simone de 128
   The Second Sex 188
Beckett, Samuel 10, 80
   Happy Days 104
   Krapp's Last Tape 42
   Play 109

   The Unnamable 37
   Waiting For Godot 22, 40, 42–3
Bell, Clive 208
Bell, Daniel, *The Cultural Contradictions of
   Capital* 48, 163
Benjamin, Walter 74
Berger, John, G 39
   Ways of Seeing 46
Bergonzi, Bernard 12, 70
Berman, Marshall 22
Berryman, John 26
Beveridge Report 8
Big Bang 18, 19
Blake, William 7, 85, 115
Blanchot, Maurice 179
Bleasdale, Alan 158
Bloomsbury 65
Bond, Edward 6, 10, 82, 84–7, 110, 120
   Bingo 85
   The Fool 86
   Lear 87
   Saved 85
Booker, Christopher 59
Booker Prize 41, 71
Borges, Jorge Luis, 'Death and the
   Compass' 194
Boyd, William 185
Bradbury, Malcolm:
   Dr. Criminale 149
   The History Man 38
   Rates of Exchange 162
   Stepping Westward 38
Brecht, Bertolt 80, 85, 111, 113–14
Brenton, Howard 168, 169
   The Churchill Play 176–7
   The Romans in Britain 177–8
Brontë, Charlotte 34
   Jane Eyre 203, 204
   Shirley 35
Brontë, Emily, *Wuthering Heights* 205
Brook, Peter 80, 81, 111–14
Brookner, Anita 185, 186–7
   Hotel du Lac 186
Brooke-Rose, Christine 71
Brophy, Brigid, *Flesh* 189

Brownjohn, Alan 116
Buber, Martin 6
Bunting, Basil, *Briggflatts* 110
Burgess, Anthony:
    A Clockwork Orange 10, 94, 145–6
    Earthly Powers 95–6, 97, 98, 197
    1985 146
Butler Education Act 117
Byatt, A. S. 40, 71
    The Game 126
    Possession 182, 185

Callaghan, James 14, 175
canon, the 40, 41, 125, 150–1
Carter, Angela 185, 190
    Nights at the Circus 195
    The Passion of New Eve 195
Cartesianism 114, 191–5, 196, 198
Catholic novel, the 94–8, 115
Caute, David, *Veronica or the Two Nations*
    33
Chatwin, Bruce 185
    The Songlines 191
Christianity 61–2, 64–6, 69, 94–8, 101,
    102, 103, 104–6
Churchill, Caryl:
    Cloud Nine 199–200
    Serious Money 19–20
    Top Girls 200
class 123–5, 158–60, 162–3, 168–78, 206,
    210
CND 123
cold war, the 95, 139, 145
condition of England novel, the 34, 63,
    101
Conquest, Robert 26, 63, 137, 211
Conrad, Joseph 204
Cooper, David 5
Coover Robert 46
cosmology 184, 185–7, 191–7, 211
Counterculture, the 5, 6, 7, 16, 58, 65, 84,
    85, 91, 109, 111, 115–19, 133–4, 168,
    209
Craig, Sandy 169
Crichton-Smith, Ian 152
critique of method 127–33
Crosland, Anthony 4

Dabydeen, David 154–5
Daniels, Sarah 200
Darwin, Charles 103, 148, 196–7, 212
Davie, Donald 128, 152
Defoe, Daniel, *Moll Flanders* 194
Dickens, Charles 34, 162, 195
Disraeli, Benjamin 34

Drabble, Margaret:
    The Millstone 181
    The Radiant Way 33
    A Summer Birdcage 181
    The Waterfall 181
Dunn, Douglas 48, 64, 123–4
Dunn, Nell 8

écriture feminine 189
Edgar, David:
    Destiny 1, 2, 3, 13, 14–16, 18, 20, 168,
        169
    Maydays 116–17, 174–6
ego psychology 146, 169
Eliade, Mercia 110
Eliot, George 93–4
Eliot, T. S. 27, 31, 106, 122, 165
    Four Quartets 149
    'The Function of Criticism' 208
    The Idea of a Christian Society 31
    Notes Toward the Definition of Culture
        117–18, 140
    'Tradition and the Individual Talent' 131
    The Waste Land 62
Encounter 3
Enterprise Culture 14, 20, 64, 141, 176, 210
entropy 102–4
environmentalism 163, 175, 183
Erikson, Erik 169
Esslin, Martin 45
Esterton, Aaron 5
existentialism 60, 66, 75, 76, 83, 91, 97, 98

Falkland War, the 18, 174–5
fantastic, the 101, 132, 139, 143, 155–6,
    181, 185
    and feminism 191–9
Farrell, J. G. 185
    The Siege of Krishnapur 201–2
fascism 74, 77
    and art 71–5, 97, 100, 101, 105, 120–1,
        185
feminism 12–13, 23, 41, 64, 66, 94, 100,
    115, 125, 134, 156, 162–3, 166–7, 175,
    185–97, 203
Fenton, James 63
Feyerabend, Paul, *Against Method* 133
Fisher, Roy, *City* 140–1
Foot Michael 175
Ford, Boris 26
Forster, E. M., *A Passage to India* 201
Foucault, Michel 153, 157, 183, 187, 191
Fowles, John 10, 37, 185
    The Aristos 75
    The Collector 123, 182

The French Lieutenant's Woman 65, 97, 110, 119, 120
The Magus 75–7
Frankfurt School, the 7, 34
Freud, Sigmund 67, 68, 69, 72, 73, 74, 101, 143, 145, 182, 194, 197, 199
Friedan, Betty 23
The Feminine Mystique 126
Fuller, Peter 64

Gadamer, Hans Georg, *Truth and Method* 130–1
Galbraith, K. 8
Gardener, Helen 50
Gaskell, Mrs. 34, 162
Gems, Pam 200
Genet, Jean 7
Giddens, Anthony 128
Ginsberg, Allen 6
Goethe 22
Goffman, Erving 37, 42, 128
and role theory 134, 135
Golding, William 10, 62, 94, 98, 99–105
Darkness Visible 33, 101–4, 110, 119, 120, 122, 185
Free Fall 98–100
Rites of Passage 33
The Spire 100–1
Goodman, Paul 6
Graham, W. S. 107–8
Gray, Alisdair 71
Lanark 197–8, 202
Greene, Graham 94, 95
The Human Factor 95
Greer, Germaine 125–6
Griffiths, Trevor 24
Comedians 158–60, 168
The Party 176–7
grotesque, the 101–4, 139, 184, 190–7
Gunn, Thom 48, 90–2, 93, 110
Jack Straw's Castle 91
The Man With the Night Sweats 92
Moly 91
My Sad Captains 92
Touch 91

Hall, Peter 80
Hall, Stuart 168
Hamilton, Ian 63
Hamilton, Richard 145
Hampshire, Stuart 168
Hancock, Tony 132
Hare, David:
Knuckle 171
Licking Hitler 170–1

Plenty 170, 171–3
Slag 171
Teeth N' Smiles 16, 20, 168
Hardy, Thomas, *Jude the Obscure* 137
Hayek, F. A. von, *The Road to Serfdom* 17
Heaney, Seamus 64, 94, 152, 164–8
'Englands of the Mind'
'Feeling into Words' 165
North 164–7
Station Island 167–8
Heath, Edward 14, 17, 142
Hegel, G. W. F. 84
Heidegger, Martin 66, 93, 143
heterotopia 191
Hill, Geoffrey 94, 98, 104–6
King Log 105, 110, 152, 164–5
Tenebrae 105
Hobsbawm, Eric 175
Hoggart, Richard, *The Uses of Literacy* 8, 48, 50, 122
Holocaust, the 60, 72, 92, 95–6, 105, 106, 110, 111, 114, 119, 137, 138–9, 148, 192
Hough, Graham 50
Hughes, Ted 10, 61, 87–90, 110, 120, 152, 164–5
Crow 88–9
Gaudete 88
Lupercal 89
Wodwo 88
Humanae Vitae 96–7

Ibsen, Henrik, *Ghosts* 170, 177
Ignatieff, Michael 208
Ionesco, Eugene 110–11
Ishiguro, Kazuo, *The Remains of the Day* 33–4

Jackson, Glenda 113
Jagger, Mick 119, 146
James, Henry 93
Jenkins, Roy 49
Jhabvala, Ruth Prawer 185
Johnson, B. S.:
Albert Angelo 38, 131–2
Christy Malry's Own Double-Entry 132
House Mother Normal 132
Travelling People 131
Trawl 132
The Unfortunates 132
Joyce, James 43, 103, 165
Ulysses 23
Jung, Karl 34, 76, 133, 148

Kant, Immanuel 79
Kelman, James, *A Disaffection* 198

Kermode, Frank, *The Sense of an Ending* 129–30
Kettle, Martin 50
Keynes J. M. 3, 8, 13, 14, 142, 210
Kott, Jan, *Shakespeare Our Contemporary* 119–20
Kristeva, Julia 187
Kuhn, Thomas 196

Lacan, Jacques 187, 195
Lady Chatterley Trial 49–51, 55–6, 134
Laing, R. D. 5, 6–7, 83, 86, 110, 111, 133–4
Larkin, Philip 10, 24, 26–30, 32, 49, 60, 123, 128, 151, 152, 164–5
Lasch, Christopher 48
Lawrence, D. H. 23, 49–51, 55–6, 62, 89
Leary, Timothy 6
Leavis, F. R. 4, 11, 46, 48, 50, 109, 117, 208
Lessing, Doris 6, 185
    Canopus in Argos 139
    The Four-Gated City 138
    The Golden Notebook 10, 133–9, 211
    The Good Terrorist 206
    Martha Quest 137–8
    The Memoirs of a Survivor 134–5, 137, 138–9, 148
Lewis, C. S., *An Experiment in Criticism* 56, 212
Littlewood, Joan 123
Lodge, David:
    The British Museum is Falling Down 96, 131
    Changing Places 151
    How Far Can You Go? 96–7
    Nice Work 24, 34–6, 94, 162
    'The Novelist at the Crossroads' 213–14
    Small World 182
Lorenz, Konrad 58
Lowell, Robert 26
Lukacs, Georg 135, 184
Lyotard, J.-F., *The Postmodern Condition* 39, 70, 185

McEwan, Ian:
    The Black Dogs 191–2
    The Child in Time 33, 191
    'Solid Geometry' 191
MacIntyre, Alisdair 183
McLuhan, Marshall 36
Macmillan, Harold 3, 8, 25, 202
magic realism 103, 139, 198
Mahon, Derek 168
Marcuse, Herbert 5, 6, 22, 60, 84, 116

Marquez, Garcia Gabriel 103, 181
Martians, the 64
Marx, Karl 6, 39, 66
Melville, Herman, *Moby Dick* 180
Mercer, David 8, 24, 46, 123
Milton, John 22
    Paradise Lost 184, 194
Moore, G. E. 65
Morris, Desmond 58
Morrison, Blake 63
Motion, Andrew 63
Movement, the 90, 128, 137
Muldoon, Paul 168
multiculturalism 156, 208, 209, 212–13
Murdoch, Iris 10, 97, 110, 119–20
    The Black Prince 68, 78
    A Fairly Honourable Defeat 78
    The Flight from the Enchanter 69, 77–9
    The Sea, The Sea 79
    A Severed Head 62, 65, 77–8, 121

Naipaul, V. S. 185, 203, 204–6
    The Enigma of Arrival 204
    Guerrillas 205–6
    A House For Mr. Biswas 205
Nairn, Tom 14
Nazism 72, 74, 87, 118, 119–21, 147
National Curriculum, the 150
national identity 122, 149–78, 184–5, 202–3
National Theatre, the 145
New Criticism 61, 62, 109
New Left 7, 14, 25, 109, 115, 119, 121–3, 133, 134, 168
New Lines 26, 137, 211
New Review 40, 63
New Society 57
Newsome Report on Secondary Education 123
Newton, Isaac 103, 114, 191, 192, 194, 196
Nichols, Grace 152
    The Fat Black Woman's Poems 154
Nietzsche, Friedrich 69, 88, 147, 153, 212
nouveau roman 39

O'Brown, Norman 6
Obscene Publications Act 49, 118
O'Connor, Flannery 183
Odyssey, The 92
Open University, the 9
Orton, Joe 10, 44–5
    What the Butler Saw 44
    Loot 45
Orwell, George 48, 150
    'England Your England' 160

Osborne, John 122, 168–9
  The Entertainer 45
  Look Back in Anger 4, 80
  Luther 169

Pazz, Octavio 24, 92
Pinter, Harold 10, 65, 69, 110
  The Caretaker 81, 82–3
  The Homecoming 84
  Old Times 84
planning 59, 108, 109, 114–15, 116–18,
    119, 129–30, 131, 135–6, 138, 139–40,
    147–8
Plath, Sylvia 10, 49, 88, 126–7, 137
Platonism 68, 79, 125, 131, 166
political theatre 158–60, 168–78
Pop Art 144–5
Popper, Karl 129–30
positivism 121–2, 129–30, 183
Potter, Dennis 24
Powell, Enoch 149, 173–4
post-colonialism 163, 166–7, 177–8, 201–7,
    210
post-industrial thesis, the 162–3, 210
post-modernism 12, 27, 33, 38, 41, 44, 46,
    53, 54, 62, 70, 100, 106, 129, 133,
    142–3, 145, 153–9, 160, 163, 181, 185,
    187, 189, 191, 196, 199, 203, 206, 210,
    211, 212
Private Eye 4, 25
psychoanalysis 66–9, 72, 97, 100–1, 169,
    195
Pynchon, Thomas 46
  The Crying of Lot 49, 180

Raban, Jonathan, *Soft City* 141–2
Race Relations Act 173
Raine, Craig 64
Read, Piers Paul 94
Reading, Peter, *Ukele Music* 140–1
Rhys, Jean, *Wide Sargasso Sea* 203–4
Riesman, David 67
Robbins Report on Higher Education 9, 38,
    123
Roberts, Michelle 94, 185, 191
Robinson, John, *Honest to God* 64, 65–6
Rorty, Richard 183
Roszak, Theodor, *The Making of a
    Counterculture* 5, 22, 116
Royal Family, the 47
Rushdie, Salman 49
  Midnight's Children 51–2
  The Satanic Verses 50–6, 103
  Shame 51, 52, 156–7, 179, 185, 191, 203,
    204, 206–7, 212

Said, Edward 152–3
  Orientalism 201
Salisbury Review 30
Sartre, J.-P., *Critique de la raison dialectique* 6
satire 24, 25, 209
science 103–4, 127–33, 147, 184, 191–7
science fiction 137
Scott, Paul, *The Raj Quartet* 201
Second Vatican Council 96
Sexton, Anne 26, 126
Shaw, G. B., *Heartbreak House* 170
Shelley, P. B. 115
situationism 120, 169
Skinner, B. F. 145–6
Snow, C. P. 4, 40
social constructivism 38, 98
Sontag, Susan, *Against Interpretation* 36, 43
Spark, Muriel 10
  The Batchelors 98
  The Comforters 181
  The Driver's Seat 143–4
  The Girls of Slender Means 115
  Not to Disturb 47–8, 62, 69, 94, 98
  The Only Problem 206
  The Prime of Miss Jean Brodie 121
Spender, Stephen, *The struggle of the
    Modern* 62
Spenser, Edmund, *The Faerie Queene* 184
  The Shepherd's Calendar 152
Spitting Image 25, 26
Steiner, George:
  The Death of Tragedy 112
  Language and Silence 112
Sterne, Laurence, *Tristram Shandy* 39
Stevens, Wallace 92
Stonewall Rebellion 199
Stoppard, Tom 10
  Jumpers 43, 44
  Professional Foul 44
  Rosencrantz and Guildenstern Are Dead
    42–3
  Travesties 43–4
Storey, David 8, 9, 65, 123
Structuralism 38, 40, 179, 203
sublime, the 155, 181, 185, 192, 194, 195,
    196, 199
Swift, Graham, *Waterland* 182–3, 211–13

television 24, 25, 46, 209
terrorism 206
That Was the Week That Was 25
Thatcher, Margaret 14, 15, 16, 18, 20, 160,
    161, 174–5
Thatcherism 13, 55, 63, 163
theatre of cruelty 111–15

Thomas, D. M., *The White Hotel* 71–5
Thompson, Denys 46
Thompson, E. P. 57, 116, 119, 122, 168
Thwaite, Anthony 88
Tillich, Paul 66
Todorov, Tzvetan 54, 92–4
Tomlinson, Charles 26, 27, 48, 92–4
  Seeing is Believing 93
  The Way of a World 93
total theatre 111, 112
Trevor, William 185
Trilling, Lionel 22, 25, 146
Troubles, the 81, 142, 160, 164–8, 177–8
Tynan, Kenneth 110–11

Unsworth, Barry 185

Vietnam War, the 116, 121
Vonnegut, Kurt 33, 70

Wain, John 122, 128
Warhol, Andy 36
Waugh, Evelyn 48, 61
Weil, Simone 77, 105
Weiss, Peter 111–15, 177
Weldon, Fay 185, 190
  The Life and Loves of a She-Devil 190
  Puffball 190

Wertenbaker, Timberlake 200
Wesker, Arnold 8, 9, 10
  and Centre 42, 123
West, Rebecca 50
White, Hayden 37
Williams, Raymond 122–3, 168
  'Culture is Ordinary' 208
  The Long Revolution 209
Williams, William Carlos, *Paterson* 140
Wilson, A. N. 94
Wilson, Angus:
  No Laughing Matter 197
  The Old Men at the Zoo 10, 71, 197
Wilson Knight, G. 104
Winters, Yvor 90, 211
Winterson, Jeanette 185, 189
  Sexing the Cherry 191, 192–5
Wittgenstein, Ludwig 37, 39
Wolfendon Report on Homosexuality 118
Woolf, Virginia 62
  Orlando 187
  To the Lighthouse 127, 187
Wordsworth, William 91, 93, 122
World War Two 1, 2, 14–16, 94, 101, 119,
  171–3, 177
Worsthorne, Peregrine 15

Yeats, W. B. 72, 105, 125, 167

OXFORD

MORE OXFORD PAPERBACKS

This book is just one of nearly 1000 Oxford Paperbacks currently in print. If you would like details of other Oxford Paperbacks, including titles in the World's Classics, Oxford Reference, Oxford Books, OPUS, Past Masters, Oxford Authors, and Oxford Shakespeare series, please write to:

UK and Europe: Oxford Paperbacks Publicity Manager, Arts and Reference Publicity Department, Oxford University Press, Walton Street, Oxford OX2 6DP.

Customers in UK and Europe will find Oxford Paperbacks available in all good bookshops. But in case of difficulty please send orders to the Cash-with-Order Department, Oxford University Press Distribution Services, Saxon Way West, Corby, Northants NN18 9ES. Tel: 0536 741519; Fax: 0536 746337. Please send a cheque for the total cost of the books, plus £1.75 postage and packing for orders under £20; £2.75 for orders over £20. Customers outside the UK should add 10% of the cost of the books for postage and packing.

USA: Oxford Paperbacks Marketing Manager, Oxford University Press, Inc., 200 Madison Avenue, New York, N.Y. 10016.

Canada: Trade Department, Oxford University Press, 70 Wynford Drive, Don Mills, Ontario M3C 1J9.

Australia: Trade Marketing Manager, Oxford University Press, G.P.O. Box 2784Y, Melbourne 3001, Victoria.

South Africa: Oxford University Press, P.O. Box 1141, Cape Town 8000.

OXFORD POETS

A PORTER SELECTED

Peter Porter

This selection of about one hundred of Porter's best poems is chosen from all his works to date, including his latest book, *Possible Worlds*, and *The Automatic Oracle*, which won the 1988 Whitbread Prize for Poetry.

What the critics have said about Peter Porter:

'I can't think of any contemporary poet who is so consistently entertaining over such a variety of material.' John Lucas, *New Statesman*

'an immensely fertile, lively, informed, honest and penetrating mind.' Stephen Spender, *Observer*

'He writes vigorously, with savage erudition and wonderful expansiveness . . . No one now writing matches Porter's profoundly moral and cultured overview.' Douglas Dunn, *Punch*

PAST MASTERS

General Editor: Keith Thomas

SHAKESPEARE

Germaine Greer

'At the core of a coherent social structure as he viewed it lay marriage, which for Shakespeare is no mere comic convention but a crucial and complex ideal. He rejected the stereotype of the passive, sexless, unresponsive female and its inevitable concommitant, the misogynist conviction that all women were whores at heart. Instead he created a series of female characters who were both passionate and pure, who gave their hearts spontaneously into the keeping of the men they loved and remained true to the bargain in the face of tremendous odds.'

Germaine Greer's short book on Shakespeare brings a completely new eye to a subject about whom more has been written than on any other English figure. She is especially concerned with discovering why Shakespeare 'was and is a popular artist', who remains a central figure in English cultural life four centuries after his death.

'eminently trenchant and sensible . . . a genuine exploration in its own right' John Bayley, *Listener*

'the clearest and simplest explanation of Shakespeare's thought I have yet read' Auberon Waugh, *Daily Mail*

OXFORD POPULAR FICTION

THE ORIGINAL MILLION SELLERS!

This series boasts some of the most talked-about works of British and US fiction of the last 150 years—books that helped define the literary styles and genres of crime, historical fiction, romance, adventure, and social comedy, which modern readers enjoy.

Riders of the Purple Sage	Zane Grey
The Four Just Men	Edgar Wallace
Trilby	George Du Maurier
Trent's Last Case	E C Bentley
The Riddle of the Sands	Erskine Childers
Under Two Flags	Ouida
The Lost World	Arthur Conan Doyle
The Woman Who Did	Grant Allen

Forthcoming in October:

Olive	Dinah Craik
The Diary of a Nobody	George and Weedon Grossmith
The Lodger	Belloc Lowndes
The Wrong Box	Robert Louis Stevenson

ILLUSTRATED HISTORIES IN
OXFORD PAPERBACKS

THE OXFORD ILLUSTRATED HISTORY
OF ENGLISH LITERATURE

Edited by Pat Rogers

Britain possesses a literary heritage which is almost unrivalled in the Western world. In this volume, the richness, diversity, and continuity of that tradition are explored by a group of Britain's foremost literary scholars.

Chapter by chapter the authors trace the history of English literature, from its first stirrings in Anglo-Saxon poetry to the present day. At its heart towers the figure of Shakespeare, who is accorded a special chapter to himself. Other major figures such as Chaucer, Milton, Donne, Wordsworth, Dickens, Eliot, and Auden are treated in depth, and the story is brought up to date with discussion of living authors such as Seamus Heaney and Edward Bond.

'[a] lovely volume . . . put in your thumb and pull out plums' Michael Foot

'scholarly and enthusiastic people have written inspiring essays that induce an eagerness in their readers to return to the writers they admire' *Economist*